The Evolution of Type

The Evolution of Type

Geometric Sans Serif
Futura (1927–1930)

Selva, a blackletter based on
medieval calligraphy (2012)

A Graphic Guide to 100 Landmark Typefaces

Examining Letters from Metal Type to OpenType

Tony Seddon Foreword by Stephen Coles

FIREFLY BOOKS

A Firefly Book

Published by Firefly Books Ltd. 2015

First printing

Publisher Cataloging-in-Publication Data (U.S.)

Seddon, Tony, 1965–
    The evolution of type : a graphic guide to 100 landmark typefaces / Tony Seddon.
[256] pages : color photographs ; cm.
Includes bibliographic references and index.
Summary: A guidebook to the development of typographic characters and their uses throughout history, including the meanings behind such landmark typefaces as used by Johannes Gutenberg in his 42-Line Bible.
ISBN-13: 978-1-77085-504-5
1. Type and type-founding — History. 2. Printing — History. I. Title.
686.224 dc23   Z250.A2.S433 2015

Library and Archives Canada Cataloguing in Publication

Seddon, Tony, 1965–, author
    The evolution of type : a graphic guide to 100 landmark typefaces / Tony Seddon. — First edition.
Includes bibliographical references and index.
ISBN 978-1-77085-504-5 (bound)
    1. Type and type-founding— History. 2. Type and type-founding.
3. Printing— history. I. Title.
Z250.A2S43 2015   686.2'24   C2015-900432-2

Published in the United States by
Firefly Books (U.S.) Inc.
P.O. Box 1338, Ellicott Station
Buffalo, New York 14205

Published in Canada by
Firefly Books Ltd.
50 Staples Avenue, Unit 1
Richmond Hill, Ontario L4B 0A7

Printed in China

Conceived, designed, and produced by
Quid Publishing
Part of the Quarto Group
Level 4 Sheridan House
114 Western Road
Hove BN3 1DD
www.quidpublishing.com

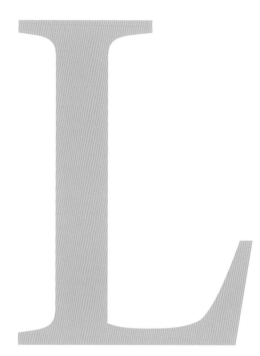

For Lily, a truly wonderful character

Contents

Foreword 10

Introduction 12

Type Classification 14

Type Anatomy 16

The Origins of Movable Type **19**

Aldus Manutius and Francesco Griffo 22

John Baskerville 23

Jenson 24

Bembo 26

Garamond 28

Plantin 30

Janson 32

Caslon 34

Fournier 36

Baskerville 38

Bell 40

Bodoni 42

Walbaum 44

Scotch Roman 46

Clarendon 48

A Line of Type **51**

Rudolf Koch 54

Eric Gill 55

Morris Fuller Benton 56

Beatrice Warde 57

Century 58

Cheltenham 60

Akzidenz-Grotesk 62

Bell Italic

Engravers	64
Eckmannschrift	66
Bookman	68
Copperplate Gothic	70
Franklin Gothic	72
News Gothic	74
Centaur	76
Goudy Old Style	78
Cooper Black	80
Wilhelm Klingspor Schrift (Gotisch)	82
Perpetua	84
Kabel	86
Futura	88
Gill Sans	90
Memphis	92
Joanna	94
DIN	96
Times New Roman	98
Albertus	100
Rockwell	102
Peignot	104
Caledonia	106
Palatino	108
Melior	110
Mistral	112
Trump Mediaeval	114
Folio	116
Univers	118
Neue Haas Grotesk/Helvetica	120
Transport	122

Rockwell

The Tech That Time Forgot   **125**

Hermann Zapf   128

Adrian Frutiger   129

Optima   130

Antique Olive   132

Amelia   134

Sabon   136

OCR-A and OCR-B   138

Americana   140

Serifa   142

Syntax   144

ITC Avant Garde Gothic   146

Frutiger   148

ITC Tiffany   150

ITC Bauhaus   152

Bell Centennial   154

ITC Galliard   156

VAG Rounded   158

Pixel Perfect   **161**

Robert Slimbach   164

Zuzana Licko   165

Tobias Frere-Jones   166

Christian Schwartz   167

Swift (Neue Swift)   168

Rotis   170

Trajan   172

ITC Officina Sans   174

Template Gothic   176

FF Scala   178

PMN Caecilia   180

FF Meta   182

HTF Didot   184

Myriad   186

Lexicon   188

HTF Didot

DTL Fleischmann	190
Mason	192
Interstate	194
Giza	196
Knockout	198
The Thesis Family	200
Verdana	202
Benton Sans	204
Base Nine & Base Twelve	206
FF Dax (FF Daxline)	208
Mrs Eaves	210
Bickham Script	212
Modesto	214
Gotham	216
Arnhem	218
Neutraface	220
MVB Verdigris	222
Brioso	224
Akkurat	226
Freight	228
Bello	230
Whitney	232
Ministry Script	234
Verlag	236
Archer	238
Vitesse	240
Heron Serif	242
Selva	244
Glossary	246
Bibliography	250
The Foundries	251
Index	252
Acknowledgments	256

Freight Micro

Foreword

Type is a fundamental part of written language in the modern world, and yet it is commonly treated as a static thing. Once cast into metal, it is fixed in time.

But type is alive!

Each typeface has an individual history. It is often born out of specific necessity, influenced by the artistic world in which its creator lives or designed to solve a particular problem. Some typefaces die soon after they fulfill this initial purpose, but others can live on far beyond their designers' intentions. They can travel through design movements, traverse formats and substrates both analog and digital, and evolve into the typographic offspring that we refer to as revivals and reinterpretations. If a typeface survives these journeys it can continue to live on as a tool in the hands of future generations, producing work its creator never imagined.

And just as music has its archetypical artists or composers who represent a given genre (be it classical, blues, folk or rock), so does type.

Certain typefaces define their classification or style; they set a standard, becoming the forebears by which all their followers are judged and compared. We know many of these classics well, whether its from the pages of our design-school textbooks (Bodoni, Garamond, Caslon, Futura) or the default font menus on our computers (Gill Sans, Times, Palatino, Helvetica). But how much do we really know about them? What was the context of the design world in which they were drawn? Were they in competition with other typefaces of the time? What life did they live after they were released? How did they survive the transition from metal to film to digital? Did they survive at all? Which typefaces followed in their shadow?

In this book, Tony Seddon makes a daring and worthwhile attempt to answer these questions. *The Evolution of Type* is a biography of these living things we call typefaces. It tells their individual stories, and while at it, tells the story of typography as a whole.

Stephen Coles

Giza

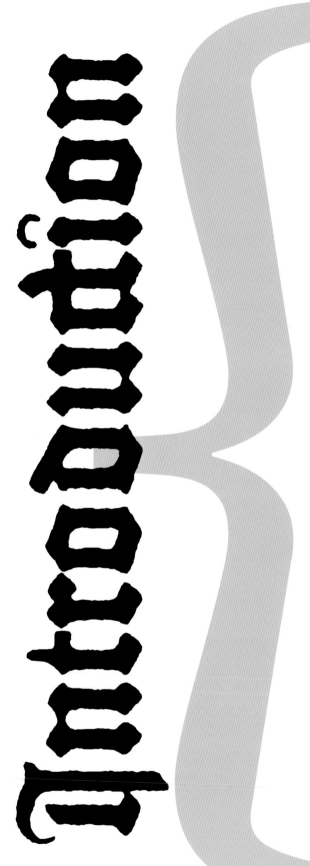

I'd like to ask you to compare the typeface on the left side of this page with the typeface on the right side of the page opposite. Hopefully there's one stand-out thing you've noticed about them—the face on the right is a whole lot easier to read. As much as anything else, this comparison visually represents the evolution of type. For the last 500 years or so, since the introduction of movable type in Europe, designers have been striving to create typefaces that are stylish but legible, space-saving yet eye-catching, fashionable or timeless. On the left we have ALOT Gutenberg A, a facsimile of Johannes Gutenberg's type from the mid 15th century, created by the Altera Littera type foundry that specializes in digital revivals of medieval script and blackletter faces. On the right we have Arnhem, a high-performance Transitional serif designed in 2001 by Fred Smeijers of the digital type foundry OurType. So what of this comparison? Well, today we're far more comfortable with the letterforms of Arnhem but, if this was the 1450s, we'd be taking a different view.

Before Gutenberg set up shop in Mainz, Germany, in 1450, anyone who could actually read would have been entirely used to seeing text written by hand in the Gothic or blackletter style. Therefore, your average educated mid-15th-century fellow, were he able to view these pages, would feel at ease with ALOT Gutenberg A but would likely feel rather confused by the letterforms of Arnhem. This neatly brackets the whole point of the evolution of type, which has always been influenced by other contemporary styles of the day. For example, architecture is a strong point of reference; think of the terms "Gothic architecture" and "Gothic type" and you have it.

The typographic timeline is an interesting one because, after an initial flurry of innovation in mid-15th-century Europe, everything effectively stalled for the best part of 450 years and the hand-setting of foundry type remained the only method for the mass production of printed text. The most significant development after Gutenberg—and prior to the invention of the first mechanized typesetting machines, Ottmar Mergenthaler's Linotype and Tolbert Lanston's Monotype—was arguably the widespread adoption of roman letterforms. The work of punch cutters such as Nicolas Jenson and Francesco Griffo drove this trend and set the standard for 200 years or more, with the likes of Robert Granjon and Jean Jannon picking up the baton in the 16th century. Then, in the mid 18th century, a successful English industrialist named John Baskerville decided to turn his attention to the printing industry and quality took a quantum leap forward—a new design standard had been set, but typesetting was still a laborious manual process.

Fast forward through the 18th and 19th centuries, during which the likes of Fournier, Bodoni and Didot were producing their great typefaces, and we encounter our friend Mergenthaler, who gave a demonstration of his Blower Linotype linecasting machine in the offices of the *New-York Tribune* in July 1886. This changed everything. The age of hot metal typesetting, where line-length "slugs" or "lines o' type" were composed using individual matrices that dropped into place from a pre-loaded magazine as an operator keyed the text, was born.

Now that typesetting was possible on an industrial scale, typeface design became big business and in our current digital age, following the move from hot metal through photosetting to PostScript and OpenType, we have many thousands of typefaces at our disposal. Not all of them are good, but over the course of the following pages I'll demonstrate how some are truly masterful examples of design.

Type Classification

During the last 100 years or so, type designers and commentators have made several serious attempts to come up with a definitive system of typeface classification. Unfortunately, none have so far been faultless and in my humble opinion (apparently shared by others who have pondered over this subject) there can never be one single system that will work across the board. This isn't to say that none of the existing systems work; on the contrary, systems such as Vox-AtypI classification, which was devised by the French historian Maximilien Vox in 1954 and adopted by the Association Typographique Internationale in 1967, works perfectly well for the majority of typefaces one throws at it but, every now and again, a face crops up that simply doesn't fit. And if the face doesn't fit …

One of the modern-day problems of typeface classification stems from the fact that many of the innovative typefaces created during a period roughly equivalent to the last 30 years or so have been designed to address a whole new set of challenges. Principal among these is the ability of a face to function well across a wide range of print and screen environments; prior to the mid 1980s the screen requirements weren't an issue, but now designers need typefaces that can work in a brochure, on a desktop computer screen, on a tablet and on the cramped screen of a smartphone. This means that it's becoming increasingly difficult to categorize many new typefaces by association with a recognized historical style; faces can bridge two or more traditional categories, meaning we may find ourselves dealing with a Humanist Transitional or Neo-Grotesque Geometric. Confusing, to say the least.

However, personally I think the best approach is to simply not get too hung up about it. Try to ensure you've got a good grounding in recognizing the tell-tale signs of a Humanist sans or a Grotesque slab, then work out for yourself where everything fits in. The Vox-AtypI system is still a good place to start despite it being a little out of date by today's standards—just take an open-minded approach and read as much as you can about other typographers' views. There are plenty of excellent online information sources, some of which I've listed in the bibliography at the back of this book.

For the purposes of this title I've used a slightly modified system that I first encountered when designing a book written by Stephen Coles, *The Anatomy of Type* (called *The Geometry of Type* for some editions). Stephen uses a "Rational Serif" category for serif faces that are "constructed" rather than written, and with even proportions and a vertically stressed structure. When you get the hang of it, it helps to tidy up the slightly gray area that hovers around the late 18th century and includes Moderns and Scotch Romans. To the right I've listed a brief explanation of each category that I hope will prove helpful as you work your way through this book. Fuller explanations of the characteristics of each classification are provided throughout the text.

- **Ancient**—before the 15th century; includes blackletter (or Fraktur) and Incised (or Antique).
- **Humanist serif** (also called Venetian)—mid 15th century onward.
- **Old Style serif** (also called Garalde)—late 15th century onward. These can be sub-divided into Italian Old Style (from 1495), French Old Style (from 1540s) and Dutch Old Style (from 1680s).
- **Transitional serif**—early 18th century onward.
- **Rational serif**—late 18th century onward; includes Moderns (also called Neoclassical or Didone) and Scotch Romans. Very bold Moderns are called Fat Face.
- **Script**—late 18th century onward and split into Formal (late 18th century), Casual (early 20th century) and Calligraphic.
- **Slab serif** (also called Square serif)—early 19th century onward. Traditionally includes Clarendons (with bracketed serifs) and Egyptians (with unbracketed serifs), but now split into Grotesque slabs, Geometric slabs and Humanist slabs.
- **Sans serif** (also called Lineals)—from the early 19th century but more prolifically early 20th century onward; includes Grotesque sans, Neo-Grotesque sans, Gothic sans, Geometric sans, Humanist sans and Neo-Humanist sans.
- **Display**—19th century onward. My interpretation doesn't include display weights of type families, just one-off typefaces designed specifically for display purposes and headlines.
- **Glyphic**—predominantly a 20th century typeface innovation, although inscriptional style letterforms date back to Roman times.
- **Contemporary serif**—a late-20th century invention, covering typefaces that feature newer innovations and therefore defy accurate or specific classification.

A note to the reader

Throughout this book Mergenthaler Linotype and Lanston Monotype refer specifically to the founding U.S. branches of each company when relevant. Otherwise, the companies are referred to simply as Linotype and Monotype. Following a number of major acquisitions over the years, Monotype Libraries now incorporate fonts from Monotype, Linotype, FontFont, ITC, Ascender and Bitstream. However, throughout this book I've referred to the originating companies where applicable.

Type Anatomy

The terminology of type anatomy can be variable, so for the sake of clarity to the largest number of readers I've listed the terms that I feel are used commonly by the majority of designers and typographers.

Typeface shown: Arnhem Display Normal

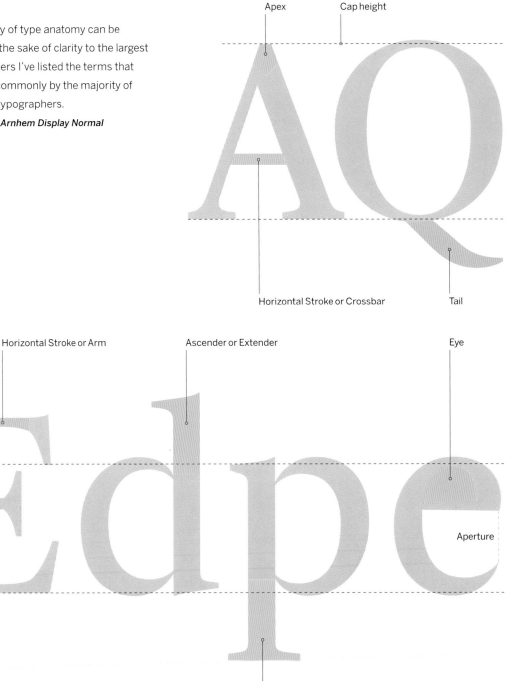

Apex

Cap height

Horizontal Stroke or Crossbar

Tail

Horizontal Stroke or Arm

Ascender or Extender

Eye

Aperture

Vertical Stroke or Stem

Descender or Extender

Spine Terminal Hook or Arch Shoulder

Spur Bowl Tail Serif Bracket

x-height Arm Link Counter Ear Dot

Leg Loop Tail

The Origins of Movable Type

To begin this precis of the earliest period of typographic endeavor, it's important to make a distinction between letterforms and type. On the one hand we have lettering or calligraphy, a form of written communication over 5,000 years old. The earliest known writing systems, Mesopotamian cuneiform and Egyptian hieroglyphs, date from around 3200 BCE with Chinese writing appearing some 2,000 years later at around 1200 BCE. However, these hand-written letterforms are not *type*—the beginning of type is synonymous with the printing techniques and technology that emerged in Europe during the 15th century.

We know that woodblock printing was created in China as early as 220 CE, and that the Chinese dabbled with a form of movable type using both ceramic and metal blocks as well as wood. However, the need to create thousands of individual characters to physically reproduce their complex ideogrammatic writing style presumably proved far too impractical and the system was not widely accepted. In any case, the nonstick water-based inks available at the time were ill-suited for use with the nonporous surfaces of printing "tiles" made from anything other than wood. Despite these early issues, people continued to use carved blocks to print images for the next 1,000 years or so, while the crucial ideas that would lead to the creation of a working movable type system continued to elude them.

During this time, two important factors came to influence the increased commercial interest in being able to print type. First, education levels began to improve with the founding of many new universities and schools throughout Western Europe. Reading and writing, previously the privilege of monastic scholars and noblemen, was seen increasingly as a necessity for anyone who wanted to get on in life and the demand for printed material shot up. Monks simply couldn't churn out their beautiful and precious handwritten books quickly enough and "ordinary" folk became professional scribes in their own right, reproducing texts for a growing market. Second, paper manufacturing techniques were rapidly improving and a cheaper alternative to the expensive calfskin vellum favored by monks was finally accessible. The only thing missing was a way to speed up the whole process.

Fast forward to the German town of Mainz in the late 1440s, where we encounter local businessman Johannes Gutenberg, the man credited with the invention of a workable movable type system. (This is despite the fact that there are a number of other claimants lurking in the background—the evidence for him simply stacks up more convincingly than it does for anyone else.) He was responsible for printing the first significant book seen in Western Europe using movable type, the 42-line Bible.

It's known as the 42-line Bible because there were 42 lines of text per page, and the printing was completed around 1455. Gutenberg used a typeface designed to resemble the style of handwritten blackletter script, which is significant because the commercial success of his Bible was vital. Make no mistake, Gutenberg was first and foremost a manufacturer and was in it for the money rather than the recognition of being the first to produce printed text on a large scale. The few people who could read were used to the blackletter style; they would have been confused by a radically different style of typeface in the same way that we find blackletter somewhat difficult to read today. So it's likely Gutenberg consciously created a product that replicated the feel of a handwritten book as

closely as possible. One can also assume that he actually had no interest in designing new letterforms, he simply went with whatever references he had ready access to, in order to save time and therefore expense. It was difficult enough for him to get his newly envisioned printing process right, so the typeface was probably one of the last things on his mind.

His printing press would have been modeled on a wooden wine press with the addition of a sliding tray containing the assembled type and paper. The tray was positioned below the hand operated screw mechanism that moved the *platen* downward to create the impression, and, crucially, he used oil-based ink that was able to adhere to the surface of the metal type. The basic design of this kind of press remained unchanged for almost 400 years, prevailing until the introduction of iron hand presses in the early 19th century. How he manufactured his metal type remains open to debate; particularly because there are obvious variations between different occurrences of the same character throughout the 42-line Bible. This implies that he didn't use the same punches and matrices to cast each and every unique character. He may have cut a number of slightly different punches to enhance the sense that the type was handwritten,

or alternatively he could have used temporary molds made from dampened sand to make different batches of type as it was needed. We'll never know for sure, but ultimately his endeavors served to kick-start a revolution in the mass dissemination of information which, significantly, removed the absolute power held by the Church over the control of knowledge. If Martin Luther hadn't been able to publish his teachings and distribute printed material to a wider audience, the Protestant Reformation may never have happened and, for good or bad, Europe would have remained immune to the onset of democracy.

Aldus Manutius and Francesco Griffo

For over 200 years, a period roughly encompassing the 16th and 17th centuries, the typefaces cut by Francesco Griffo for the famous and prolific Renaissance printer Aldus Manutius set the benchmark for practically all type designed and manufactured throughout Western Europe. Manutius was born in 1449 to a well-heeled family in Bassiano, some 40 miles south-east of Rome, and following a scholarly education and a financial covenant from his friend Giovanni Pico's family he founded the Aldine Press in Venice in 1494. He subsequently embarked on a project to improve on the Humanist designs of Nicolas Jenson's typefaces, acquiring the services of punch cutter Griffo, and the resulting roman face was first used to print Cardinal Pietro Bembo's De Aetna in 1495. Griffo's skills as a punch cutter undoubtedly cemented Manutius' reputation as a printer of excellence; his work demonstrates a degree of abstraction from the calligraphic influences so obviously present in Jenson's designs which give us the original Old Style serifs, typefaces exhibiting a greater level of precision with more refined detailing in the serifs and strokes. Further success came with the publication of an edition of Francesco Colonna's Hypnerotomachia Poliphili in 1499, which again used type cut by Griffo.

Manutius' enduring reputation is enhanced by his connection with the invention, along with Griffo of course, of italic type. The first appearance of their Aldine type, based on a Niccolò de' Niccoli script found in a papal chancery of the 1420s, is in a 1501 edition of Virgil's Opera. The word "italic" derives from the Italian origin of the first italic faces, designed primarily to preserve space on the page in order to save on the cost of paper, which was extremely expensive in the 16th century. He's also known for his use of the cost-saving octavo book format, where a large sheet of paper is printed with 16 separate pages that are then folded and gathered to form an eight-leaf (or 16-page) section. His smaller and cheaper "pocket" editions helped to make books more accessible to ordinary people, rather like paperbacks did in the early 19th century. Manutius died in 1515 and his firm was taken over by his grandson, Aldus Manutius the Younger.

Griffo's good fortune appears to have run out by 1516 when, after a previous dispute with Manutius over the level of accreditation he received, he returned to his native Bologna and was charged with the murder of a relative during a fight. His death in 1518 or 1519 is likely to have been linked to his execution for this crime.

John Baskerville

Like many of his contemporaries, John Baskerville wasn't known during his lifetime specifically as a typeface designer. Type was a part of the toolkit necessary for him to ply his main area of trade as a printer in the days when typefaces were not treated as a commercial product in quite the same way as they are today. Independent type foundries did exist in the 18th century, but the more successful printers like Baskerville tended to cut and cast type for their own use, occasionally employing artisan punch cutters for the specialist work. Baskerville was himself a skilled engraver, having left the English county of Worcestershire in 1725 to work in Birmingham as a writing master and engraver. Ever the entrepreneur, he established a successful business manufacturing japanware (Japanese-style lacquerwork) before starting his printing firm around 1750.

Keen to improve on the accepted quality of type reproduction, Baskerville embarked on a period of experimentation with an aim to refine the styling of the dominant Dutch-influenced typefaces that were popular in the mid 18th century. He realized that the quality of both paper stock and ink was vital to this process and embraced the newly invented technique for manufacturing wove paper, pioneered by British manufacturer James Whatman. Wove paper has a much flatter surface as it's made using a mold with cross-woven wires, whereas laid paper is made using parallel wires which creates a ribbed surface. He coupled this with his own ink formulations that were much blacker and more opaque than other commercial offerings, enabling him to direct his punch cutter John Handy to cut type with finer strokes and serifs, details which would otherwise have been lost during printing. He also introduced heated copper rollers to his printing process to dry the ink more quickly, lessening the detrimental effect of ink soak.

Baskerville counted the Cambridge University Press among his prestigious clients and produced a highly regarded folio Bible for them in 1763, as well as an edition of the New Testament for the Oxford University Press. The American inventor and statesman Benjamin Franklin was an admirer of Baskerville's typefaces and introduced them to the U.S., where they achieved equal success despite some detractors complaining that they were "too thin and narrow and hurt the eye." On his death in 1775 his punches were sold by his former housekeeper and widow Sarah (née Eaves), but are now in the collection of Cambridge University Press after they were presented to them by the French type foundry Deberny & Peignot in 1953.

Jenson

| **Country of origin:** Italy | **Classification:** Venetian Humanist Serif
| **Designer:** Nicolas Jenson

*c.*1470

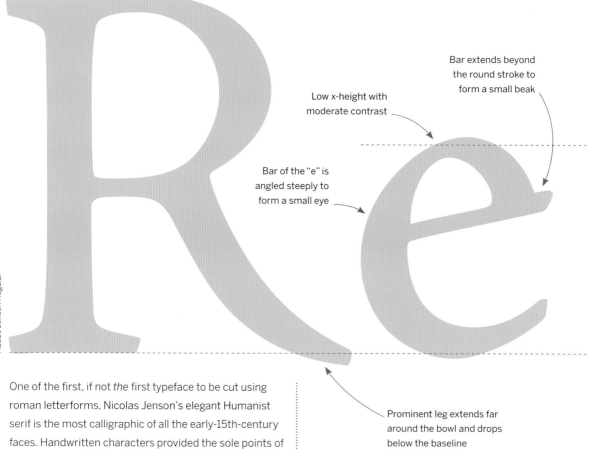

Adobe Jenson Regular

Low x-height with
moderate contrast

Bar extends beyond
the round stroke to
form a small beak

Bar of the "e" is
angled steeply to
form a small eye

Prominent leg extends far
around the bowl and drops
below the baseline

One of the first, if not *the* first typeface to be cut using roman letterforms, Nicolas Jenson's elegant Humanist serif is the most calligraphic of all the early-15th-century faces. Handwritten characters provided the sole points of reference at this time.

9/12pt Adobe Jenson Regular

LOREM IPSUM DOLOR SIT AMET, CONSECTETUER ADIPISCING ELIT, SED DIAM nonummy nibh euismod tincidunt ut laoreet dolore magna aliquam erat volutpat. ut wisi enim ad minim veniam, quis nostrud exerci tation ullamcorper suscipit lobortis nisl ut aliquip ex ea commodo consequat. Duis autem vel eum iriure dolor in hendrerit in vulputate velit esse molestie consequat,

12/15pt Adobe Jenson Regular

LOREM IPSUM DOLOR SIT AMET, CONSECTETUER ADIPISCING ELIT, sed diam nonummy nibh euismod tincidunt ut laoreet dolore magna aliquam erat volutpat. Ut wisi enim ad minim veniam, quis nostrud exerci tation ullamcorper suscipit lobortis nisl ut aliquip ex ea commodo consequat. Duis

Nicolas Jenson was born in France in 1420 and worked as an engraver at the French Royal Mint until, in 1458, King Charles VII dispatched him to Mainz in Germany to learn about the new movable-type technology that Johannes Gutenberg had developed a few years earlier. By 1470 Jenson had relocated to Venice, still a separate Republic during the Renaissance period, and opened his own printing shop where he cut one of the earliest typefaces to use roman characters rather than the more familiar blackletter style. In those days, typefaces were not named as they are now because they weren't traded commercially; each printer cut and owned his own set of punches that were used exclusively by the business, but the face became known as Jenson over subsequent years. Jenson's success and technological innovation helped establish Venice as a center of publishing excellence in 15th-century Italy and the typeface, because of its fine design qualities and its pedigree, has retained its influence over the years.

Jenson is classified as a Humanist serif (sometimes more specifically a Venetian Humanist serif) because of its close stylistic ties to calligraphic lettering; the oblique stress typical of Humanist serif faces is very evident, especially with the lowercase "e" with its distinctive beak.

Jenson's face was cut without an accompanying italic style—Aldus Manutius (see page 22) introduced italics to the printing world a few decades later—but subsequent versions did benefit from the introduction of italics. An early revival that carried the Jenson name was J.W. Phinney's 1893 design for American Type Founders (ATF), which in turn was based on William Morris' Golden Type cut in 1890 for The Kelmscott Press. Monotype produced another version, naming it Italian Old Style and adding a companion bold style, and Frederic W. Goudy's redesign for Monotype added some swash capitals to the italic.

Notable (and finer) faces that draw inspiration from Jenson include Centaur, designed by Bruce Rogers in 1914, and Cloister, designed by Morris Fuller Benton a year earlier in 1913. The best interpretation of the original face available today is Adobe Jenson, designed by Robert Slimbach for Adobe and first issued in 1995. Slimbach manages to recapture much of the spirit of Jenson's original design and utilizes four subfamilies of differing optical sizes (Roman, Caption, Subhead and Display) to replicate the size-specific design of the original metal typeface. The italic styles are based on the lettering of the 15th-century writing master Ludovico Vincentino degli Arrighi.

Adobe Jenson Regular *Adobe Jenson Caption* *Adobe Jenson Display*

Bembo

| **Country of origin:** Italy | **Classification:** Old Style Serif
| **Designers:** Aldus Manutius and Francesco Griffo

1495

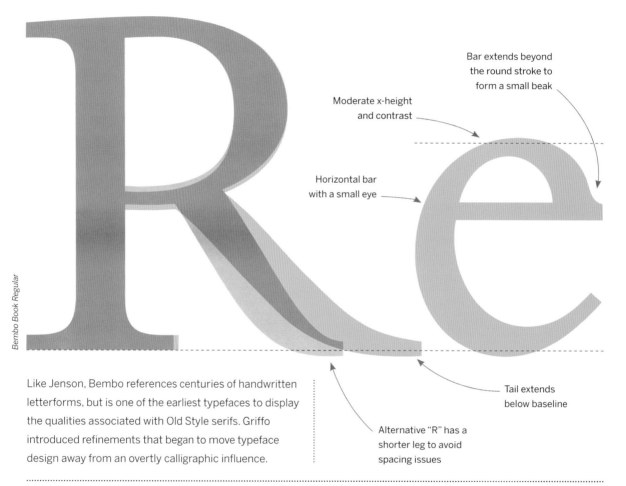

Bembo Book Regular

Moderate x-height and contrast

Bar extends beyond the round stroke to form a small beak

Horizontal bar with a small eye

Tail extends below baseline

Alternative "R" has a shorter leg to avoid spacing issues

Like Jenson, Bembo references centuries of handwritten letterforms, but is one of the earliest typefaces to display the qualities associated with Old Style serifs. Griffo introduced refinements that began to move typeface design away from an overtly calligraphic influence.

9/12pt Bembo Book Regular (Monotype)

LOREM IPSUM DOLOR SIT AMET, CONSECTETUER ADIPISCING ELIT, SED DIAM NONUMMY NIBH euismod tincidunt ut laoreet dolore magna aliquam erat volutpat. Ut wisi enim ad minim veniam, quis nostrud exerci tation ullamcorper suscipit lobortis nisl ut aliquip ex ea commodo consequat. Duis autem vel eum iriure dolor in hendrerit in vulputate velit esse molestie consequat, vel illum

12/15pt Bembo Book Regular (Monotype)

LOREM IPSUM DOLOR SIT AMET, CONSECTETUER ADIPISCING ELIT, sed diam nonummy nibh euismod tincidunt ut laoreet dolore magna aliquam erat volutpat. Ut wisi enim ad minim veniam, quis nostrud exerci tation ullamcorper suscipit lobortis nisl ut aliquip ex ea

Bembo is the first of the Old Style typefaces. Cut in Italy by Francesco Griffo under the direction of printer Aldus Manutius (see page 22), it was first used to set the type of Pietro Bembo's book *De Aetna*, a 60-page text about a journey to Mount Aetna (the Latin name of Mount Etna) that was published by Manutius in 1495. Griffo is arguably the first typeface designer to begin to consciously move away from the calligraphic influence of the Humanist serif style that Nicolas Jenson had favored in 1470; his typeface exhibits a greater level of precision, with serifs more refined than the earlier face. The ascenders of Bembo's lowercase characters are distinctively higher than the uppercase and, like Jenson, when first cut by Griffo there was no accompanying italic style for the typeface.

The first commercial release of Bembo was cut by the English branch of Monotype in 1929 under the direction of Stanley Morison, with an American version coming from Lanston Monotype shortly afterward. An italic style was added at this time, styled partly from a typeface designed in 1524 by Giovanni Taglienti but perhaps influenced more by a face designed by Ludovico Vicentino degli Arrighi around 1526. At this point it's interesting to compare Bembo with Monotype's earlier typefaces from 1923,

Poliphilus and its accompanying italic Blado. Monotype Poliphilus was styled after another Griffo/Manutius typeface similar to that used in *De Aetna*, but was drawn directly from surviving letterpress impressions, crucially retaining many of the imperfections that might otherwise be pared away by the draftsman. In this way they created letterforms that were less refined than they would have been if styled straight from the punches. Comparison of the two typefaces reveals broadly similar letterforms, but if you want the feel of Bembo with a more rustic quality, Poliphilus and Blado make good choices. Bembo also received bold styles courtesy of Monotype, but they're not especially successful as they detract somewhat from the elegance of the original face.

Monotype have subsequently released photo and digital versions of Bembo over the years but, until fairly recently, the offerings failed to capture the true nature of the original face. However, in 2005 Monotype decided to address these issues and released Bembo Book, which does a much better job of replicating the original correctly. The face remains an extremely popular choice for designers, especially for use in setting type for books, as its proportions provide a very even color when set in large blocks of running text.

Rjfw Rjfw

Poliphilus

Blado

Garamond

| **Country of origin:** France | **Classification:** Old Style Serif
| **Designers:** Claude Garamond and Robert Granjon

1532

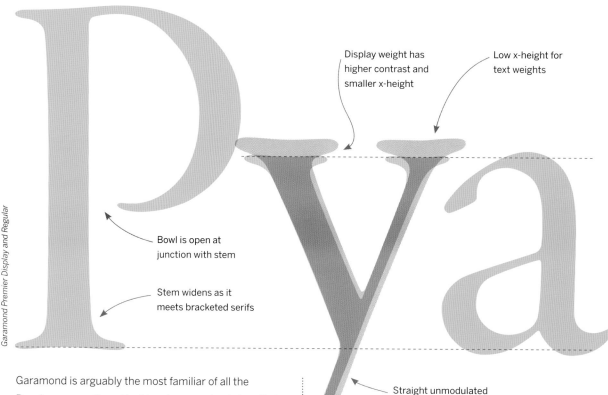

Garamond Premier Display and Regular

Display weight has higher contrast and smaller x-height

Low x-height for text weights

Bowl is open at junction with stem

Stem widens as it meets bracketed serifs

Straight unmodulated tail with a ball terminal

Ball terminal of Regular weight much larger

Garamond is arguably the most familiar of all the Renaissance serifs as the Monotype version is bundled with Microsoft Office. Garamond Premier Display, shown above, is one of four optical sizes included in Adobe's contemporary family of fonts.

9/12pt Garamond Premier Regular (Adobe)

LOREM IPSUM DOLOR SIT AMET, CONSECTETUER ADIPISCING ELIT, SED DIAM NONUMMY NIBH euismod tincidunt ut laoreet dolore magna aliquam erat volutpat. ut wisi enim ad minim veniam, quis nostrud exerci tation ullamcorper suscipit lobortis nisl ut aliquip ex ea commodo consequat. duis autem vel eum iriure dolor in hendrerit in vulputate velit esse molestie consequat, vel illum

12/15pt Garamond Premier Regular (Adobe)

LOREM IPSUM DOLOR SIT AMET, CONSECTETUER ADIPISCING ELIT, sed diam nonummy nibh euismod tincidunt ut laoreet dolore magna aliquam erat volutpat. Ut wisi enim ad minim veniam, quis nostrud exerci tation ullamcorper suscipit lobortis nisl ut aliquip ex ea commodo consequat. Duis

Claude Garamond (or Garamont) worked in Paris as a master punch cutter during the early half of the 16th century, drawing much of his personal influences from the earlier work of Francesco Griffo (see page 22), which arguably makes Bembo and Garamond the two most important typefaces of the Renaissance period. A good many typefaces have been linked to Garamond over the years and have subsequently been named for him—inaccurately in some cases, according to typographic scholars—but he was without doubt a major influence for typeface designers throughout Europe during the 16th and 17th centuries.

Identifying contemporary versions of typefaces as true Garamond revivals can be problematic because of his prolificacy; he was one of the first punch cutters to commercially produce type for retail to other customers. Another issue lies in the fact that, although he personally cut some wonderful italics as stand-alone fonts, the practice of actually paring an italic with its own roman style was not yet fashionable. Garamond revivals comprising complete families often contain italics that were not cut by Garamond, but rather by another prolific French punch cutter from the same period, Robert Granjon.

To add to the confusion, some 60 years after Garamond's death a talented Protestant punch cutter named Jean Jannon, who cut typefaces with a strong leaning toward Garamond's original designs, had his matrices confiscated by the Catholic authorities. Jannon's characters are more asymmetrical than Garamond's, but after being stored for a couple of centuries, the matrices were incorrectly identified as Garamond's work and some Garamond revivals are actually Jannon typefaces. Thanks to research carried out by Beatrice Warde (see page 57) we now know that Monotype Garamond (1922), Simoncini Garamond (1958) and Garamond 3 (from ATF's cut of 1918) are all based on Jannon's type rather than Garamond's.

One of the best digital options available today is Robert Slimbach's Garamond Premier, an update of his earlier Adobe Garamond family that's now drawn with subfamilies of four differing optical sizes, a treatment similar to that he gave to Adobe Jenson a few years earlier. The Regular and Caption options cover the bases for text setting, while the Display and Subhead options retain the delicacy of the letterforms when set at larger point sizes. Stempel Garamond, another true Garamond first issued in digital format by Linotype, is also worthy of consideration as it's based on an original 16th-century specimen sheet, but overall the face isn't quite as successful as Adobe's offering.

Garamond Premier Regular   Garamond Premier Caption   Garamond Premier Subhead

Plantin

| **Country of origin:** The Netherlands | **Classification:** Old Style Serif
| **Designer:** Robert Granjon

1557–1590

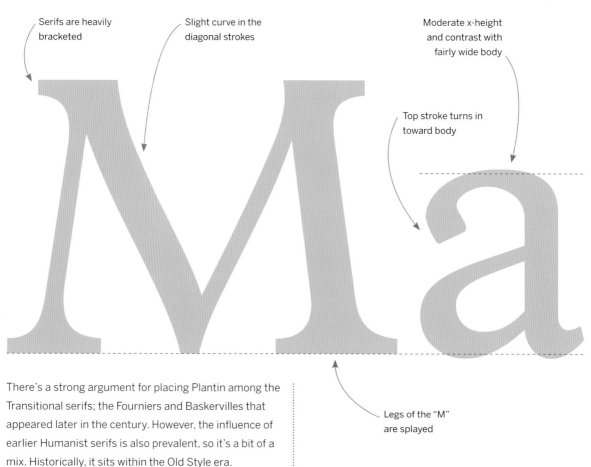

Serifs are heavily bracketed

Slight curve in the diagonal strokes

Moderate x-height and contrast with fairly wide body

Top stroke turns in toward body

Plantin Regular

Legs of the "M" are splayed

There's a strong argument for placing Plantin among the Transitional serifs; the Fourniers and Baskervilles that appeared later in the century. However, the influence of earlier Humanist serifs is also prevalent, so it's a bit of a mix. Historically, it sits within the Old Style era.

9/12pt Plantin Regular (Monotype)

LOREM IPSUM DOLOR SIT AMET, CONSECTETUER ADIPISCING ELIT, SED diam nonummy nibh euismod tincidunt ut laoreet dolore magna aliquam erat volutpat. ut wisi enim ad minim veniam, quis nostrud exerci tation ullamcorper suscipit lobortis nisl ut aliquip ex ea commodo consequat. Duis autem vel eum iriure

12/15pt Plantin Regular (Monotype)

LOREM IPSUM DOLOR SIT AMET, CONSECTETUER ADIPISCING elit, sed diam nonummy nibh euismod tincidunt ut laoreet dolore magna aliquam erat volutpat. Ut wisi enim ad minim veniam, quis nostrud exerci tation ullamcorper suscipit lobortis nisl

Plantin is an Old Style serif face based on type cut in the 16th century by the French punch cutter Robert Granjon. It was named after the influential printer and publisher Christophe Plantin, who was born in France around 1520 but who set up his business in the Belgian town of Antwerp, which at that time had grown to become one of the most successful commercial centers in the whole of Europe. Curiously, it appears that Plantin never actually used Granjon's type in any of his publications; it's rather the association with the period that links Plantin with Granjon's typeface design. Granjon was, of course, influential across the board during the 16th century and there are few typefaces from the period that don't bear at least some of the hallmarks of his style.

Monotype were responsible for the earliest revival of Granjon's type in 1913, entrusting Frank Hinman Pierpont with the project. Pierpont's specialty was adapting older typeface designs specifically for use on the Monotype machine, and Plantin was one of the first typefaces to be developed specifically to meet the demands of mechanical composition. It features a slightly heavier stroke width than other earlier faces from the period, because paper manufacturing technology, particularly in the area of coating or calendering, meant that ink spread during printing was becoming less of an issue.

Type designers had previously tended toward designing their faces with thinner strokes to help compensate for ink spread. Plantin also features a fairly narrow character width, short ascenders and descenders, and a large x-height, so is both space-saving and highly legible at smaller sizes. This made it an extremely popular choice for publication design during the first half of the 20th century. Significantly, the Monotype cut of Plantin was chosen as the principal prototype for Times New Roman, confirming its importance as a model of excellence for space-saving but legible typeface design. This is doubly interesting if you take into account that Pierpont, and Stanley Morison (the man responsible for the development of Times New Roman), were reportedly often not on good terms, with Pierpont regarding the younger Morison as a threat to his authority at Monotype.

Today, Monotype's digital version remains faithful to the original design and has experienced something of a resurgence in popularity after falling out of favor during the latter half of the 20th century. A more condensed version, News Plantin, was developed for London-based newspaper *The Observer* and is now commercially available, as is the even narrower Plantin Headline.

Plantin Regular   Times New Roman Regular

Janson

| **Country of origin:** The Netherlands | **Classification:** Old Style Serif
| **Designer:** Miklós (Nicholas) Kis

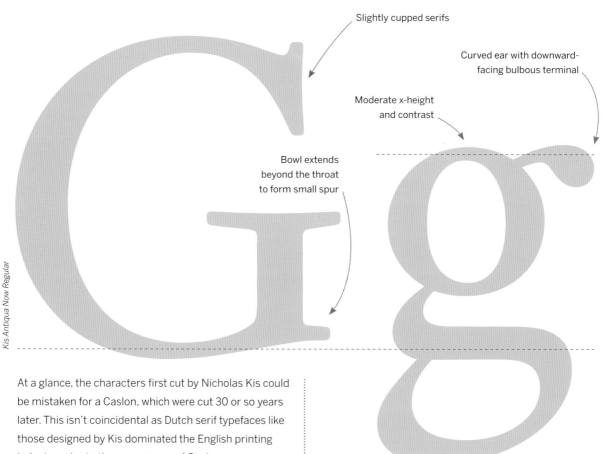

Slightly cupped serifs

Curved ear with downward-facing bulbous terminal

Moderate x-height and contrast

Bowl extends beyond the throat to form small spur

Kis Antiqua Now Regular

At a glance, the characters first cut by Nicholas Kis could be mistaken for a Caslon, which were cut 30 or so years later. This isn't coincidental as Dutch serif typefaces like those designed by Kis dominated the English printing industry prior to the appearance of Caslon.

9/12pt Kis Antiqua Now Regular (Elsner+Flake)

LOREM IPSUM DOLOR SIT AMET, CONSECTETUER ADIPISCING ELIT, SED DIAM nonummy nibh euismod tincidunt ut laoreet dolore magna aliquam erat volutpat. ut wisi enim ad minim veniam, quis nostrud exerci tation ullamcorper suscipit lobortis nisl ut aliquip ex ea commodo consequat. Duis autem vel eum iriure dolor in hendrerit in vulputate velit

12/15pt Kis Antiqua Now Regular (Elsner+Flake)

LOREM IPSUM DOLOR SIT AMET, CONSECTETUER ADIPISCING elit, sed diam nonummy nibh euismod tincidunt ut laoreet dolore magna aliquam erat volutpat. Ut wisi enim ad minim veniam, quis nostrud exerci tation ullamcorper suscipit lobortis nisl ut

Like some of the Garamonds mentioned on the previous spread, Janson is another typeface that ought to be named differently—in this case, it should really be called Kis. Modern revivals of Janson were adapted from type that had for many years been attributed to the 17th-century Dutch punch cutter Anton Janson, but contemporary research has shown that in reality the original punches were cut by a Hungarian punch cutter and printer named Miklós (Nicholas) Kis. Kis spent time in Amsterdam during the 1680s learning the tricks of his chosen trade and unfortunately his subsequent work was somehow linked with Janson, even though the latter worked some 400 miles away in Leipzig, Germany. In the case of some contemporary revivals, the name Janson has stuck, but in recent years the misrepresentation of Kis' work has been addressed.

Kis' original punches survived and in 1919 were acquired by the Stempel foundry in Frankfurt, Germany. They subsequently manufactured matrices for Linotype in 1937, making this version the truest to Kis' original typeface. Stempel had maintained close ties with Linotype since 1900 as one of the principal suppliers of matrices for the Linotype machine, and the project was overseen by the American type designer and Linotype stalwart Chauncey H. Griffith. Around the same time, Monotype released a version of Janson adapted by Sol Hess with input from Bruce Rogers, and it's worth noting that the design of Monotype Ehrhardt, cut between 1937 and 1938, is also derived from Kis' type. Linotype went on to release an update to Janson in 1954 that was redrawn by Hermann Zapf.

There are a couple of worthy digital versions of Janson available today. Linotype's 1985 release, Janson Text, was supervised by Adrian Frutiger and maintains a close link to the original metal type. Alternatively, Kis Antiqua Now, designed by Hildegard Korger and Erhard Kaiser and released in 2008 by Elsner+Flake, is an excellent contemporary interpretation of Kis' classic Dutch Baroque design.

The letterforms of Kis Antiqua Now (in yellow) are geometrically a little more precise than Janson Text, particularly at junctions

Janson Text and Kis Antiqua Now Regular

Caslon

| **Country of origin:** United Kingdom | **Classification:** Old Style Serif
| **Designer:** William Caslon

1725

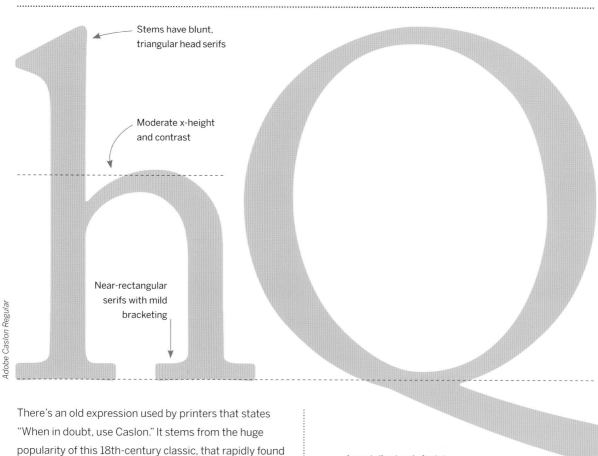

Adobe Caslon Regular

Stems have blunt, triangular head serifs

Moderate x-height and contrast

Near-rectangular serifs with mild bracketing

Long tail extends far into neighboring space

There's an old expression used by printers that states "When in doubt, use Caslon." It stems from the huge popularity of this 18th-century classic, that rapidly found its way into practically every print shop in England and its overseas territories upon its commercial release.

9/12pt Adobe Caslon Regular

LOREM IPSUM DOLOR SIT AMET, CONSECTETUER ADIPISCING ELIT, SED DIAM nonummy nibh euismod tincidunt ut laoreet dolore magna aliquam erat volutpat. ut wisi enim ad minim veniam, quis nostrud exerci tation ullamcorper suscipit lobortis nisl ut aliquip ex ea commodo consequat. Duis autem vel eum iriure dolor in hendrerit in vulputate velit

12/15pt Adobe Caslon Regular

LOREM IPSUM DOLOR SIT AMET, CONSECTETUER ADIPISCING elit, sed diam nonummy nibh euismod tincidunt ut laoreet dolore magna aliquam erat volutpat. ut wisi enim ad minim veniam, quis nostrud exerci tation ullamcorper suscipit lobortis nisl ut aliquip

Caslon is a giant among typefaces and is regarded by many designers as the default choice for a serif typeface when no other comes forward as the more obvious choice. William Caslon, one-time gunsmith and typeface designer, was born in Worcestershire, England, in the early 1690s and moved to London in 1716 to start his business as an engraver and type founder. Caslon is rightly regarded as the father of English type founding; he cut all his own punches, many of which still survive in the collection of the St Bride Library in London, and the veracity of his original typeface has remained intact over the years. There is, however, a raft of variations on the Caslon theme, some of which are far less successful than others, making it a little difficult to keep track of the true Caslon. A face bearing the name Caslon is no guarantee that it will share any genuine links with the original design.

When Caslon's typeface first appeared, in 1725, it was an instant hit and found its way into the collections of printers throughout England, overwhelming the previous dominance of Dutch types. Furthermore, the face gained a rapid foothold throughout the English colonial territories, including America, where it was used to set the Declaration of Independence. Benjamin Franklin was a fan of the face; he met Caslon while visiting London and used it in many of his own publications. After 1858, when Philadelphian type founder Lawrence Johnson acquired duplication rights to Caslon, the face became known as Old Style in the U.S. It was later renamed Caslon Old Style by Henry Lewis Bullen of American Type Founders, following the huge 1892 merger of 23 independent type foundries to form ATF. Caslon, although classified as an Old Style serif, is one of the first typefaces to demonstrate a tendency away from penned shapes, toward the constructed letterforms that characterize Transitional serifs. Some would even argue that Caslon is in fact an early Transitional, predating Baskerville by some 25 years.

Many variations were to follow, often in response to tweaked versions released by rival foundries that claimed to have improved the original design, or to have successfully reproduced a more faithful version of the original. Today, typing Caslon into the search field of a large online retailer such as MyFonts produces 20 separate choices. To help navigate this myriad selection, Adobe Caslon, first drawn by Carol Twombly in 1989 and developed over the following few years, is the best choice if the spirit of the original design is desired.

The larger x-height, sharper serifs and greater contrast of Big Caslon make it more suitable for headline use

Adobe Caslon Regular

Big Caslon Roman

Fournier

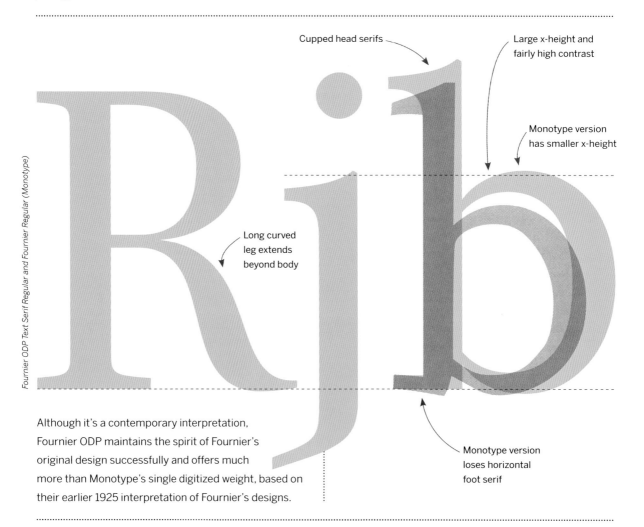

Fournier ODP Text Serif Regular and Fournier Regular (Monotype)

Cupped head serifs

Large x-height and fairly high contrast

Monotype version has smaller x-height

Long curved leg extends beyond body

Monotype version loses horizontal foot serif

Although it's a contemporary interpretation, Fournier ODP maintains the spirit of Fournier's original design successfully and offers much more than Monotype's single digitized weight, based on their earlier 1925 interpretation of Fournier's designs.

9/12pt Fournier ODP Text Serif Regular (Production Type)

LOREM IPSUM DOLOR SIT AMET, CONSECTETUER ADIPISCING ELIT, SED DIAM NONUMMY NIBH euismod tincidunt ut laoreet dolore magna aliquam erat volutpat. ut wisi enim ad minim veniam, quis nostrud exerci tation ullamcorper suscipit lobortis nisl ut aliquip ex ea commodo consequat. Duis autem vel eum iriure dolor in hendrerit in vulputate velit esse molestie

12/15pt Fournier ODP Text Serif Regular (Production Type)

LOREM IPSUM DOLOR SIT AMET, CONSECTETUER ADIPISCING ELIT, SED diam nonummy nibh euismod tincidunt ut laoreet dolore magna aliquam erat volutpat. Ut wisi enim ad minim veniam, quis nostrud exerci tation ullamcorper suscipit lobortis nisl ut aliquip ex ea

Pierre-Simon Fournier, known alternatively as Pierre le Jeune because his father Jean Claude was involved in the same industry, was a highly respected punch cutter and type founder who worked in France during the mid 18th century. Alongside his elegant typeface designs and his early use of initials and ornaments in his work, he devised and introduced the point system for type measurement that we still use today. His typefaces number among the earliest to fall under the Transitional classification, slightly preceding John Baskerville's work in England, if documented dates are to be trusted. One can certainly pick out visual links between the works of the two men when comparing the details of certain letterforms. However, there's an enhanced degree of airy lightness to Fournier's original typefaces; the character widths of his roman style are slightly narrower than Baskerville's and Fournier employs a greater variation of axis, which makes his type feel somewhat more playful on the page without losing its poise.

Until recently, the sole version to be digitized was Monotype's 1925 cut; not an insurmountable problem as, on the whole, it's faithful to the metal version and to the principles of Fournier's original design. There are a few oddities; for some reason the lowercase roman "b" and "d" have lost their flat foot serifs and the curved strokes of the lowercase italic characters feel a little misshapen and angular, but it works all the same. Interestingly, Fournier cut the roman and italic styles with a fairly significant difference in x-height—the italic is smaller—and this feature was faithfully carried over by Monotype so, if you're using Monotype Fournier, mixing roman and italic in one line can create the impression that the italics are set too small. This won't bother everyone but it's something to look out for when setting up your text styling.

However, we should soon have access to a contemporary interpretation of this most classic of Transitional typeface, Fournier ODP, designed by Jean-Baptiste Levée of the French digital foundry Production Type with assistance from Yoann Minet, Mathieu, Laurent Bourcellier and Roxane Gataud. Originally commissioned as the corporate typeface for the Orchestre de Paris (hence the inclusion of ODP in the name), Levée has expanded the original single-weight typeface into a 45-style family with corresponding weights adhering to the same proportions. A full set of sans serifs have been introduced alongside the familiar serifed styles, a Graphique series much closer to a Modern with increased contrast and hairlines is also present, and a set of Gothic styles complete the family. The spirit of Fournier's original work is still very much in evidence, making Fournier ODP a compelling update. Unfortunately at the time of writing the fonts are still licensed exclusively to the Orchestre de Paris, but they should be commercially available at some point in the (hopefully) near future.

Fournier ODP Text Serif Regular and
Fournier ODP Graphique Serif Regular

Fournier ODP Text Sans Regular and
Fournier ODP Graphique Sans Regular

Baskerville

| **Country of origin:** United Kingdom | **Classification:** Transitional Serif
| **Designer:** John Baskerville

1757

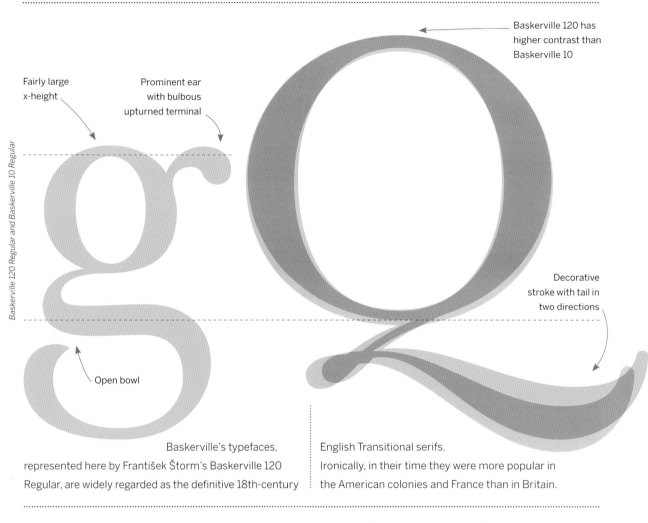

Baskerville 120 has higher contrast than Baskerville 10

Fairly large x-height

Prominent ear with bulbous upturned terminal

Decorative stroke with tail in two directions

Open bowl

Baskerville 120 Regular and Baskerville 10 Regular

Baskerville's typefaces, represented here by František Štorm's Baskerville 120 Regular, are widely regarded as the definitive 18th-century English Transitional serifs.

Ironically, in their time they were more popular in the American colonies and France than in Britain.

9/12pt Baskerville 10 Regular (Storm)

LOREM IPSUM DOLOR SIT AMET, CONSECTETUER ADIPISCING ELIT, SED diam nonummy nibh euismod tincidunt ut laoreet dolore magna aliquam erat volutpat. Ut wisi enim ad minim veniam, quis nostrud exerci tation ullamcorper suscipit lobortis nisl ut aliquip ex ea commodo consequat. Duis autem vel eum iriure

12/15pt Baskerville 10 Regular (Storm)

LOREM IPSUM DOLOR SIT AMET, CONSECTETUER adipiscing elit, sed diam nonummy nibh euismod tincidunt ut laoreet dolore magna aliquam erat volutpat. Ut wisi enim ad minim veniam, quis nostrud exerci tation ullamcorper

John Baskerville was born in Worcestershire, England, in 1706 and was essentially an 18th-century entrepreneur as type founding was not his sole area of business. He involved himself in various enterprises, one being the lucrative manufacture of Japanese-style lacquerwork, which made him a wealthy man, but it's for his printing and typeface design endeavors that he's best remembered. Basing himself in Birmingham, an important center for commerce both then and now, Baskerville established his printing business around 1750 and embarked on a project to improve the styling of the dominant Dutch-influenced typefaces of the time, such as Caslon. The driving force behind his ideas was his own work in improving the technology behind both paper and ink manufacturing. He embraced the newly invented technique (pioneered by James Whatman) for making wove paper, which was much smoother than laid paper, and created his own ink that was much blacker and more opaque than the offerings from other suppliers. He also modified his printing process, introducing heated copper rollers that dried the ink more quickly and lessened the effect of ink soak, allowing the letterforms to hold their shapes more readily. Bringing these elements together created a call for a finer typeface with sharper serifs and an increased contrast between the thickest and thinnest strokes.

Baskerville designed his first typeface in the early 1750s and oversaw the cutting, which was carried out by the punch cutter John Handy. As well as refining overall detail, his design pulled the axis of the rounded letterforms to a more upright position. This represents the first step toward the Rational styles of Bodoni and Didot that emerged at the end of the 18th century, and the first English serif face to be classified as Transitional—the bridge between the Old Style and Rational (or Modern) serifs. Ironically, not everyone approved of the new style of typeface; in a letter to Baskerville from his friend Benjamin Franklin (who seemed to know everybody at that time) it was reported that one individual complained that "the Strokes of your Letters being too thin and narrow, hurt the eye, and he could never read a Line of them without Pain …" However, the face was extremely successful, particularly in France and the U.S. if not initially at home in the British Isles.

Just about every digital type foundry that ever did business created a version of Baskerville at one time or another, and many fall a little short of the qualities of the original. However, František Štorm of the Czech Republic-based digital foundry Storm has designed a well-crafted version, with several optical size choices, that captures much of the refined yet full-bodied feel of the original.

ITC's version differs considerably from Storm's offering, particularly in the styling of the numerals

Cw27Cw27

ITC New Baskerville Roman

Baskerville 120 Regular

Bell

| **Country of origin:** United Kingdom | **Classification:** Rational Serif
| **Designer:** Richard Austin

1788

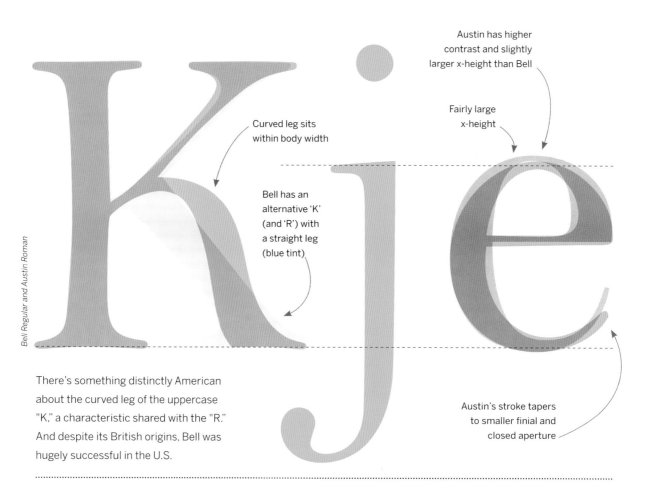

Bell Regular and Austin Roman

Austin has higher contrast and slightly larger x-height than Bell

Fairly large x-height

Curved leg sits within body width

Bell has an alternative 'K' (and 'R') with a straight leg (blue tint)

Austin's stroke tapers to smaller finial and closed aperture

There's something distinctly American about the curved leg of the uppercase "K," a characteristic shared with the "R." And despite its British origins, Bell was hugely successful in the U.S.

9/12pt Austin Text Roman No.2 (Commercial Type)

LOREM IPSUM DOLOR SIT AMET, CONSECTETUER ADIPISCING ELIT, SED DIAM NONUMMY NIBH euismod tincidunt ut laoreet dolore magna aliquam erat volutpat. ut wisi enim ad minim veniam, quis nostrud exerci tation ullamcorper suscipit lobortis nisl ut aliquip ex ea commodo consequat. Duis autem vel eum iriure dolor in hendrerit in vulputate velit esse molestie consequat, vel

12/15pt Austin Text Roman No.2 (Commercial Type)

LOREM IPSUM DOLOR SIT AMET, CONSECTETUER ADIPISCING ELIT, sed diam nonummy nibh euismod tincidunt ut laoreet dolore magna aliquam erat volutpat. Ut wisi enim ad minim veniam, quis nostrud exerci tation ullamcorper suscipit lobortis nisl ut aliquip ex ea

The Rational serif Bell is regarded as the first British Modern; Stanley Morison described it this way when Monotype revived the face in 1932 and the distinction has been accepted ever since. Bell was first cut in 1788 by Richard Austin for the printer and publisher John Bell. Born in London, Austin had trained as a wood engraver before he joined Bell's type founding operation as a punch cutter, and after spending 10 years with the firm he went on to cut Scotch Roman for William Miller's Edinburgh foundry some 25 years later. Bell was an instant hit and sold well on both sides of the Atlantic, enjoying particular success in the publishing houses of Boston and Philadelphia during the late 18th and early 19th centuries.

As mentioned above, Monotype manufactured a version of Bell that was released in England in 1932, and Lanston Monotype followed with a U.S. release a few years later in 1940. Interestingly, Lanston marketed the face as a more refined reworking of Scotch Roman, which for me effectively describes the feel of the original Bell. While the letterforms share many shape characteristics, Bell displays a little less contrast than Scotch Roman and is slightly narrower, creating a slightly paler color when set as running text.

The face is particularly useful for evoking an American feel, given its runaway success in the U.S. following its first release in 1788. The digital version of Monotype's 1932 release is a decent facsimile of the original, particularly when one uses the alternate swash variants for the italic uppercase characters. However, as an alternative you may like to take a look at Austin from Commercial Type, a digital foundry launched as a joint venture between Paul Barnes and Christian Schwartz. Named for its original creator, Austin was designed for the British style magazine *Harpers & Queen*. It's described on Commercial's site as a loose revival of Richard Austin's typefaces and while it doesn't claim to be a steadfastly accurate revival of Bell, it does include the horizontal top serifs on the lowercase, that Monotype's version lacks. Plus, it has a slightly more modern sheen to it that may be more appropriate for some projects. There is also a useful hairline weight.

Some glyph options for Bell Italic

The same options for Austin Text Italic

Bodoni

| **Country of origin:** Italy | **Classification:** Rational Serif
| **Designer:** Giambattista Bodoni

*c.*1790

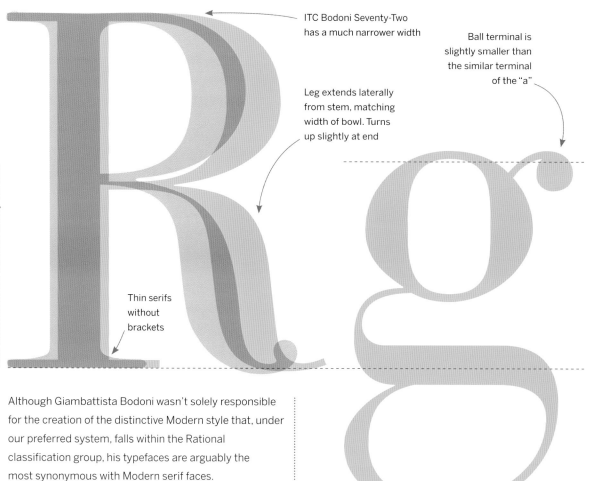

Bauer Bodoni Roman and ITC Bodoni Seventy-Two Book

ITC Bodoni Seventy-Two has a much narrower width

Ball terminal is slightly smaller than the similar terminal of the "a"

Leg extends laterally from stem, matching width of bowl. Turns up slightly at end

Thin serifs without brackets

Although Giambattista Bodoni wasn't solely responsible for the creation of the distinctive Modern style that, under our preferred system, falls within the Rational classification group, his typefaces are arguably the most synonymous with Modern serif faces.

9/12pt ITC Bodoni Six Book

LOREM IPSUM DOLOR SIT AMET, CONSECTETUER ADIPISCING ELIT, SED diam nonummy nibh euismod tincidunt ut laoreet dolore magna aliquam erat volutpat. Ut wisi enim ad minim veniam, quis nostrud exerci tation ullamcorper suscipit lobortis nisl ut aliquip ex ea commodo consequat. Duis autem

12/15pt ITC Bodoni Twelve Book

LOREM IPSUM DOLOR SIT AMET, CONSECTETUER ADIPISCING ELIT, sed diam nonummy nibh euismod tincidunt ut laoreet dolore magna aliquam erat volutpat. Ut wisi enim ad minim veniam, quis nostrud exerci tation ullamcorper suscipit lobortis nisl ut

Giambattista Bodoni was born in Saluzzo, a town and former province in the Piedmont region of Italy, in February, 1740. Both his father and grandfather worked in the printing trade and at the age of 18 he moved to Rome to work as a pupil at the Vatican's Propoganda Fide (Propagation of the Faith) printing house. He relocated to Parma in 1768, where he masterminded the establishment of Parma's ducal printers, the Stamperia Reale, under the employment of Duke Ferdinand of Bourbon-Parma. His rapid success and considerable output (more than 25,000 of his original punches are preserved in Parma's Bodoni Museum) led to the establishment of his own print shop in 1791, Officina Bodoni. His earliest typefaces were inspired by the work of Pierre-Simon Fournier and he was an admirer of John Baskerville (see page 23), but by the early 1790s he had moved away from the Transitional style toward the more geometric style that we now call Modern. His beautiful typefaces, typified by a high contrast and vertical axis with abrupt hairline serifs and a small x-height, are considered to be among the earliest Rational serif faces. Look for a very subtle bracketing of the serifs, a detail omitted from a number of later copies, to identify a classic Bodoni-inspired face.

There have been numerous attempts over the years to capture the essence of Bodoni's elegant letterforms in the digital format but, as per usual, not all of them have been totally successful. However, in the case of Bodoni there are two that stand out; one is better suited for setting running text and general publication design, whereas the other is more suitable for stand-alone applications such as packaging designs or poster work. For text setting, go for ITC Bodoni, designed by Janice Fishman, Holly Goldsmith, Jim Parkinson and Sumner Stone in 1994. It's drawn from three specific sizes of the metal type; size Six for smaller running text and captions, size Twelve for larger text, and size Seventy-Two for display and headline setting. The text weights feature a reduction in the contrast from sizes Twelve to Six to ensure the hairline serifs don't disappear when the type is set at small point sizes, whereas size Seventy-Two ramps up the contrast considerably and displays a much narrower width to increase the character count per line.

For anything else Bodoni-related take a look at Bauer Bodoni, a version that represents Bodoni's original ideas more typically. The digital version is available from Adobe and is a good facsimile of the Bauer Foundry's metal type, designed by Heinrich Jost in 1926. Its moderate x-height and narrow width means it works well at larger sizes, but it isn't recommended for setting text as the fine serifs can break up when printed.

Moderate contrast compared to the Seventy-Two weight

Thicker serifs are slightly irregular for Six

A much higher contrast compared to the Six weight, with increased vertical stress and a narrower body

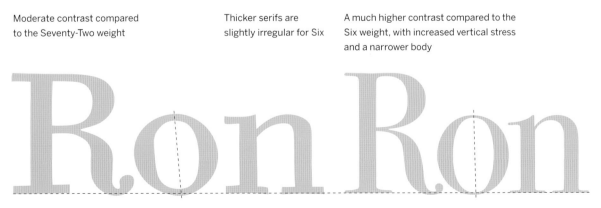

ITC Bodoni Six Roman

ITC Bodoni Seventy-Two Roman

Walbaum

| **Country of origin:** Germany | **Classification:** Rational Serif
| **Designer:** Justus Erich Walbaum

*c.*1805

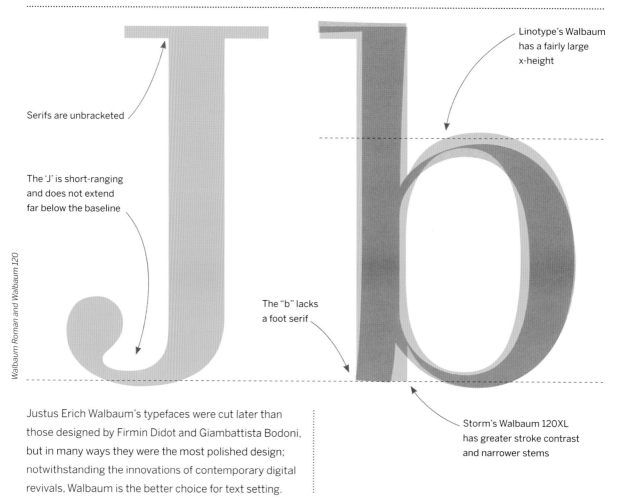

Serifs are unbracketed

The 'J' is short-ranging and does not extend far below the baseline

Walbaum Roman and Walbaum 120

Linotype's Walbaum has a fairly large x-height

The "b" lacks a foot serif

Storm's Walbaum 120XL has greater stroke contrast and narrower stems

Justus Erich Walbaum's typefaces were cut later than those designed by Firmin Didot and Giambattista Bodoni, but in many ways they were the most polished design; notwithstanding the innovations of contemporary digital revivals, Walbaum is the better choice for text setting.

9/12pt Walbaum Roman (Linotype)

LOREM IPSUM DOLOR SIT AMET, CONSECTETUER ADIPISCING ELIT, SED DIAM nonummy nibh euismod tincidunt ut laoreet dolore magna aliquam erat volutpat. Ut wisi enim ad minim veniam, quis nostrud exerci tation ullamcorper suscipit lobortis nisl ut aliquip ex ea commodo consequat. Duis autem

12/15pt Walbaum Roman (Linotype)

LOREM IPSUM DOLOR SIT AMET, CONSECTETUER ADIPISCING elit, sed diam nonummy nibh euismod tincidunt ut laoreet dolore magna aliquam erat volutpat. Ut wisi enim ad minim veniam, quis nostrud exerci tation ullamcorper

From around 1784, so perhaps slightly earlier than Giambattista Bodoni (or Richard Austin, for that matter), a French type founder named Firmin Didot was also producing and using Rational serif typefaces. His faces generally featured slightly finer hairlines, flatter top serifs, and no bracketing where a hairline meets a serif. It's on Didot's, rather than Bodoni's, work that Walbaum is more closely based.

Justus Erich Walbaum was a self-taught German punch cutter who in the late 1790s purchased the established type foundry of Ernst Wilhelm Kircher in Goslar. In 1802, Goslar became part of the Kingdom of Prussia, prompting Walbaum to relocate to Weimar where his business continued to flourish. Around a century later, in 1919, a number of Walbaum's original matrices were acquired by the Berthold foundry, making their metal version of his typeface a true original. Berthold's version was introduced to the English market by the Curwen Press in 1925 and a Monotype version followed shortly afterward in 1934.

A comparison of the digitized versions of Berthold Walbaum and Monotype Walbaum reveals two distinctly different typefaces, despite the fact that they're both based on Walbaum's original designs. The visual differences come about because each is based on type cut by Walbaum at different point sizes. Monotype Walbaum was derived from a 10-point sample and is considerably lighter and smaller on the body than Berthold Walbaum, which is now sold as Linotype Walbaum. The latter was based on a 16-point sample but ironically it tends to be the more common choice for text setting, as visually, it's a little more typical of a Walbaum original and it colors darker on the page. Either way, among the classic Modern serifs Walbaum is generally considered to be a better choice for text setting than a Bodoni or a Didot because of its lower contrast; it is less likely to break up when printed at smaller point sizes.

A newer version of Walbaum designed by František Štorm of digital type foundry Storm, Walbaum 2010, was released a few years ago. His ideas produced a range of styles split over two optical sizes: Walbaum 10 for setting from 6-point to around 30-point type, and Walbaum 120 Pro for anything larger than 30-point. Both sizes are accompanied by corresponding XL styles that feature a slightly larger x-height, and to round things off there is Walbaum Grotesk, a brand new idea for a complementary Grotesque sans with metrics that align perfectly with the 120XL styles. Storm's design doesn't attempt to modernize or duplicate the original design, but rather to offer a newly interpreted solution for use in both text and headline setting.

Linotype's Walbaum is fairly sturdy with moderate contrast

Monotype's Walbaum is more fragile with less contrast. The serifs are slightly irregular

Rafgy Rafgy

Walbaum Roman (Linotype)

Walbaum Regular (Monotype)

Scotch Roman

| **Country of origin:** United Kingdom | **Classification:** Rational Serif
| **Designer:** Richard Austin

1813

Serifs are bracketed

High contrast, aligning the Scotch Roman alongside Moderns under the Rational Serif classification

Miller is narrower on the body and features an alternative "R" with a more prominent upturned tail

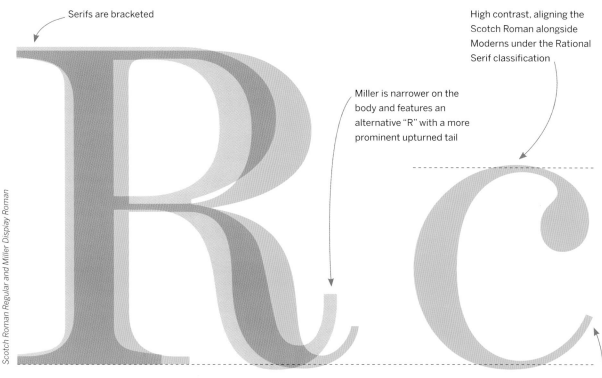

Scotch Roman Regular and Miller Display Roman

Monotype's digital release Scotch Roman is based on the first modern adaptation of 1903, which in turn was based on Miller's specimen sheet of 1813. A progression of earlier Modern styles, Scotch Roman was enormously influential throughout the 19th century.

The outstroke of the "c" and "e" end slightly beyond the body to create a more circular letterform

9/12pt Scotch Roman (Monotype)

LOREM IPSUM DOLOR SIT AMET, CONSECTETUER ADIPISCING ELIT, SED diam nonummy nibh euismod tincidunt ut laoreet dolore magna aliquam erat volutpat, ut wisi enim ad minim veniam, quis nostrud exerci tation ullamcorper suscipit lobortis nisl ut aliquip ex ea commodo consequat. Duis autem vel eum iriure dolor

12/15pt Scotch Roman (Monotype)

LOREM IPSUM DOLOR SIT AMET, CONSECTETUER ADIPISCING elit, sed diam nonummy nibh euismod tincidunt ut laoreet dolore magna aliquam erat volutpat. Ut wisi enim ad minim veniam, quis nostrud exerci tation ullamcorper suscipit lobortis nisl

Is it a typeface, or is it a typographic classification? Well, the term Scotch Roman is certainly used as a general description for a style of Rational serif popular during the early half of the 19th century, particularly in the U.S., despite its British origins. However, a typeface by the name of Scotch Roman also exists, so the answer is—both.

There are a couple of theories regarding the precise derivation of the typeface Scotch Roman. This is not especially unusual per se, but it's important to cite both possible sources for a style that inspired so many other popular faces from the period, creating a subclassification for Rational serifs in the process. The earliest source is the Edinburgh type foundry of William Miller; a specimen sheet printed by the foundry in 1813 features a Rational serif that is believed to be the work of Richard Austin, the punch cutter responsible for Bell. Some 20 years or so later, a second possible source emerges; the Glasgow foundry of Alexander Wilson & Son, which cut and manufactured a typeface sharing many of the characteristics of Miller's earlier typeface. Contemporary versions of Scotch Roman could potentially be considered as derivations of both the above sources as there's little to distinguish one from the other when studying printed samples, but given that Miller's face is the earliest it gets my vote as the original.

The first contemporary version was adapted from Miller's specimen sheet and manufactured in 1903 by the New York foundry of A.D. Farmer and Sons, a business that went on to become part of the giant American Type Founders. This is the first instance of the term "Scotch Roman" entering common use after a much earlier (although different) design for a Rational serif by Boston type founder Samuel Nelson Dickinson had been known as "Scotch-face." A Monotype version from 1908, based on the A.D. Farmer face, included modified cuts for larger display sizes and in 1924 Sol Hess designed Scotch Roman Italic. Linotype also had their own version of Scotch Roman, marketed from 1931 as Scotch No.2.

Monotype's digital version is acceptable enough but its uses are limited, notwithstanding the fact that there are only the two styles that struggle a little at smaller text sizes because of their fairly high contrast. For greater flexibility it's worth looking at Miller, designed by Matthew Carter with Tobias Frere-Jones and Cyrus Highsmith for Font Bureau and released in 1997. The face is by no means a facsimile of the earlier Scotch Roman, but rather a rethinking of the style to match the requirements of the modern publishing industry. The family includes optical sizes for both text and display settings, plus some additional specialist variations designed specifically for publication design.

Miller is more robust than Scotch Roman, with a moderate contrast

Straight legs feature in Monotype's Scotch Roman

Miller Text Roman

Scotch Roman

Clarendon

| **Country of origin:** United Kingdom | **Classification:** Grotesque Slab
| **Designer:** Robert Besley

1845

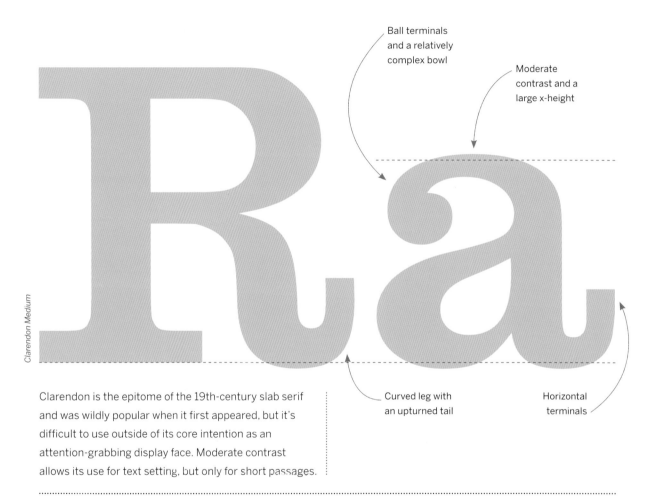

Clarendon Medium

Ball terminals and a relatively complex bowl

Moderate contrast and a large x-height

Curved leg with an upturned tail

Horizontal terminals

Clarendon is the epitome of the 19th-century slab serif and was wildly popular when it first appeared, but it's difficult to use outside of its core intention as an attention-grabbing display face. Moderate contrast allows its use for text setting, but only for short passages.

18pt Clarendon Medium (Linotype)

Rcyrg237

36pt Clarendon Medium (Linotype)

Rcyrg237

72pt Clarendon Medium (Linotype)

Rcyrg237

Like Scotch Roman on the previous spread, Clarendon can be used to describe a subclassification of the larger Grotesque slab group that commonly features heavy, bracketed serifs and ball terminals. The original Clarendon was designed by Robert Besley and cut by Benjamin Fox in 1845 for London-based R. Besley & Co., previously the Fann Street Foundry. The success of this proclamatory typeface was swift; it became the substance of Victorian era poster typography and was copied by many other foundries once the patent (the first ever applied to a typeface design) had expired after only 3 years. This rapid take-up for Clarendon-style typefaces on both sides of the Atlantic contributed to the name of the original font becoming the byword for all those cut in the style.

The original Clarendon was designed to operate as a display face from the very beginning and was normally paired with completely different fonts for text; the idea of creating large typeface families with a broad range of weights and styles for integrated use still hadn't taken hold in the mid 19th century. Even today it has a limited number of truly useful weights, none of which include an italic, and it only works properly at relatively large point sizes so is a no-go area for the majority of situations where smaller text setting is required. Perhaps this contributed to its falling out of fashion by the end of the 19th century. However, by the 1950s its popularity had increased once more and in 1953 English foundry Stephenson Blake issued a sloped version that they named Consort. A condensed roman version of Consort, designed by Steve Jackaman, survives today in digital format. Other notable revivals include the Eduard Hoffmann and Hermann Eidenbenz design for the Swiss Haas Foundry from 1953, now available in digital format from Linotype, and Craw Clarendon, Freeman Craw's 1955 version for American Type Founders.

There have been several attempts to further address the limitations of Clarendon since the advent of digital type. David Berlow of The Font Bureau designed the eight-style family Belizio, based on Haas Clarendon via Aldo Novarese's 1955 typeface Egizio, in 1998, and a similar offering that takes its inspiration from the same source material was drawn by Patrick Griffin of Canada Type in 2007. However, the most complete digital family available today is arguably Sentinel, released by Hoefler & Co. in 2009. It includes 12 styles—six weights from Light through to Black—and was designed to be used flexibly for both display and text setting. It doesn't claim to be a faithful revival (serifs are unbracketed) but rather offers a contemporary solution in the spirit of the 19th century.

Clarendon has bracketed serifs that are lighter than the stems

Sentinel has unbracketed serifs that are lighter than the stems

Each weight of Sentinel includes a "true" italic style, atypical of a traditional Grotesque slab

Clarendon Medium

Sentinel Semi Bold

Sentinel Semi Bold Italic

A Line of Type

Johannes Gutenberg's role in bringing together the technologies of the hand-operated screw-press, oil-based inks and movable type in the mid 15th century marks the emergence of the first practical system for reproducing text on a relatively large scale. His original techniques were improved on during the following decades, enhanced by advances in the quality of both ink and paper, but the skills required to cut the punches for each character and to cast the type, and the hand compositing skills required to set type, changed very little over the next 400 years.

An individual piece of type, known as a sort, was made by handcutting a punch consisting of a steel peg with the letter or glyph cut in relief and in reverse at one end. Punch cutting was a highly skilled profession that could take years to master, and many of the early typefaces were cut by established engravers working in conjunction with the typeface's designer. Considering how labor intensive and skillful the punch cutting process was, original punches were extremely valuable and closely guarded by their owners. To make a sort, the punch was first driven into a copper bar at a precise depth to form a matrix that was then inserted into an adjustable and reusable mold for casting. The two-part molds could be set to different widths, meaning the width of each sort could be adjusted in order to determine inter-character spacing. In the early days of movable type the casting was often done by the printers themselves; specialist foundries commissioning their own typefaces for sale under license appeared later as the demand for fonts grew. The exceptions to this process were larger display fonts that were sometimes cast in sand molds or simply carved from wooden blocks.

Did you ever wonder why capitals are referred to as uppercase and small letters as lowercase? Once the sorts were ready for use, they had to be arranged in a regulated way so a compositor could easily identify and select each character. This problem was solved through the use of a type drawer, or case, divided into a set of standardized compartments that each contained a specific letter or glyph. When in use, the case containing the capitals was placed in a rack above the case containing the small letters, hence the terms uppercase and lowercase. The compositor would select the individual sorts and arrange them in rows on a special tray called a composing stick; words were separated by blank spacers and strips of metal or wood (called leads) were sometimes inserted between lines to provide greater interlinear spacing, or leading. All of this was ultimately assembled as a page in a special tray or frame called a galley, which was placed directly on the press for proofing and then printing. The term galley proof is derived from this and is still used today to describe running text that requires an editorial check prior to layout and production.

By the beginning of the 19th century the design of printing presses had improved with the introduction of mechanized iron hand presses. Initially these were still hand operated but were capable of producing a much cleaner single impression—older wooden presses often needed several step-by-step impressions to produce a solid image. However, steam-driven presses using a cylinder instead of a platen were introduced as early as 1814. Increasing production rates created a demand for a more efficient typesetting system, and by the late 1880s not one but two solutions had emerged— the Linotype and Monotype hot metal typesetting machines.

The machines were developed independently of one another at around the same time in the U.S.; the Linotype was invented by Ottmar Mergenthaler, a German immigrant based in Baltimore, and the Monotype by Tolbert Lanston in Washington. Both machines used a broadly similar approach; instead of simply automating the hand-composition process using precast sorts, they used matrices to cast fresh type for each new job. The term "hot metal" is derived from the fact that, once each print run was completed, the used type was melted down and reused, providing the additional advantage of no longer having to laboriously distribute individual sorts back into their type cases. There were a couple of significant differences between the machines. The Linotype was an all-in-one keyboard-driven device that assembled matrices from a preloaded magazine before casting each line of type as a solid slug (or a "line o' type," hence the name). Once each line had been cast, an assembly arm collected the matrices and sorted them back into the top of the magazine, ready to be used again. Putting together galleys with Linotype slugs was a quick and easy process, but the Linotype had a downside; proof corrections were difficult to make as complete lines (and often full paragraphs) had to be reset from scratch—a compositor couldn't simply adjust a few sorts by hand. This might be why the Linotype was popular with newspapers that needed a quick turnaround and were less concerned about the odd typo. Additionally, Linotype setting on a solid slug couldn't be kerned; the machines could cast two different weights in any one line but only if they were exactly the same width. Most typefaces needed a redraw in order to work on the system, leading to visual compromises where italics often looked too wide and bolds appeared too narrow.

Unlike the Linotype, the Monotype machine had two separate components: a keyboard with a punch system that output coordinates to a paper spool, and a completely separate casting machine. Once a galley had been input by the keyboard operator, the paper spool (annotated with information about font choice and point size) was transferred to a caster. Rather than a magazine-style loading system, each Monotype font was arranged in a matrix case, a grid of matrices with standardized coordinates for each character that corresponded to the punched coordinates on the paper spool. The matrix case moved rapidly above an adjustable mold while each separate matrix was propelled downward into the mold by a pin using compressed air. The freshly cast sorts were then assembled into lines of type, ready to be brought together in a galley for proofing. The technical restraints imposed by the Linotype machine didn't apply to the Monotype system; significantly, type could be spaced (or kerned) more flexibly and the widths of different styles didn't have to match.

There were a few additional advantages to the Monotype system, despite it being slower than the Linotype. First, having separate keyboards and casters meant a production line using extra casters could be kept busy by fewer keyboard operators. Second, paper spools could be stored and reused or sent to other locations to produce the same galleys of text without being re-keyed. Third, Monotype casters could also be used to manufacture extra sorts for hand compositing and proof correction.

On that subject, both machines, particularly the Linotype, needed a large number of matrices to operate proficiently. Handcut punches (which couldn't last for ever and would eventually wear down or break) couldn't be made quickly enough to meet demand so a more efficient

manufacturing method was needed. It was provided by a Milwaukee-based type founder named Linn Boyd Benton, who came up with the idea of a matrix and punch cutting machine that used a pantograph to control a very fine engraving drill while the operator traced character outlines from large-scale drawings. The invention sped up the punch cutting process considerably and the technique was simple enough for operators to master without years of practice. As usual, there was a downside; punch cutters working at actual size would introduce small variations for faces cut at different point sizes (such as slightly larger counters in smaller point sizes to prevent them filling in when printed), but this couldn't happen if only one set of master drawings was used to cut all the point sizes for one typeface. The more conscientious manufacturers produced extra sets of drawings to compensate, but not everyone was quite so scrupulous. However, the machine provided a means for many more type designers to get their typefaces manufactured, a fundamental element in the evolution of typeface design.

Ultimately, hot metal type-casters were hugely successful and it was only the advent of phototypesetting in the 1950s to 1960s that began to push the technology aside. Linotype and Monotype manufactured their last hot metal machines in the 1970s when phototypesetting technology had extended to smaller users and the commercial demand for hot metal type disappeared. Furthermore, by this time letterpress printing had largely been replaced by offset lithography, so metal type was no longer fully compatible with the modern printing plant. Despite this, there are still many machines around the world that are kept in good working order by museums and enthusiastic individuals, and type purists still maintain that the finest quality typesetting is that produced using hot metal or hand-composed foundry type.

Rudolf Koch

In the early 20th century, German type foundries were world leaders in terms of innovative typeface design, and Frankfurt's Bauer type foundry was particularly advanced in its support of commissioning new designs from artists and graphic designers rather than type specialists. Lucien Bernhard's eponymous faces, Emil Rudolf Weiss' Weiss Antiqua and Paul Renner's Futura are notable examples. The commercial production of these designs as fully developed typefaces was usually completed by craftsmen employed by the foundry, but Rudolf Koch provides us with a notable exception to this practice; as a type designer he spent most of his career working as an employee of the Klingspor foundry in Offenbach and personally drafted and cut all of his typeface designs.

Born in Nuremberg in 1876, Koch was a gifted calligrapher who had several years of experience as a freelance designer by the time he joined the staff at Klingspor in 1906. He'd mastered the art of broadpen calligraphy while eking out a living as a freelancer in Leipzig, and his skills marked him out when he answered the advertisement for the position at Klingspor. At least half of Koch's designs were blackletter faces derived from his own lettering style, with the marvelous Wilhem Klingspor Schrift representing the pinnacle of his achievements in this area. However, by the late 1920s the blackletter tradition was waning in Germany and the modernist influence of the Bauhaus (not initially favored by Koch) heralded a sea-change for German type foundries. Overcoming his own personal reservations, Koch designed the Geometric sans serif face Kabel, a massive stylistic departure that he was said to have ultimately enjoyed. Kabel manages to feel somewhat livelier than most other Geometric sans faces of the time, which bears testament to Koch's skills as a calligrapher as well as a type designer, and remains a timeless and popular choice.

As a type designer Koch is interesting because (with the possible exception of Kabel) his faces were on the whole roughly hewn; he never lost his flair for the free-flow calligraphic style he came from and his type designs reflect this. They may not all be perfect, but they never lack personality. He stayed with Klingspor for the remainder of his life, despite lucrative offers from other foundries. He stated that the creative and collaborative support of foundry owner Carl Klingspor was worth far more to him than any question of business and he would never seek another position, a resolve that he stuck to until his death in 1934.

Eric Gill

Arthur Eric Rowton Gill was many things: a stone carver, sculptor, engraver, illustrator, print maker, essayist and, of course, type designer. He was also a controversial figure and something of a sexual predator, according to Fiona MacCarthy's excellent 1989 biography, but I'll stick to the less salacious side of his achievements. Gill was born in Brighton, England, in 1882 and showed artistic promise at an early age. He attended art school in Chichester and later, in London, attended lettering classes given by Edward Johnston, the designer of the famous typeface used to this day by London Underground. His apprenticeship at the architecture practice of W.H. Caroë, architect to the Ecclesiastical Commissioners in Westminster, led to letter-carving commissions and soon afterwards Gill embarked on his lifelong career as a freelance craftsman.

Gill established workshops in various locations during his career, moving from his first in London's Hammersmith to Ditchling in East Sussex in 1907. It was here that he further developed his talent for sculpture and commissions from prestigious clients such as the BBC and Westminster Cathedral made him famous. By 1924 Gill had tired of the artistic community that had grown around him in Ditchling and moved to a remote abandoned monastery in the Welsh mountains at Capel-y-ffin. It was here that he produced his designs for Perpetua, after prolonged insistence from Stanley Morison at Monotype. At first Gill had been reluctant to become commercially involved with Morison, saying that typography was "not his country," but Morison wanted unique new typefaces to add to the Monotype repertoire of classic revivals and he saw Gill as the man to provide them. Gill was persuaded by the argument that the finest typefaces were the result of the expertise of the artisan punch cutters, honed over centuries of artistic endeavor, a view that appealed to his sense of place as a carver. Gill clearly changed his mind about typography during this period, as he began to design characters for a number of clients including Army & Navy Stores, and in 1926 painted the signage for the Bristol bookshop owned by Douglas Cleverdon. Morison was acquainted with Cleverdon and happened to see Gill's work, which led to the commission that became the famous Gill Sans.

By 1928 Gill had moved once again to Pigotts, a farmhouse near High Wycombe in Buckinghamshire, so he could be nearer to his London clients, and designed his other best known face Joanna for use at Hague & Gill, the failed printing firm he established with his son-in-law René Hague. It was his personal favorite—he called it "type with no frills"—and it was eventually released commercially by Monotype in 1958. Several further faces followed, but none have stood the test of time as well as his earlier efforts, which in the case of Gill Sans represents one of the most successful sans serifs faces ever designed. Gill died in Middlesex, in 1940.

Morris Fuller Benton

By all accounts, Morris Fuller Benton was a very unassuming and retiring character, but in reality he was the most prolific type designer of the early 20th century. In terms of his output, he is rivaled only by the likes of contemporary designers such as Tobias Frere-Jones; he designed 221 typefaces covering 23 separate families, many of which were revivals of historical classics, between 1900 and his retirement in 1937. To put this in context, he produced around twice as many faces as Frederic Goudy, yet Goudy was a high profile "name" in the typographic sphere; Benton simply preferred to keep his head down and get on with his work.

Morris Fuller Benton was the son of Linn Boyd Benton, the inventor (among many other innovative typesetting technologies) of the Benton Pantograph, an engraving machine that revolutionized the production of matrices for the new Linotype typesetting machines. The Pantograph was capable of scaling a single engineered drawing of a character to produce a variety of font sizes, and could also condense, expand and slant the design. Benton Sr. headed up the type design department of the newly established conglomerate American Type Founders and Morris Fuller joined his father there in 1896, taking over as senior in-house designer in 1900. The fact that Benton Sr. continued working for ATF for many more years

may have served to enhance the anonymity of the younger Benton's work, but it certainly didn't suppress the volume of his contribution to the ATF catalog. The pair were close and were known to walk to and from work together until Linn Boyd's retirement (only two weeks prior to his death) in 1932.

Aside from his design work, Morris Fuller Benton is credited as the originator of the typeface family concept. In the earliest days of type design different faces with similar attributes were paired visually, regardless of who designed them, particularly in the case of choosing an italic to complement a roman. Benton's accreditation isn't strictly true, but he certainly produced much of his work by adding complementary weights and styles to existing faces—for example, he drew 18 variations of Century which was his father's sole type design—so contributed heavily to the promotion of the idea of the cohesively designed family. Despite his large output, Benton is arguably best known for his earliest work which included Franklin Gothic and News Gothic, classic sans serif faces that became the mainstay of American typesetting for years and are still enormously popular today. Benton died in 1948.

Beatrice Warde

A group photograph taken at a lunch party for ATF's senior archivist and librarian Henry Lewis Bullen. Beatrice Warde is seated next to Bullen in the front row. From The Inland Printer, *January 1924.*

Technically speaking, Beatrice Warde shouldn't get a mention here as she wasn't a type designer. However, I wanted to include her because her overall contribution to typeface design is as great as, and perhaps even greater than, many professional type designers. Warde was born Beatrice Becker in New York in 1900, and developed a fascination for calligraphy at an early age. This interest grew throughout her time at college to encompass all forms of typography and type design and, through a connection with the designer Bruce Rogers (see page 76), Warde was appointed to the post of assistant librarian for American Type Founders following her graduation.

Her principal task involved assisting Henry Lewis Bullen, ATF's senior archivist, in the compilation of the company's extensive specimen books. The position allowed Warde to build an encyclopedic knowledge of typefaces and type design, which would serve her well throughout her developing career as a communicator on all things typographic. Warde worked for ATF for 4 years, marrying the talented printer and type designer Frederic Warde in 1922 just a year after joining the company. The Wardes moved to Europe in 1925 to engage in further typographic studies, but a year later their marriage ended. They divorced in 1926, but the break-up was amicable and the pair remained on fair terms until Warde's early death in New York at the age of 45.

In the 1920s it was extremely rare to find a woman working in the male-dominated typographic industry; in a group portrait taken in 1923 at a lunch party in honor of Bullen, Warde is the only female among the 37 people in the photograph. This explains why her first contributions to British typography journal *The Fleuron*, commissioned by founder Stanley Morison, were written under the male pen-name Paul Beaujon; she felt her opinions wouldn't otherwise be taken seriously. It was during this time that Warde uncovered the evidence that connected the work of punch cutter Jean Jannon to several contemporary versions of Garamond, the sources of which had been incorrectly attributed to specimens thought to have been produced by Claude Garamond. The executives at Monotype were so impressed that they invited "Paul Beaujon" to edit their corporate magazine *The Monotype Recorder*, and Morison didn't divulge Warde's secret until she arrived at the Monotype's London offices. Once the executives had regained their composure, Warde was appointed to the position and rose to become Monotype's publicity manager. Her subsequent contributions to the promotion of good typography, including her famous Crystal Goblet essays, were invaluable and she remained with the company until her retirement in 1960. Warde, the "First Lady of Typography," died in 1969.

Century

| **Country of origin:** United States | **Classification:** Rational Serif
| **Designer:** Linn Boyd Benton

1894

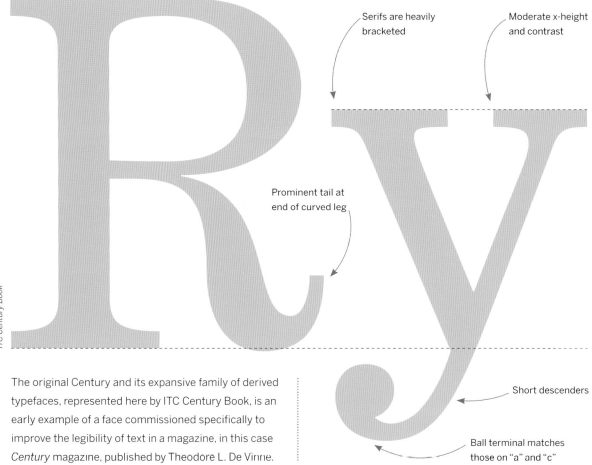

Serifs are heavily bracketed

Moderate x-height and contrast

Prominent tail at end of curved leg

ITC Century Book

Short descenders

Ball terminal matches those on "a" and "c"

The original Century and its expansive family of derived typefaces, represented here by ITC Century Book, is an early example of a face commissioned specifically to improve the legibility of text in a magazine, in this case *Century* magazine, published by Theodore L. De Vinne.

9/12pt ITC Century Book

LOREM IPSUM DOLOR SIT AMET, CONSECTETUER ADIPISCING ELIT, SED DIAM nonummy nibh euismod tincidunt ut laoreet dolore magna aliquam erat volutpat. ut wisi enim ad minim veniam, quis nostrud exerci tation ullamcorper suscipit lobortis nisl ut aliquip ex ea commodo consequat. Duis autem vel eum iriure dolor in

12/15pt ITC Century Book

LOREM IPSUM DOLOR SIT AMET, CONSECTETUER ADIPISCING ELIT, sed diam nonummy nibh euismod tincidunt ut laoreet dolore magna aliquam erat volutpat. Ut wisi enim ad minim veniam, quis nostrud exerci tation ullamcorper suscipit lobortis nisl

Century, or Century Roman as it was originally known when it was designed at American Type Founders in 1894 by Linn Boyd Benton, came from a commission submitted by Theodore L. De Vinne. De Vinne, the publisher of the well-known illustrated monthly magazine *Century*, wasn't happy with the typefaces he had at his disposal, stating that, "Readers of failing eyesight rightfully ask for types that are plain and unequivocal, that reveal the entire character at a glance, and are not discerned with difficulty by body marks joined to hairlines and serifs that are half seen or not seen at all." He wanted a legible face with a darker color, and with a relatively narrow width, allowing a similar amount of text to fit the double-column layout of the magazine as with previous editions. Benton designed the face with a large x-height to enhance the condensed feel of the typeface.

Century made its debut in 1895 and was considered a success by De Vinne, although it experienced a limited take-up from other printers as it was seen as a little too condensed for general tastes. However, the original design went on to spawn a raft of additional weights and styles, most of which were designed by L.B. Benton's son Morris Fuller Benton after he joined ATF as chief type designer in 1900. The first new styles to emerge were Century Expanded and Italic, which proved to be a lot more popular than the original face, followed by Century Bold and Bold Italic in 1904, then Century Bold Condensed and Extended in 1906 (and released in 1909 and 1910 respectively). Collectively, Century represents one of the first "type families." Benton's principal commission at ATF involved the unification of the myriad typefaces inherited by the new company following its formation via the merger of 23 independent type foundries in 1892. Mention should also be made here of Century Old Style (1906) and of course Century Schoolbook (1918–21), both of which are closely related to Century but quite different; Century Old Style features distinctive Old Style serifs and Century Schoolbook has wider strokes and is spaced more generously.

ITC Century, the digitized version of which is shown on this spread, was commissioned by the International Typeface Corporation in 1975 and designed by Tony Stan. It's not an identikit of Benton's original design—Stan tightened up the letterspacing and increased the x-height slightly in line with the contemporary visual sensibilities—but a good range of weights and styles cover most of the historical versions.

Century Schoolbook features notched serifs on the "C" and "S"

ITC Century features a greater contrast and feels a little finer

Cgk Cgk

Century Schoolbook Roman

ITC Century Book

Cheltenham

| **Country of origin:** United States | **Classification:** Old Style Serif
| **Designers:** Bertram Grosvenor Goodhue and Ingalls Kimball

1896

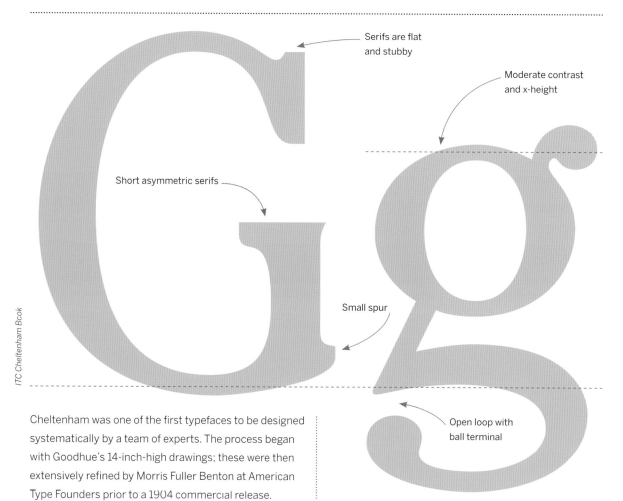

ITC Cheltenham Book

Serifs are flat and stubby

Moderate contrast and x-height

Short asymmetric serifs

Small spur

Open loop with ball terminal

Cheltenham was one of the first typefaces to be designed systematically by a team of experts. The process began with Goodhue's 14-inch-high drawings; these were then extensively refined by Morris Fuller Benton at American Type Founders prior to a 1904 commercial release.

9/12pt ITC Cheltenham Book

LOREM IPSUM DOLOR SIT AMET, CONSECTETUER ADIPISCING ELIT, SED DIAM NONUMMY NIBH euismod tincidunt ut laoreet dolore magna aliquam erat volutpat. Ut wisi enim ad minim veniam, quis nostrud exerci tation ullamcorper suscipit lobortis nisl ut aliquip ex ea commodo consequat. Duis autem vel eum iriure dolor in hendrerit in

12/15pt ITC Cheltenham Book

LOREM IPSUM DOLOR SIT AMET, CONSECTETUER ADIPISCING ELIT, sed diam nonummy nibh euismod tincidunt ut laoreet dolore magna aliquam erat volutpat. Ut wisi enim ad minim veniam, quis nostrud exerci tation ullamcorper suscipit lobortis

Cheltenham is a bit of an odd fellow. It's one of those typefaces that, from the very start following the completion of its design in 1902 and its patented commercial release in 1904, has been either loved or loathed by printers and designers alike. It was designed not by a professional typeface designer but by architect Bertram Grosvenor Goodhue, although Ingalls Kimball, director of the Cheltenham Press in New York, provided advice throughout the design process. Each character was drawn at around 14 inches high, modified extensively by the designer, then modified even further at the foundry, in this case the all-powerful American Type Founders. It's unclear if this latter stage was overseen by Morris Fuller Benton or by Joseph W. Phinney at the Boston offices of ATF, but suggestions that the face was first known as Boston Old Style may provide a clue.

Detractors cite several design features as problematic; it has long ascenders but short descenders, combined with a rather small x-height, uppercase characters are quite wide, and there are several unusual character shapes. The "A" has an extension at the apex of its thicker stroke, the "G" has an extension to its lower curved stroke, and the "g" has a curiously angled and broken loop. ATF's original weights and styles also contained a peculiar alternative lowercase "r" with its arm raised above the x-height, but the character appears to have been omitted from cuts released by other foundries. The fact is, these features were designed into the face to help create better legibility and on the whole they manage to do just that. It's perhaps not helpful that, despite Goodhue's intention for Cheltenham Old Style (the Old Style element of the original was only retained on versions of the typeface based directly on the original single weight) to be used primarily for text setting, the large range of weights and styles designed by Morris Fuller Benton at ATF over the next 10 years encouraged its use as a display face. Setting at larger point sizes only served to highlight the unusual features of the typeface even more.

Of course, one man's poison is another man's meat and the typeface enjoyed success despite its quirks. Versions were released in metal by a number of other foundries including Monotype and Linotype, and in 1975 ITC released the version that has subsequently become the most widely available digitized font family with four weights including a condensed width, all of which have an accompanying italic style.

Cheltenham ATF Old Style differs considerably from the newer ITC release, and has a much smaller x-height

Cheltenham ATF Old Style Regular　　　　　*ITC Cheltenham Book*

Akzidenz-Grotesk

| **Country of origin:** Germany | **Classification:** Grotesque Sans
| **Designers:** H. Berthold AG staff

1898

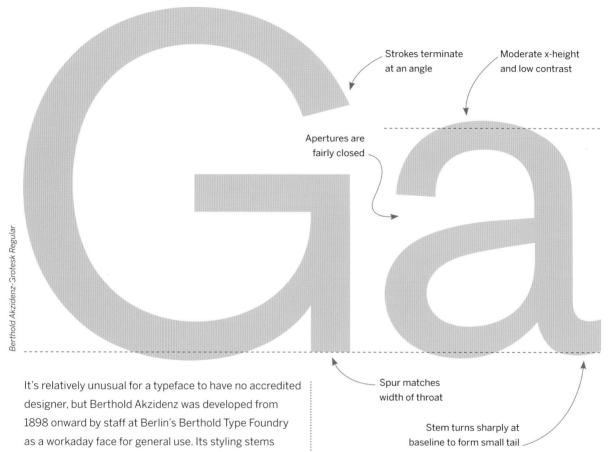

Berthold Akzidenz-Grotesk Regular

Strokes terminate
at an angle

Moderate x-height
and low contrast

Apertures are
fairly closed

Spur matches
width of throat

Stem turns sharply at
baseline to form small tail

It's relatively unusual for a typeface to have no accredited designer, but Berthold Akzidenz was developed from 1898 onward by staff at Berlin's Berthold Type Foundry as a workaday face for general use. Its styling stems from typical mid-19th-century display faces.

9/12pt Berthold Akzidenz-Grotesk Regular

LOREM IPSUM DOLOR SIT AMET, CONSECTETUER ADIPISCING ELIT, SED DIAM nonummy nibh euismod tincidunt ut laoreet dolore magna aliquam erat volutpat. Ut wisi enim ad minim veniam, quis nostrud exerci tation ullamcorper suscipit lobortis nisl ut aliquip ex ea commodo consequat. Duis autem vel eum iriure dolor in hendrerit in vulputate velit

12/15pt Berthold Akzidenz-Grotesk Regular

LOREM IPSUM DOLOR SIT AMET, CONSECTETUER ADIPISCING ELIT, sed diam nonummy nibh euismod tincidunt ut laoreet dolore magna aliquam erat volutpat. Ut wisi enim ad minim veniam, quis nostrud exerci tation ullamcorper suscipit lobortis nisl ut

We can identify the names of the designers of most of the typefaces featured in this book, but in the case of this extremely important sans serif typeface it's a different story. All we know for sure is that it was designed at the Berthold Type Foundry of Berlin for H. Berthold AG itself, as an everyday typeface for general use, and existed as a single weight in its earliest form. Its styling is close in nature to display faces typical to the mid 19th century, that appeared frequently in advertisements, but the specific origin of the face is often cited as Royal Grotesk by the punch cutter Ferdinand Theinhardt, cut around 1880. Originally known as Accidenz-Grotesk, its name derives from the German word *Akzidenzschrift*, which can be translated variously as "display type" or "jobbing type." In England and the U.S., Akzidenz was marketed under the alternative name of Standard.

The original single weight was added to piecemeal in the years following the 1898 release, often by pairing up existing sans serifs of differing weights when they happened to be acquired from other foundries. The resulting "family," if one could call it that, was therefore a bit of a mishmash and it would be some time before it was consolidated into a more cohesive set of weights and styles. It really started to find its feet with the emergence of the Swiss Style (or the International Typographic Style) following World War II. The growth in popularity for sans serif faces led Berthold to recut an improved and expanded Akzidenz-Grotesk series under the direction of Günter Gerhard Lange.

Looking at Akzidenz-Grotesk today, it's difficult to reconcile with the fact that it was designed almost 120 years ago. It still looks very contemporary, very Modernist in fact, and it's unlikely that the staff at Berthold had any idea how much of an impact their typeface would have in the future in terms of influencing the design of a raft of iconic sans serifs. Most significantly, it's credited as the inspiration for Neue Haas Grotesk, which later became Helvetica, and it takes a trained eye to distinguish between the two at a glance. Akzidenz-Grotesk is still published by Berthold and there are a couple of good digitized options: 2006's Akzidenz-Grotesk Next by Bernd Möllenstädt and Dieter Hofrichter, which references the original typeface closely but cleans up the discrepancies, and the Akzidenz-Grotesk Pro family, which includes normal, condensed and extended widths.

Details like the curved leg and greater width of Neue Haas Grotesk help distinguish it from Akzidenz-Grotesk

Rgsr Rgsr

Berthold Akzidenz Grotesk Regular

Neue Haas Grotesk Text 55 Roman

Engravers

| **Country of origin:** United States | **Classification:** Rational Serif
| **Designer:** Robert Wiebking

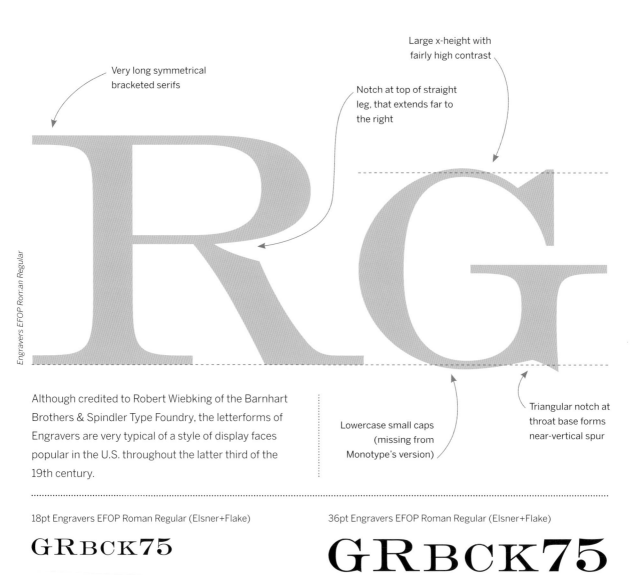

Large x-height with
fairly high contrast

Very long symmetrical
bracketed serifs

Notch at top of straight
leg, that extends far to
the right

Engravers EFOP Roman Regular

Lowercase small caps
(missing from
Monotype's version)

Triangular notch at
throat base forms
near-vertical spur

Although credited to Robert Wiebking of the Barnhart
Brothers & Spindler Type Foundry, the letterforms of
Engravers are very typical of a style of display faces
popular in the U.S. throughout the latter third of the
19th century.

18pt Engravers EFOP Roman Regular (Elsner+Flake)

GRBCK75

36pt Engravers EFOP Roman Regular (Elsner+Flake)

GRBCK75

72pt Engravers EFOP Roman Regular (Elsner+Flake)

GRBCK75

Robert Wiebking produced all his work in the U.S. but was born in Germany, emigrating to America in 1881, where he took up an apprenticeship as an engraver with Chicago manufacturer C.H. Hanson. He subsequently established an independent career and worked with many of the major American type foundries of the day, cutting a large number of Frederic W. Goudy's typefaces as well as working with Bruce Rogers on the development of Centaur. Wiebking is credited with the design of Engravers Roman, one of only a few faces he designed personally, but it would be fair to say that the design is in part a realization of a popular style of copperplate or steel-engraved type used frequently throughout the latter part of the 19th century.

Engravers Roman was first issued by the Chicago type foundry Barnhart Brothers & Spindler in 1899. BB&S was an interesting foundry; known for working with innovative designers such as Oswald Cooper and Will Ransom, like many others it was bought by American Type Founders in 1911, but the contract included a proviso that the merger would be delayed for 20 years, giving employees the chance to either find alternative employment or retire. I doubt this would have happened if the merger was being pushed through today. The foundry marketed Engravers Roman under the banner headline "latest design—the only genuine," which indicates that the foundry accepted there were other similar faces on offer from their competitors. The face proved to be a success and was soon supplemented with additional weights, Engravers Roman Condensed and Engravers Titling. The Titling weight was soon replaced by Engravers Bold, designed by Morris Fuller Benton at American Type Founders and cast by BB&S. Wiebking designed a couple of additional weights in 1914–15 that were named Engravers Litho Bold and Bold Condensed, but the face was visually quite different so it wouldn't be confused with the original design.

There are a number of digitized versions of Engravers available today. Monotype, URW++ and Elsner+Flake all have offerings that are respectful of Wiebking's original design, retaining the sharp serifs and high contrast. Another version designed by Bitstream is marketed as Engravers' Roman but looks substantially different.

KEQ5

Engravers EFOP Roman Regular

Elsner+Flake's version of Engravers features less contrast than other similar versions

KEQ5

Engravers Regular

Monotype's version of Engravers doesn't substitute small caps for lowercase characters

Eckmannschrift

| **Country of origin:** Germany | **Classification:** Display
| **Designer:** Otto Eckmann

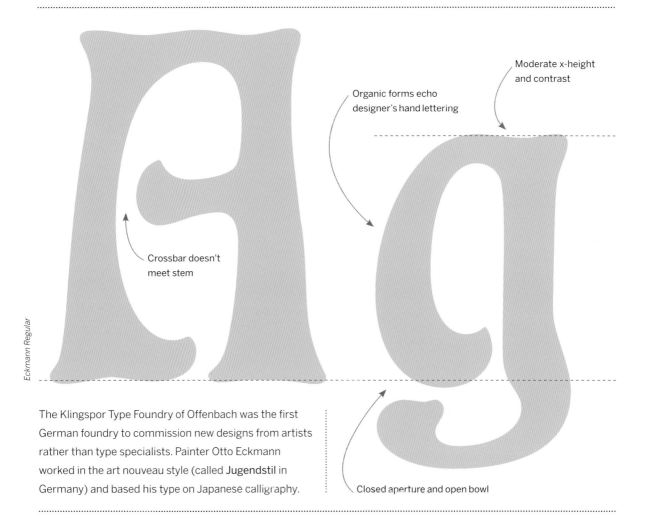

Eckmann Regular

Organic forms echo
designer's hand lettering

Moderate x-height
and contrast

Crossbar doesn't
meet stem

Closed aperture and open bowl

The Klingspor Type Foundry of Offenbach was the first
German foundry to commission new designs from artists
rather than type specialists. Painter Otto Eckmann
worked in the art nouveau style (called **Jugendstil** in
Germany) and based his type on Japanese calligraphy.

18pt Eckmann Regular (Linotype)

ELTbkps43

36pt Eckmann Regular (Linotype)

ELTbkps43

72pt Eckmann Regular (Linotype)

ELTbkps43

Eckmannschrift, which is generally referred to simply as Eckmann, was born out of the Jugendstil movement, the German equivalent of art nouveau. Art nouveau experienced its heyday between the years 1890 and 1914, the year that saw the start of World War I. It was considered a "total style;" all the visual elements of an art nouveau piece, be it a poster or a piece of furniture, were heavily influenced by the signature look of the movement with its flowing, organic sensibilities. Japanese *Ukiyo-e* woodblock printing provided one of the main historical points of reference for the style; this is particularly evident in Eckmann's design, which employs elements of Japanese calligraphy.

Otto Eckmann began his career as a painter, but he subsequently abandoned painting in favor of graphic and typographic design. This was a fairly common occurrence at this time; the opportunities for artists to carve out profitable careers for themselves in the burgeoning field of graphic design (or commercial art, as it was known at the time) was a big draw for Eckmann and many of his contemporaries. He designed Eckmannschrift in 1900 as a commission from Carl Klingspor of the Klingspor Type Foundry

of Offenbach am Main, Germany, basing the styling of the letterforms on his personal lettering style developed while creating covers for books and magazines. Although the brush-drawn face is heavily influenced by art nouveau, it also attempts to retain some of the structure of a Fraktur or blackletter typeface. Germans were still very passionate about preserving the use of Frakturs during the early part of the 20th century and the commercial success of the typeface would likely have relied in part on the design referencing that fact. The face does succeed in that respect; the calligraphy of the strokes manages to echo those of a classic Fraktur fairly well while removing many of the flourishes typical of a blackletter face.

Eckmann tragically died of tuberculosis in 1902 at the age of 37, only 2 years after his sole typeface design was released. There are a couple of digital options available today by Linotype and URW++, both of which are faithful to the original design.

A comparison of Eckmann with the style of a typical Fraktur face shows distinct structural similarities in the letterforms

Eckmann Regular   *Fette Fraktur Regular*

Bookman

| **Country of origin:** United States | **Classification:** Old Style Serif
| **Designer:** Alexander Phemister

1901

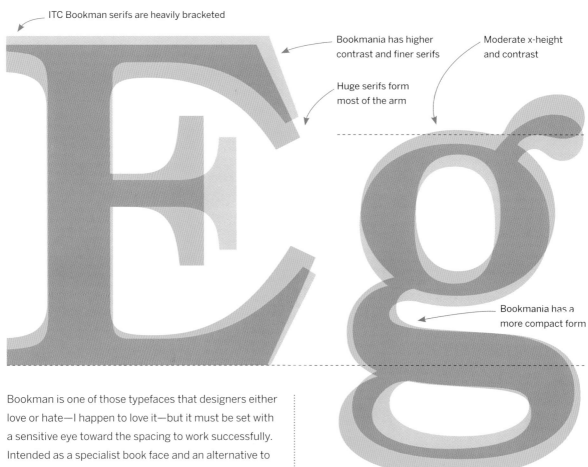

ITC Bookman serifs are heavily bracketed

Bookmania has higher contrast and finer serifs

Moderate x-height and contrast

Huge serifs form most of the arm

Bookmania has a more compact form

ITC Bookman Medium and Bookmania Semi Bold

Bookman is one of those typefaces that designers either love or hate—I happen to love it—but it must be set with a sensitive eye toward the spacing to work successfully. Intended as a specialist book face and an alternative to Caslon, it's also been used extensively in advertising.

9/12pt Bookmania Regular (Mark Simonson)

LOREM IPSUM DOLOR SIT AMET, CONSECTETUER ADIPISCING ELIT, SED DIAM nonummy nibh euismod tincidunt ut laoreet dolore magna aliquam erat volutpat. Ut wisi enim ad minim veniam, quis nostrud exerci tation ullamcorper suscipit lobortis nisl ut aliquip ex ea commodo consequat. Duis autem vel eum iriure dolor in

12/15pt Bookmania Regular (Mark Simonson)

LOREM IPSUM DOLOR SIT AMET, CONSECTETUER ADIPISCING elit, sed diam nonummy nibh euismod tincidunt ut laoreet dolore magna aliquam erat volutpat. Ut wisi enim ad minim veniam, quis nostrud exerci tation ullamcorper suscipit lobortis nisl

Bookman began as Antique Old Style No.7, a typeface designed by Alexander Phemister for the Scottish type foundry Miller & Richard in 1858 or thereabouts. Phemister based his Old Style on Caslon (a common practice for designers at that time) but thickened the strokes to create a slightly darker weight. This face was subsequently copied by the Bruce Type Foundry who released Antique No.310, then followed it up in 1901 with Bartlett Old Style. In the same year, Bruce became part of American Type Founders and Bartlett was renamed Bookman Old Style by ATF director Wadsworth A. Parker. Parker was also responsible for adding the first swash characters to Bookman, providing the relatively unique flavor that champions of the face love so much. It's not common for roman faces to include swash characters, particularly when they're as flamboyant as Bookman's, which may help explain why there are detractors who dislike using the face. Spacing can be a little tricky, too, with serifs projecting far to the right with the "E," "F" and "L," but careful kerning can produce wonderfully rich typography.

A raft of additional Bookmans were issued over the years, and today we have ITC Bookman, digitized from the 1975 revival designed by Ed Benguiat and comprised of four weights and eight styles. The swashes and alternative characters, previously a separate font named ITC Bookman Swash, are now integrated in the OpenType version. In the pursuit of legibility, Benguiat increased the x-height and introduced a more moderate contrast, plus he drew a cursive italic for each weight that differs completely from the mechanically sloped italics of the older design. The result is still a Bookman, but the true essence of the older design became a little diluted in the process. Enter Bookmania, the 2011 revival from Mark Simonson. His take on the face is based on a combination of the larger cuts of Bookman Old Style combined with an anonymous version from the 1960s, the source of which remains a tantalizing mystery. Simonson's theory follows that it was a custom redraw for an ad campaign that somehow found its way into the typographic food chain—he refers to it as "Sixties Bookman." Bookmania is by no means a facsimile of an older design, but it recaptures much of the spirit of the original and of course now includes the modern OpenType niceties: small caps, old style, proportional and tabular figures; swash ligatures and even swash small caps. The all-important oblique roman is also back, but it's been optically corrected and features a couple of stylistic adjustments.

Bookmania Regular

Bookman is all about exuberant swashes, and Bookmania has lots of them. The oblique roman is also true to the original design   *Bookmania Italic*

Copperplate Gothic

| **Country of origin:** United States | **Classification:** Glyphic
| **Designer:** Frederic W. Goudy

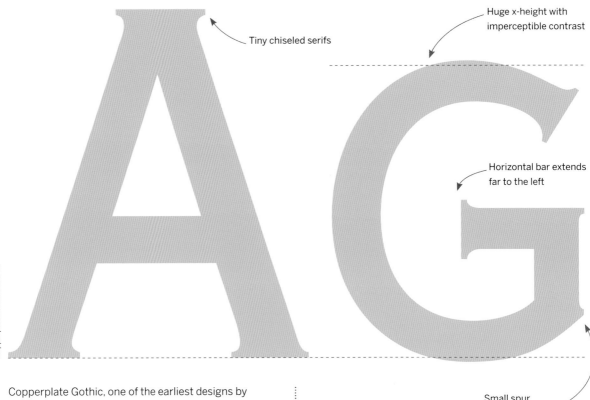

Copperplate Gothic 30 AB

Tiny chiseled serifs

Huge x-height with imperceptible contrast

Horizontal bar extends far to the left

Small spur matches serifs

Copperplate Gothic, one of the earliest designs by Frederic W. Goudy, isn't a Gothic at all. A cursory glance may fool one into thinking it's a sans serif, but tiny chiseled serifs make this a Glyphic, meaning a face that appears to have been carved in stone.

18pt Copperplate Gothic 30 AB (Adobe)

QURES345

36pt Copperplate Gothic 30 AB (Adobe)

QURES345

72pt Copperplate Gothic 30 AB (Adobe)

QURES345

Copperplate Gothic, one of Frederic W. Goudy's earliest designs, was created in 1901 and first released by American Type Founders. It's not a typical Goudy typeface and is an unusual departure for a designer much better known for his classic roman serif faces. Following on from Goudy's Copperplate Gothic Heavy, additional weights were drawn by ATF's Clarence C. Marder, with Morris Fuller Benton pitching in a single extra weight, Copperplate Gothic Shaded, in 1912. The face is in fact not a Gothic, despite its name. Tiny serifs that almost disappear completely when the face is set at smaller point sizes adorn the ends of the horizontal and vertical strokes, making the font a Glyphic. Glyphic typefaces are so called because they appear as though they could have been carved out of stone or etched into metal, an indication of how Copperplate Gothic acquired its name. The serifs do in fact also perform a practical function, sharpening up the stroke edges which would otherwise appear soft when set below 8 point.

Copperplate Gothic has the distinction of being the all-time best-selling typeface ever released by American Type Founders, which is quite an achievement considering the output of ATF at its height. The face proved to be incredibly popular for use on stationery and formal announcement cards, the kind of material produced by practically every print shop regardless of size. It's safe to surmise that there wasn't a single print shop across the U.S. that didn't own the face. Other near-identical faces were marketed by Monotype and Stephenson Blake (as Spartan), Ludlow (as Lining Plate Gothic), and the Italian type foundry Nebiolo (as Atalante).

The contemporary digital version from Adobe is styled accurately from the original typeface, but offers an altogether different package. Small capitals stand in for the lack of a lowercase, and the old naming convention has been switched to a coded numbering system. There are five weights with nine styles in total, numbered from 29 to 33 with each number indicating a change in both width and weight. Font names are also appended with either AB or BC, indicating the relative size of the uppercase to the small capitals.

Copperplate Gothic 29 AB, 30 AB, 31 AB and 32 AB

The numerical order of Copperplate Gothic's naming can be confusing, as it combines changes in both weight and width

Copperplate Gothic 29 BC, 30 BC, 31 BC, 32 BC and 33 BC

Franklin Gothic

| **Country of origin:** United States | **Classification:** Gothic Sans
| **Designer:** Morris Fuller Benton

1902–1912

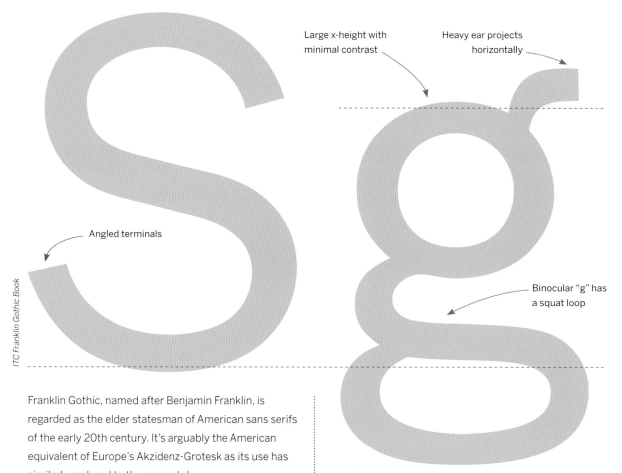

Large x-height with minimal contrast

Heavy ear projects horizontally

Angled terminals

Binocular "g" has a squat loop

ITC Franklin Gothic Book

Franklin Gothic, named after Benjamin Franklin, is regarded as the elder statesman of American sans serifs of the early 20th century. It's arguably the American equivalent of Europe's Akzidenz-Grotesk as its use has similarly endured to the present day.

9/12pt ITC Franklin Gothic

LOREM IPSUM DOLOR SIT AMET, CONSECTETUER ADIPISCING ELIT, SED DIAM NONUMMY NIBH euismod tincidunt ut laoreet dolore magna aliquam erat volutpat. Ut wisi enim ad minim veniam, quis nostrud exerci tation ullamcorper suscipit lobortis nisl ut aliquip ex ea commodo consequat. Duis autem vel eum iriure dolor in hendrerit in vulputate

12/15pt ITC Franklin Gothic

LOREM IPSUM DOLOR SIT AMET, CONSECTETUER ADIPISCING ELIT, SED diam nonummy nibh euismod tincidunt ut laoreet dolore magna aliquam erat volutpat. Ut wisi enim ad minim veniam, quis nostrud exerci tation ullamcorper suscipit lobortis nisl ut aliquip ex ea

Franklin Gothic is *the* modern-era American Gothic; it's an Akzidenz-Grotesk for the United States. Indeed it's been proposed, and it's highly likely that, Morris Fuller Benton was influenced by Akzidenz-Grotesk when he designed and cut the first weights of Franklin Gothic in 1902 but the theory can only be speculative. It was one of the first of many 19th-century revivals Benton worked on, having joined American Type Founders a couple of years earlier as their in-house typeface designer.

The use of the word "Gothic" for typefaces drawn in this style is an Americanism and shouldn't be confused with the European usage of the term when applied to blackletter faces. Gothic was traditionally used in the United States to denote a sans serif typeface and probably derives from the fact that sans serif faces were so closely associated with Germany during the late 19th and early 20th centuries. The equivalent classification in Europe is Grotesque sans serif.

Most (but not all) sources state that Franklin Gothic was named for Benjamin Franklin, and I see no reason to doubt this, given Franklin's historical status and his close associations with type and type founding.

Benton went on to design Franklin Gothic Condensed and Extra Condensed in 1906, adding an italic style in 1910. A wide version was begun and abandoned by Benton, then revisited by Bud Renshaw in 1952, although it appears to have never made it as far as a digital release from any of the major foundries.

There are a number of digital versions of Franklin Gothic available today. ITC Franklin Gothic is a good option that sticks closely to Benton's original design and includes a broad range of styles. It was digitized from the redrawn and expanded set of weights designed by Victor Caruso in 1980, and David Berlow added the Compressed and Condensed weights in 1991. It retains the subtle contrasts of thick and thin strokes, although in line with many other contemporary revivals there's a slight increase in x-height and a subtle narrowing in the width to allow a greater economy of space. URW Franklin Gothic is almost identical with an even larger selection of weights and styles in four widths and, at the time of writing, it's available to Adobe Creative Cloud subscribers via Typekit.

Franklin Gothic URW Medium, Medium Condensed, Demi Compressed and Demi Extra Compressed

News Gothic

| **Country of origin:** United States | **Classification:** Gothic Sans
| **Designer:** Morris Fuller Benton

1908

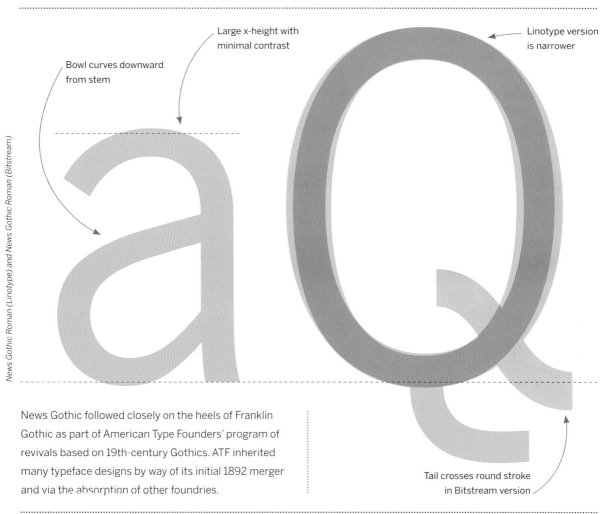

News Gothic Roman (Linotype) and News Gothic Roman (Bitstream)

Bowl curves downward from stem

Large x-height with minimal contrast

Linotype version is narrower

Tail crosses round stroke in Bitstream version

News Gothic followed closely on the heels of Franklin Gothic as part of American Type Founders' program of revivals based on 19th-century Gothics. ATF inherited many typeface designs by way of its initial 1892 merger and via the absorption of other foundries.

9/12pt News Gothic Roman (Linotype)

LOREM IPSUM DOLOR SIT AMET, CONSECTETUER ADIPISCING ELIT, SED DIAM NONUMMY NIBH EUISMOD tincidunt ut laoreet dolore magna aliquam erat volutpat. Ut wisi enim ad minim veniam, quis nostrud exerci tation ullamcorper suscipit lobortis nisl ut aliquip ex ea commodo consequat. Duis autem vel eum iriure dolor in hendrerit in vulputate velit esse molestie consequat, vel illum dolore eu

12/15pt News Gothic Roman (Linotype)

LOREM IPSUM DOLOR SIT AMET, CONSECTETUER ADIPISCING ELIT, SED DIAM nonummy nibh euismod tincidunt ut laoreet dolore magna aliquam erat volutpat. Ut wisi enim ad minim veniam, quis nostrud exerci tation ullamcorper suscipit lobortis nisl ut aliquip ex ea commodo consequat. Duis

Like Franklin Gothic, discussed on the previous spread and designed 6 years earlier, News Gothic is a very "American" sans serif and enjoyed enormous success in the early decades of the 20th century. Another Morris Fuller Benton typeface for American Type Founders, it was designed in 1908 and for a while became the most popular sans serif in use throughout the U.S. It was designed intentionally as a jobbing typeface that could be employed across a wide range of applications, but as its name suggests, the principal target usage was newspaper publishing. The number, and the size, of newspapers had increased steadily ever since the invention and introduction of mechanical composition some 20 or so years earlier.

News Gothic was just the typeface for this kind of work, but initially Benton designed only three weights in three widths and without italics; Regular, Condensed and Extra Condensed. Although there are a number of differences in the details of the letterforms, News Gothic is essentially a lighter version of Franklin Gothic and printers could pair News Gothic text setting with bolder Franklin Gothic styles for headlines. Despite the unrivaled success enjoyed by News Gothic (and American Gothics in general), it suffered a loss in popularity during the 1930s in the face of competition from the newly popular sans serif faces arriving from Europe. This may have been due to the influx of European, and in particular German, designers emigrating to the States to escape the increasing threat of Nazism, but new faces such as Kabel and Futura were all the rage during the years leading up to World War II.

Following a resurgence in popularity for the American Gothic, Linotype released their version of News Gothic, Jackson Burke's Trade Gothic, in 1948. ATF and Monotype countered by expanding their News Gothic families, adding bold weights and italic styles to the existing widths during the 1950s and 1960s, and the face has remained in favor ever since as a solid, no-nonsense sans serif workhorse. There are many digital versions available today; the Linotype version closely resembles Intertype's cut released in 1955, whereas Monotype's is considerably wider. Bitstream's version is the one to go for if you want to capture the essence of the original ATF release most accurately. For contemporary alternatives look at Source Sans, Adobe's first open-source typeface released in 2012, which draws inspiration from the classic American Gothic typeface style, or Benton Sans, featured later in this book.

Adobe's Source Sans draws inspiration from News Gothic—note the angle of the terminals and the styling of the tail on the "Q"

Qes8 Qes8

News Gothic Roman

Source Sans Regular

Centaur

| **Country of origin:** United States | **Classification:** Humanist Serif
| **Designer:** Bruce Rogers

Centaur Regular

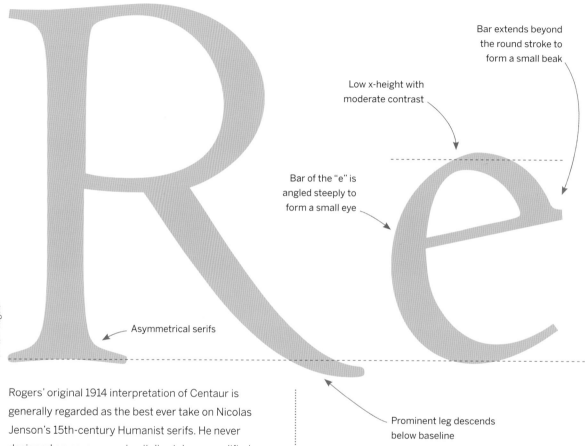

Bar extends beyond the round stroke to form a small beak

Low x-height with moderate contrast

Bar of the "e" is angled steeply to form a small eye

Asymmetrical serifs

Prominent leg descends below baseline

Rogers' original 1914 interpretation of Centaur is generally regarded as the best ever take on Nicolas Jenson's 15th-century Humanist serifs. He never designed an accompanying italic style—a modified version of Arrighi italic was used instead.

9/12pt Centaur Roman (Monotype)

LOREM IPSUM DOLOR SIT AMET, CONSECTETUER ADIPISCING ELIT, SED DIAM NONUMMY NIBH euismod tincidunt ut laoreet dolore magna aliquam erat volutpat. ut wisi enim ad minim veniam, quis nostrud exerci tation ullamcorper suscipit lobortis nisl ut aliquip ex ea commodo consequat. Duis autem vel eum iriure dolor in hendrerit in vulputate velit esse molestie consequat, vel illum

12/15pt Centaur Roman (Monotype)

LOREM IPSUM DOLOR SIT AMET, CONSECTETUER ADIPISCING ELIT, sed diam nonummy nibh euismod tincidunt ut laoreet dolore magna aliquam erat volutpat. Ut wisi enim ad minim veniam, quis nostrud exerci tation ullamcorper suscipit lobortis nisl ut aliquip ex ea commodo consequat. Duis autem

Centaur has long been regarded as the finest modern interpretation of the Humanist serifs of Nicolas Jenson, designed during the second half of the 15th century. It was designed by Bruce Rogers, first and foremost a book designer, as a 1914 commission from the Metropolitan Museum of Art for a custom typeface they could employ for signage and display setting. As well as it being an interpretation of Jenson's work, Rogers also referenced and refined Montaigne, a typeface he'd designed a decade earlier for a 1903 limited edition of *The Essays of Montaigne*. Rogers originally drew the face as titling characters, given the intended use, creating the first draft by working quickly over enlarged characters taken from Jenson's original type. Perhaps it was this relatively relaxed approach that gave the characters their natural flow; with minimal adjustments, Rogers succeeded in creating a face that captured the essence of Jenson's calligraphy without literally copying it.

Around a year later, Rogers used the typeface in a limited edition of Maurice de Guérin's *The Centaur*, published by the Metropolitan Museum of Art. He worked on the text version of Centaur with the engraver Robert Wiebking (on the advice of Frederic W. Goudy, who had also worked with Wiebking) and in part attributed the typeface's success to Wiebking's skill. However, there was still no italic style and when, in 1929, he finally allowed Monotype to release the face commercially, Rogers lacked the confidence to design one. Instead, an italic designed by Frederic Warde in 1925 named Arrighi (named for the Italian writing master Ludovico Vicentino degli Arrighi) was paired with the roman weight. Centaur was to remain Rogers' final typeface design.

There is only one digital version available today and sadly it's not held in high esteem by many designers, so it tends not to make too many appearances in high-quality book publishing. There have been attempts by various designers over the years to create an acceptable digital version that successfully marries the weights while creating a more harmonious relationship between the roman and italic styles, but success has proved to be elusive. The legendary beauty of the books set with the original metal type surely adds to this problem as digital setting can never quite capture the true essence of a great typeface printed with letterpress. In a way, it's a good thing to have a typeface that will forever represent an aspirational goal for type designers, but perhaps one day someone will crack the problem and create the perfect digital version of Centaur.

Centaur Regular

Adobe Jenson Regular

Centaur is a good deal finer in terms of its color than Adobe Jenson, a highly regarded interpretation of Jenson's style

Goudy Old Style

| **Country of origin:** United States | **Classification:** Old Style Serif
| **Designer:** Frederic W. Goudy

1915–1916

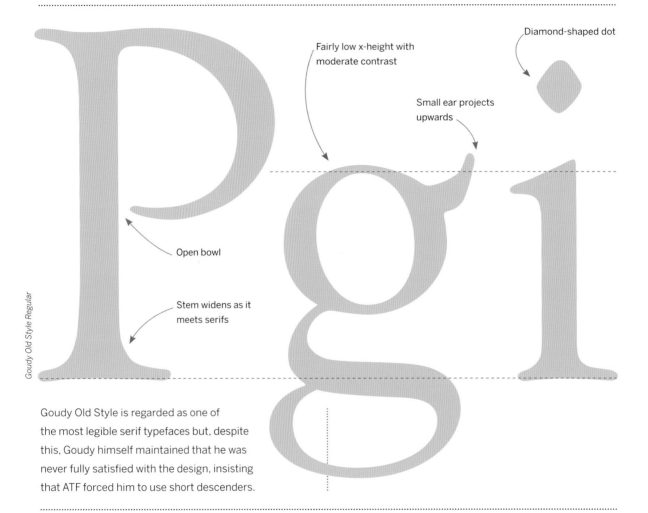

Goudy Old Style Regular

Fairly low x-height with moderate contrast

Diamond-shaped dot

Small ear projects upwards

Open bowl

Stem widens as it meets serifs

Goudy Old Style is regarded as one of the most legible serif typefaces but, despite this, Goudy himself maintained that he was never fully satisfied with the design, insisting that ATF forced him to use short descenders.

9/12pt Goudy Old Style Regular (URW++)

LOREM IPSUM DOLOR SIT AMET, CONSECTETUER ADIPISCING ELIT, SED DIAM NONUMMY NIBH euismod tincidunt ut laoreet dolore magna aliquam erat volutpat. Ut wisi enim ad minim veniam, quis nostrud exerci tation ullamcorper suscipit lobortis nisl ut aliquip ex ea commodo consequat. Duis autem vel eum iriure dolor in hendrerit in vulputate velit esse molestie consequat, vel

12/15pt Goudy Old Style Regular (URW++)

LOREM IPSUM DOLOR SIT AMET, CONSECTETUER ADIPISCING ELIT, sed diam nonummy nibh euismod tincidunt ut laoreet dolore magna aliquam erat volutpat. Ut wisi enim ad minim veniam, quis nostrud exerci tation ullamcorper suscipit lobortis nisl ut aliquip ex ea

Frederic W. Goudy was a prolific perfectionist, and something of a late starter. Born in Bloomington, Illinois, in 1865, at the age of 24 he relocated to Chicago and found work as a clerk for various companies, a job that he found unrewarding. Goudy had always been interested in lettering and, following the sale of his share of a small printing firm he had helped establish in the late 1890s, he sent drawings for a set of capitals to the Dickinson Type Foundry in Boston, that had become part of American Type Founders during the original 1892 merger. The drawings found favor and became his first commercial design, a typeface named Camelot. As well as setting up a new printing firm with fellow designer Will Ransom in 1903, named the Village Press, Goudy made the decision to devote time to a career as a freelance lettering artist and went on to design (by his own reckoning) over 120 separate weights and styles of type, making him one of the most prolific typeface designers of all time.

Following the success of Kennerley Old Style, designed in 1911 for an H.G. Wells anthology published by Mitchell Kennerley, Goudy's reputation was firmly established. More commercial designs followed and in 1915 ATF commissioned him to design a brand new typeface, Goudy Old Style. ATF insisted on alterations to Goudy's design to make it fit their common line, a standard measurement established to ensure that all their typefaces could be aligned with one another, and he wasn't pleased. Goudy was well known for making his feelings known, a fact that often set him at odds with his contemporaries and occasionally his clients. To quote Goudy himself, "The face, as finally produced was, I felt, almost as great an innovation in type as my Kennerley … I am almost satisfied that the design is a good one, marred only by the short descenders which I allowed the American Type Founders to inveigle me into giving p, q, g, j and y—though only under protest." Goudy Old Style Italic, modeled on Aldus Manutius' 16th-century Humanist type, followed in 1918, and in 1930 Monotype added alternative long descenders to their version of Goudy Old Style, but it's likely the adaptation wasn't overseen by Goudy.

Digital versions of Goudy Old Style have been released by most of the major publishers, including Monotype, Lanston Type Co. (now part of the P22 Type Foundry), Bitstream, URW++, Linotype and Adobe. In comparison, the Monotype version is a little wider than others, whereas the URW++ release is more economical in terms of width and spacing.

Monotype's version is slightly wider than others

Goudy Old Style Regular

Cooper Black

| **Country of origin:** United States | **Classification:** Display
| **Designer:** Oswald B. Cooper

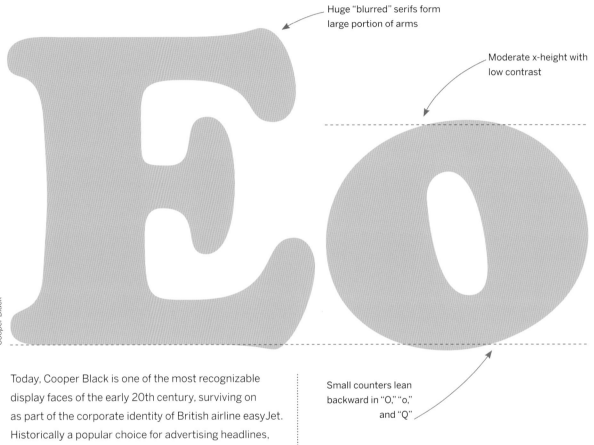

Huge "blurred" serifs form large portion of arms

Moderate x-height with low contrast

Cooper Black

Small counters lean backward in "O," "o," and "Q"

Today, Cooper Black is one of the most recognizable display faces of the early 20th century, surviving on as part of the corporate identity of British airline easyJet. Historically a popular choice for advertising headlines, its influence on later typographic trends is palpable.

18pt Cooper Black (Adobe)

EQcgsx3

36pt Cooper Black (Adobe)

EQcgsx3

72pt Cooper Black (Adobe)

EQcgsx3

Oswald Cooper, the designer of Cooper Black as well as a number of other typefaces that bear his name, studied under Frederic Goudy at the Frank Holme School of Illustration in Chicago and was associated with several other important typeface designers established in the Chicago area, including Will Ransom and William Addison Dwiggins. In 1904, Cooper formed Bertsch & Cooper in partnership with Fred Bertsch. In 1913, the Barnhart Brothers & Spindler Type Foundry commissioned Cooper to design his first typeface, an Old Style serif based on his lettering style, which was eventually released in 1918 as the single weight Cooper Old Style; an italic style was added in 1924.

The follow-up, Cooper Black, was released in 1922 and immediately made an impact; it was quite different from anything else available at that time and is rightly regarded as the first of the 20th century "super-bolds." BB&S marketed it with the line "the selling type supreme, the multibillionaire sales type," and Cooper himself quipped that it was "for far-sighted printers with near-sighted customers." The face sparked a new trend for super-bold display faces and became BB&S's best-selling typeface in their history. In fact, it also remains American Type Founders second-best-selling face (Copperplate Gothic occupies the top spot) following the completion of their merger with BB&S. Cooper Black Italic was completed in 1926 with the unusual inclusion of a dozen alternative swash capitals. Other weights that existed as metal type include Cooper Hilite, designed in 1925, and Cooper Black Condensed, designed in 1926 and described by Cooper as "condensed but not squeezed."

Sadly, the swash characters have been omitted from contemporary digitized versions; a search reveals that a font named Cooper Black Italic Swash appears to exist but buying options are elusive, although a web font version is available at Fontdeck. Versions of Cooper Black have been released in the digital format by a number of foundries and distributors including Linotype, Adobe, URW++, Elsner+Flake, and Bitstream. Cooper BT, designed at Bitstream in 1986, adds Light, Medium and Bold weights with corresponding italics to the standard Black.

Bitstream Cooper Bold

Bitstream Cooper Bold Italic

Wilhelm Klingspor Schrift (Gotisch)

| **Country of origin:** Germany | **Classification:** Blackletter
| **Designer:** Rudolf Koch

1919–1925

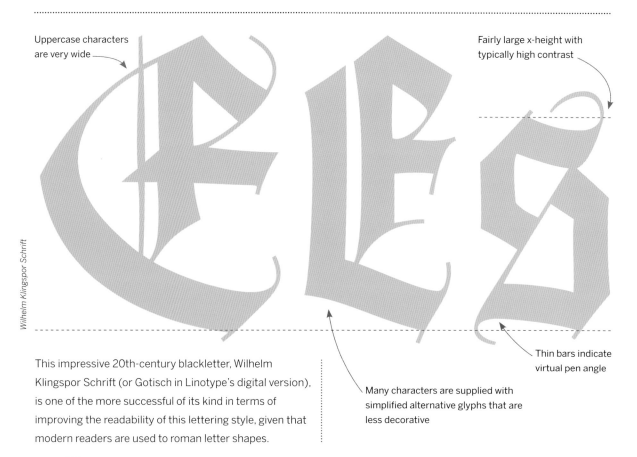

Wilhelm Klingspor Schrift

Uppercase characters are very wide

Fairly large x-height with typically high contrast

Thin bars indicate virtual pen angle

Many characters are supplied with simplified alternative glyphs that are less decorative

This impressive 20th-century blackletter, Wilhelm Klingspor Schrift (or Gotisch in Linotype's digital version), is one of the more successful of its kind in terms of improving the readability of this lettering style, given that modern readers are used to roman letter shapes.

18pt Wilhelm Klingspor Schrift (Alter Littera)

FFKKbgjprz36

36pt Wilhelm Klingspor Schrift (Alter Littera)

FFKKbgjprz36

72pt Wilhelm Klingspor Schrift (Alter Littera)

FFKKbgjprz36

Wilhelm Klingspor Schrift is a textura style of blackletter typeface, meaning it belongs to the most calligraphic group of faces used in the earliest books, which take their style from formal handwriting. It was designed by the great German calligrapher and type designer Rudolf Koch (see page 54) for the Klingspor Type Foundry of Offenbach am Main between 1919–25 and is regarded as one of the finest 20th-century blackletters. Originally known as Missal Schrift, it was named for Wilhelm Klingspor, the recently deceased co-owner of the foundry who was the son of the firm's founder, Carl Klingspor.

It's a beautiful example of a blackletter that is elegant rather than heavy, with sharp elements of decoration and hairline strokes at the terminals of both uppercase and lowercase. Blackletter faces generally thrive when used as display faces set at larger point sizes but Klingspor and Koch addressed this by designing and casting alternative optical sizes for smaller text setting. The fine decoration was pared back to improve legibility, stroke widths were increased slightly and the x-height was made slightly larger.

The digital versions of the face, called Wilhelm Klingspor Gotisch by Linotype and Adobe, are not without their problems and the designer and design historian Paul Shaw has documented them in his article "Paean to Wilhelm Klingspor Schrift: Textura in Pinstripes." He points out that the digitization of the face is still beautiful but not entirely faithful; some characters have been redesigned in an attempt to improve legibility for modern readers not used to blackletter faces. However, Shaw's biggest disappointment stems from the fact that so many of the original characters designed by Koch have been omitted from the full character set. The two original sets of capitals, one normal and one condensed, have been reduced to a single choice with an arbitrary mix of the two previous widths, many alternate lowercase characters and decorative glyphs are missing, and the 35 ligatures of the original now number only 15. This is a shame given the flexibility of the OpenType format. Stepping into the breach is a new version from José Alberto Mauricio of Alter Littera, a Madrid-based digital type foundry run as a personal project to faithfully revive medieval scripts and classic faces. The missing glyphs have all been reinstated along with a few extra characters to further improve the usability of the face.

The unfamiliarity of blackletter faces for some can be confusing, given that there are often multiple letterforms for each character

Wilhelm Klingspor Schrift Regular

Perpetua

| **Country of origin:** United Kingdom | **Classification:** Transitional Serif
| **Designer:** Eric Gill

1925–1932

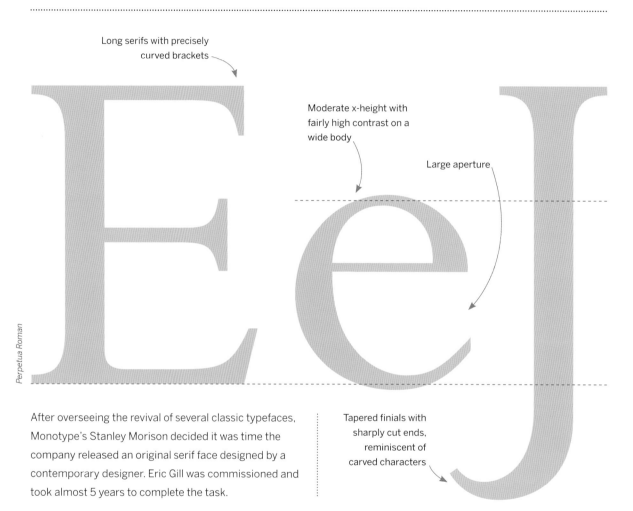

Long serifs with precisely curved brackets

Moderate x-height with fairly high contrast on a wide body

Large aperture

Perpetua Roman

Tapered finials with sharply cut ends, reminiscent of carved characters

After overseeing the revival of several classic typefaces, Monotype's Stanley Morison decided it was time the company released an original serif face designed by a contemporary designer. Eric Gill was commissioned and took almost 5 years to complete the task.

9/12pt Perpetua Regular (Monotype)

LOREM IPSUM DOLOR SIT AMET, CONSECTETUER ADIPISCING ELIT, SED DIAM NONUMMY NIBH EUISMOD tincidunt ut laoreet dolore magna aliquam erat volutpat. Ut wisi enim ad minim veniam, quis nostrud exerci tation ullamcorper suscipit lobortis nisl ut aliquip ex ea commodo consequat. Duis autem vel eum iriure dolor in hendrerit in vulputate velit esse molestie consequat, vel illum dolore eu feugiat nulla facilisis at

12/15pt Perpetua Regular (Monotype)

LOREM IPSUM DOLOR SIT AMET, CONSECTETUER ADIPISCING ELIT, SED diam nonummy nibh euismod tincidunt ut laoreet dolore magna aliquam erat volutpat. Ut wisi enim ad minim veniam, quis nostrud exerci tation ullamcorper suscipit lobortis nisl ut aliquip ex ea commodo consequat. Duis autem

Designed at around the same period as his famous and eponymous face Gill Sans, Perpetua is one of two important Transitional serif faces designed by the multitalented Arthur Eric Rowton Gill (the other being Joanna). The first ideas for the face were begun in 1925 at the request of Stanley Morison, the principal typographic consultant at Monotype. Throughout the 1920s and 1930s Morison oversaw a number of important revivals on behalf of Monotype, including classics such as Baskerville and Bembo. But, he was also keen to commission completely new typefaces for the corporation. He was a founder member of the Fleuron Society, a group dedicated to the furtherance of all things typographic, and outlined his views in an article for the society's journal. Morison wanted to combine the talents of a living designer of repute with those of an expert punch cutter, and he'd already decided that a man with Gill's prerequisite skills would be an excellent choice for the task to hand.

In an effort to retain as much as possible of the chiseled quality of Gill's design for Perpetua, Morison selected a French punch cutter named Charles Malin to cut the face in the traditional way, handing actual punches over to Monotype to manufacture the matrices and type. The decision was almost certainly also taken as a way to avoid dealings with Frank Hinman Pierpont, the director of Monotype's Salfords works near Redhill in Surrey, England; the two men didn't enjoy a good working relationship and were often at odds with one another. As it turned out, Gill was unhappy with several details; he made changes to the design after Malin had begun work on the punches and the process broke down. This was further complicated by a reciprocal (and embarrassing) agreement Gill had made to design an italic for Robert Gibbings of the Golden Cockerel Press that he could use with his stock of Caslon. However, despite the various issues, an amiable conclusion was somehow reached and Perpetua's first appearance came in 1928 when it was used to set the text for a translated edition of a book called *The Passion of Perpetua and Felicity*, providing the eventual name for the face. The italic was originally named Felicity and treated as a separate paired typeface, but eventually (and after even further alteration) the Perpetua family came into being with Bold weights added some 30 years later. It's ironic that, after all the problems surrounding its creation, Morison and Gill have received all the credit when in fact Pierpont and his staff at Salfords contributed much to the final stages of perfecting and manufacturing the typeface.

Monotype's digitized version, also published by Adobe, is the only commercially available version and it's a faithful adaptation, including titling weights from the original metal release.

Perpetua Titling Regular

Perpetua Italic

Kabel

| **Country of origin:** Germany | **Classification:** Geometric Sans
| **Designer:** Rudolf Koch

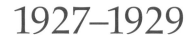

1927–1929

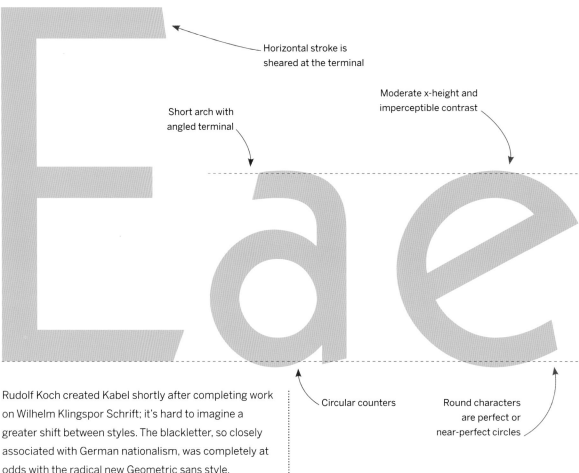

Horizontal stroke is
sheared at the terminal

Moderate x-height and
imperceptible contrast

Short arch with
angled terminal

Kabel Book

Circular counters

Round characters
are perfect or
near-perfect circles

Rudolf Koch created Kabel shortly after completing work on Wilhelm Klingspor Schrift; it's hard to imagine a greater shift between styles. The blackletter, so closely associated with German nationalism, was completely at odds with the radical new Geometric sans style.

9/12pt Kabel Book (Linotype)

LOREM IPSUM DOLOR SIT AMET, CONSECTETUER ADIPISCING ELIT, SED DIAM NONUMMY NIBH EUISMOD tincidunt ut laoreet dolore magna aliquam erat volutpat. Ut wisi enim ad minim veniam, quis nostrud exerci tation ullamcorper suscipit lobortis nisl ut aliquip ex ea commodo consequat. Duis autem vel eum iriure dolor in hendrerit in vulputate velit esse molestie consequat, vel illum dolore eu feugiat nulla facilisis at vero eros et accumsan et iusto

12/15pt Kabel Book (Linotype)

LOREM IPSUM DOLOR SIT AMET, CONSECTETUER ADIPISCING ELIT, SED diam nonummy nibh euismod tincidunt ut laoreet dolore magna aliquam erat volutpat. Ut wisi enim ad minim veniam, quis nostrud exerci tation ullamcorper suscipit lobortis nisl ut aliquip ex ea commodo consequat. Duis autem vel eum iriure dolor in

Rudolf Koch designed Kabel, one of the two classic Geometric sans serif faces to emerge from late 1920s Germany, around the same time Paul Renner was working on Futura. Influenced strongly by the ideas emanating from Germany's Bauhaus art school, Kabel contains a raft of ideas that give away the fact that Koch was first and foremost a calligrapher. Despite its Geometric classification, the face displays a degree of calligraphic impulse; the mild contrast seen in some strokes and the angled terminals provide Kabel with a livelier feel that other strictly Geometric sans serifs don't possess.

Working with geometric drawing tools must have been quite a departure for Koch, given that he was accustomed to designing blackletter display faces and Humanist type developed from his own hand lettering. He'd just completed work on the blackletter face Wilhelm Klingspor Schrift and noted that he enjoyed the challenge of switching from the impulsively driven calligraphic style to the stricter rules of the engineered sans serif. Koch drew Kabel Light and its accompanying italic style first, and followed up with three additional weights: Medium, Bold and Extra Bold. Corresponding condensed weights were also produced in metal but seem not to have made it as far as the digital platform.

In the U.S., Kabel was released by Monotype with the rather uninspiring name Sans Serif, and the face was also named Cable for some markets. There are various attributions for the name; some sources report its connection to the 1926 opening of the first cable car running to the summit of the Zugspitze mountain, which lies on Germany's border with Austria. Others connect it with the installation of a new Berlin–Vienna telephone line in 1927, and even with the laying of the transatlantic telephone cable—perhaps it was actually none of these and was merely intended to convey a metaphorical sense of technology and communication.

Digitized versions are available from a few sources, but none appear to match the original Klingspor version, which featured a single-story "a" and "g" and an "e" with a horizontal bar. Linotype's family follows the design of Monotype's U.S. release (mentioned above) with four weights—Light, Book, Heavy and Black—corresponding to the original four drawn by Koch. Victor Caruso's ITC Kabel, drawn in 1976 under license from Stempel (who bought the rights to the Klingspor catalog after the foundry's closure), is an interpretation and is comprised of five rather than four individual weights (Book, Medium, Demi, Bold and Ultra).

The significant differences in the styling of ITC Kabel provide a good example of ITC's penchant for increasing x-heights considerably

QRgi QRgi

Kabel Book   *ITC Kabel Book*

Futura

| **Country of origin:** Germany | **Classification:** Geometric Sans
| **Designer:** Paul Renner

1927–1930

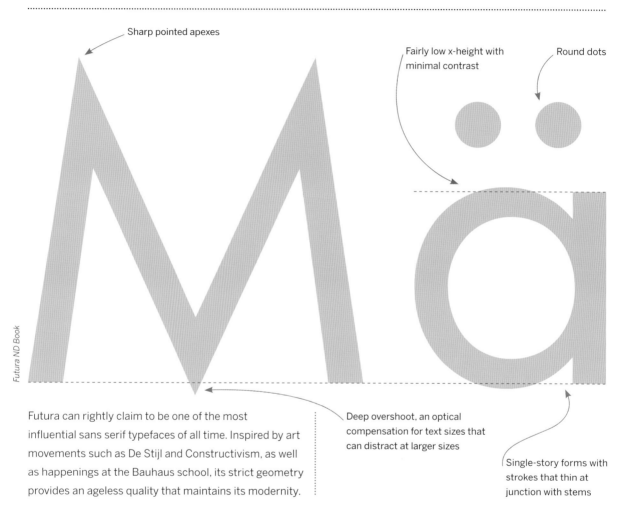

Sharp pointed apexes

Fairly low x-height with minimal contrast

Round dots

Futura ND Book

Futura can rightly claim to be one of the most influential sans serif typefaces of all time. Inspired by art movements such as De Stijl and Constructivism, as well as happenings at the Bauhaus school, its strict geometry provides an ageless quality that maintains its modernity.

Deep overshoot, an optical compensation for text sizes that can distract at larger sizes

Single-story forms with strokes that thin at junction with stems

9/12pt Futura ND Book (Neufville)

LOREM IPSUM DOLOR SIT AMET, CONSECTETUER ADIPISCING ELIT, SED DIAM nonummy nibh euismod tincidunt ut laoreet dolore magna aliquam erat volutpat. Ut wisi enim ad minim veniam, quis nostrud exerci tation ullamcorper suscipit lobortis nisl ut aliquip ex ea commodo consequat. Duis autem vel eum iriure dolor in

12/15pt Futura ND Book (Neufville)

LOREM IPSUM DOLOR SIT AMET, CONSECTETUER ADIPISCING ELIT, sed diam nonummy nibh euismod tincidunt ut laoreet dolore magna aliquam erat volutpat. Ut wisi enim ad minim veniam, quis nostrud exerci tation ullamcorper suscipit lobortis nisl

Futura is the classic Geometric sans serif that has never really gone out of fashion since its first appearance in 1927. Designed for Frankfurt's Bauer Type Foundry by Paul Renner, Futura was in typographic terms a game changer. Renner was a member of the modernist-leaning Deutscher Werkbund (German Association of Craftsmen), was an advocate of the Bauhaus (although he wasn't directly associated with the school), and held strong views on the inappropriateness of blackletter typefaces for everyday modern use. He also intensely disliked the associations of traditional blackletter faces with the rise of National Socialism in pre-war Germany and openly criticized the Nazis' cultural policies in his published work *Kulturbolschewismus*, an act that precipitated his dismissal from his post as director of the Meisterschule für Deutchlands Buchdrucker (Master School for German Printers).

Futura is a model of geometric simplicity with round characters drawn as near-perfect circles and practically no stroke contrast. Renner's first design used only triangles, circles and squares, but this proved to be problematic in terms of legibility so he was persuaded to adjust some glyphs to bring their proportions more in line with classic roman characters. When first issued, the large family consisted of six weights with accompanying italic style, three condensed weights with italics, and an inline. The face was very successful and was also licensed to France's Deberny & Peignot for European distribution. A face named Spartan was jointly produced by American Type Founders and Linotype in the U.S. between 1939 and 1955 and was practically indistinguishable from Futura. There are digital versions of a similarly named face that reference Futura's influence, but on inspection I can't find any reason to recommend them.

There are many legitimate digitized versions of Futura available—all the significant digital foundries and a number of smaller independents have the face in their collections—but one in particular stands out as a fine example of a truly accurate revival. The rights to the typeface catalog of the Bauer Type Foundry are now owned by Barcelona's Fundición Tipográfica Neufville, previously a subsidiary of the foundry before it closed its Frankfurt headquarters. Neufville Digital, a company established to create and distribute new versions of classic Bauer faces directly from the original sources, have Futura ND, which has been faithfully rendered by Marie-Therésè Koreman from Renner's original drawings. The family contains the full range of weights with their italic styles. In the absence of the Neufville revival, the versions offered by Linotype or Adobe are perfectly acceptable and carry the full range of weights and styles.

Round characters (including the "C") are formed from perfect circles

OGOQ

Futura ND Book

Gill Sans

| **Country of origin:** United Kingdom | **Classification:** Humanist Sans
| **Designer:** Eric Gill

1928–1930

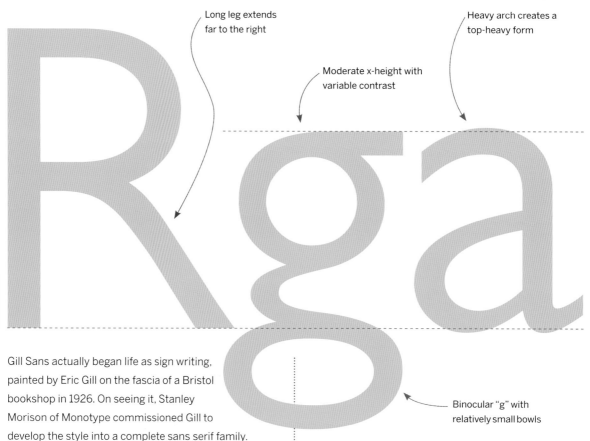

Long leg extends far to the right

Heavy arch creates a top-heavy form

Moderate x-height with variable contrast

Gill Sans Book

Binocular "g" with relatively small bowls

Gill Sans actually began life as sign writing, painted by Eric Gill on the fascia of a Bristol bookshop in 1926. On seeing it, Stanley Morison of Monotype commissioned Gill to develop the style into a complete sans serif family.

9/12pt Gill Sans Book (Monotype)

LOREM IPSUM DOLOR SIT AMET, CONSECTETUER ADIPISCING ELIT, SED DIAM NONUMMY NIBH euismod tincidunt ut laoreet dolore magna aliquam erat volutpat. Ut wisi enim ad minim veniam, quis nostrud exerci tation ullamcorper suscipit lobortis nisl ut aliquip ex ea commodo consequat. Duis autem vel eum iriure dolor in hendrerit in vulputate velit esse molestie consequat, vel

12/15pt Gill Sans Book (Monotype)

LOREM IPSUM DOLOR SIT AMET, CONSECTETUER ADIPISCING ELIT, SED diam nonummy nibh euismod tincidunt ut laoreet dolore magna aliquam erat volutpat. Ut wisi enim ad minim veniam, quis nostrud exerci tation ullamcorper suscipit lobortis nisl ut aliquip ex ea commodo consequat.

Gill Sans, despite its fame and widespread use by large corporations such as the British Broadcasting Corporation (BBC), is a bit of an oddity. On the one hand it's clearly a Geometric sans serif, but then you come across characters like the double-story "a" with its relatively high contrast, and the binocular form "g," that Gill himself referred to as a "pair of spectacles." It's almost as if Gill couldn't resist throwing in the odd Humanist touch here and there just to be awkward and it makes Gill Sans a little tricky to classify, but it's a Humanist sans.

Gill was designed partly in response to the flood of new sans serif typefaces being produced by the German type foundries during the early decades of the 20th century. Another Stanley Morison commission for Monotype and influenced in part by Edward Johnston's classic typeface designed for the London Underground (Gill was apprenticed to Johnston for a time), the full character set is built around lettering painted by Gill above the shop front of a Bristol store owned by radio producer and bookseller Douglas Cleverdon. Conceived as a display face that would work equally well when set at smaller sizes in publications such as timetables or price lists, the face was quickly adopted as a corporate face by the London and North Eastern Railway. The rest of the British rail network soon followed

suit, and the publisher Penguin helped raise the face's profile even further by using it on all the covers of their famous paperbacks.

It can be a cantankerous face to work with and seasoned typographers will testify to the spacing problems it can generate, thanks to features like the extended leg of the "R," and manual kerning is required when the lowercase "l" occurs as a pair (as in the face's name, ironically). This has done nothing to turn designers away from its worldly charm and its use remains widespread, particularly as it's included as part of the Macintosh operating system and the Microsoft Office package, and its popularity shows no signs of abating.

Gill Sans has remained steadfastly Monotype and the digital version available today is just that. Digital weights break down into seven weights and 12 styles in the standard width, with three condensed weights for text, four display weights and a couple of shadow styles. There's also Gill Sans Infant, a family with simplified letterforms designed specifically for younger readers and featuring a single-story roman "a" that moves the design closer in appearance to Futura.

Gill Sans Medium

Gill Sans Infant Regular

Memphis

| **Country of origin:** Germany | **Classification:** Geometric Slab
| **Designer:** Rudolf Wolf

1929

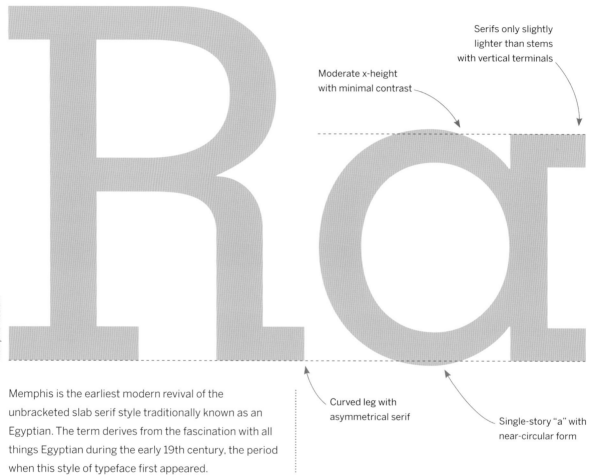

Memphis Medium

Serifs only slightly
lighter than stems
with vertical terminals

Moderate x-height
with minimal contrast

Curved leg with
asymmetrical serif

Single-story "a" with
near-circular form

Memphis is the earliest modern revival of the unbracketed slab serif style traditionally known as an Egyptian. The term derives from the fascination with all things Egyptian during the early 19th century, the period when this style of typeface first appeared.

9/12pt Memphis Medium (Linotype)

LOREM IPSUM DOLOR SIT AMET, CONSECTETUER ADIPISCING ELIT, SED DIAM nonummy nibh euismod tincidunt ut laoreet dolore magna aliquam erat volutpat. Ut wisi enim ad minim veniam, quis nostrud exerci tation ullamcorper suscipit lobortis nisl ut aliquip ex ea commodo consequat. Duis autem

12/15pt Memphis Medium (Linotype)

LOREM IPSUM DOLOR SIT AMET, CONSECTETUER ADIPISCING ELIT, sed diam nonummy nibh euismod tincidunt ut laoreet dolore magna aliquam erat volutpat. Ut wisi enim ad minim veniam, quis nostrud exerci tation ullamcorper suscipit

If you happen to carry out any of your own research on this typeface, don't be surprised if you come across conflicting design accreditation. Memphis has often been attributed to the German calligrapher and painter Emil Rudolf Weiss, who designed a number of typefaces bearing his name for the Bauer Type Foundry in Frankfurt. This is an incorrect attribution; it was designed by the similarly named Rudolf Wolf. He worked for Stempel, which was also located in Frankfurt, and it was this foundry rather than Bauer that released Memphis in 1929, representing the earliest modern revival of an Egyptian slab serif. Further examination of Weiss' overtly Humanist design style proves beyond doubt that Memphis is the work of another designer.

The term Egyptian, when applied to a typeface style, is derived from the intense interest in Europe for all things Egyptian sparked by Napoleon's early-19th-century Northeast Africa campaign. Ancient Egyptian architecture exhibits a distinctly slab-like horizontal aesthetic, and the heavy square slabs of the new style of display type that emerged around the same time picked up the moniker through this visual association. It was common in the early 1900s to find slab serifs with names such as Cairo or Pharaoh, and Memphis continued this tradition, picking up the alternative name Girder in the U.S. Today Memphis is more commonly classed as a Geometric slab.

Egyptian slab serifs remained popular through the 19th and into the early 20th centuries, a fact that almost certainly prompted Stempel to consider commissioning a revival in the same style with the benefit of a more modern design concept. Wolf was able to draw inspiration from the Geometric sans serif faces (such as Futura) that were emerging in Germany around the same time and Memphis has often been referred to as "Futura with serifs." The Stempel Type Foundry enjoyed a close relationship with Linotype throughout its existence, being the sole manufacturer of matrices for the Linotype machine in Europe and one of the few worldwide. Because of this, it was Linotype that introduced Memphis Light and Bold by 1933, with further weights and condensed widths appearing between 1933 and 1938. Chauncey H. Griffith designed the Extra Bold.

Linotype acquired the rights to Stempel's library of typefaces in 1985 and was subsequently responsible for the digitization of the face, which is the most complete and most accurate digital version available today. The family consists of five weights running from Light to Extra Bold, with italic styles accompanying all except the Extra Bold weight. The condensed weights haven't yet progressed to the digital format.

A quick comparison between Memphis and Futura reveals a source of inspiration

Memphis Medium

Futura ND Medium

Joanna

| **Country of origin:** United Kingdom | **Classification:** Transitional Serif
| **Designer:** Eric Gill

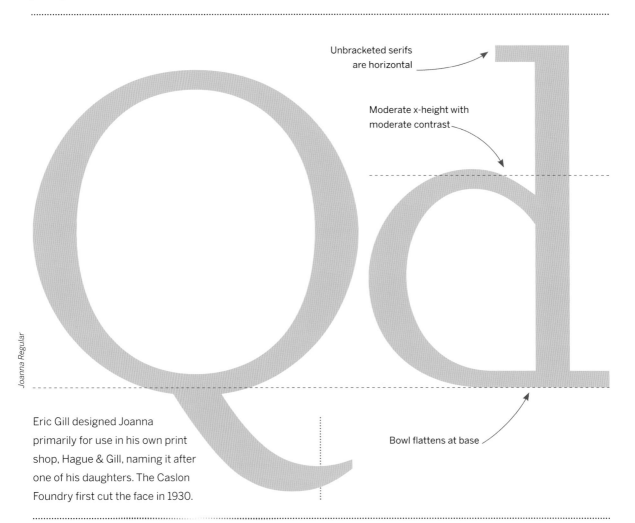

1930

Unbracketed serifs are horizontal

Moderate x-height with moderate contrast

Joanna Regular

Bowl flattens at base

Eric Gill designed Joanna primarily for use in his own print shop, Hague & Gill, naming it after one of his daughters. The Caslon Foundry first cut the face in 1930.

9/12pt Joanna Regular (Monotype)

LOREM IPSUM DOLOR SIT AMET, CONSECTETUER ADIPISCING ELIT, SED DIAM NONUMMY NIBH EUISMOD tincidunt ut laoreet dolore magna aliquam erat volutpat. Ut wisi enim ad minim veniam, quis nostrud exerci tation ullamcorper suscipit lobortis nisl ut aliquip ex ea commodo consequat. Duis autem vel eum iriure dolor in hendrerit in vulputate velit esse molestie consequat, vel

12/15pt Joanna Regular (Monotype)

LOREM IPSUM DOLOR SIT AMET, CONSECTETUER ADIPISCING ELIT, SED diam nonummy nibh euismod tincidunt ut laoreet dolore magna aliquam erat volutpat. Ut wisi enim ad minim veniam, quis nostrud exerci tation ullamcorper suscipit lobortis nisl ut aliquip ex ea commodo

From August 1924 to October 1928, Eric Gill and his entourage lived and worked in a former monastery in the hamlet of Capel-y-ffin, located on the English–Welsh border in Powys. It was here that the designs for his other best known faces, Perpetua and Gill Sans, were begun. Difficulties stemming from the remoteness of the location prompted Gill to move to Piggots farm near High Wycombe in Buckinghamshire. In 1930, his daughter Joanna married an aspiring printer named René Hague and the firm Hague & Gill was established at the farm. Needing type to use at the press, Gill designed Joanna, naming it after his daughter.

It was first used to set Gill's *An Essay on Typography,* which was published in 1931, and is in part a reinventing of Perpetua with a little additional influence from an earlier typeface designed for Monotype by Gill in 1929, named Solus (not digitized until a 2004 revival by Keith Bates of K-Type). It's been said that it was a personal favorite of Gill's; he called it "type with no frills," wanting to create a practical, engineered quality for the face. It was cut and cast for hand composition at the Caslon foundry and is a really rather beautiful and fairly unusual typeface with its Transitional structure and unbracketed serifs. The italic style aligns with Stanley Morison's general dislike of the cursive over the oblique roman—both Morison and Gill agreed that an oblique roman italic paired more successfully with its counterpart weight—but Gill limited the slope to just 3 degrees and introduced some cursive features to the lowercase "a," "e" and "g," meaning Joanna Italic works just as well when used on its own as it does when paired with the roman. The same can be said of Perpetua Italic.

Hague & Gill wasn't a success and the type was sold to publisher J.M. Dent in 1938. They commissioned Monotype to produce a version for machine composition, maintaining exclusivity until Monotype was able to release Joanna commercially in 1958. Like all of Gill's typefaces that aren't relatively recent digital interpretations of the original cuts, the digital version of Joanna is a Monotype face, also available from Adobe as Joanna MT. The original roman has been expanded into four weights: Regular, Semi Bold, Bold and Extra Bold, with italic styles for all but the Extra Bold.

Joanna Regular

Perpetua Regular

Joanna is effectively a close reworking of Gill's earlier Transitional serif Perpetua

The bowl of the "b" and the small eye of the "e" are key features that tie the two faces

DIN

| **Country of origin:** Germany | **Classification:** Geometric Sans
| **Designers:** German Institute for Standardization (Deutsches Institut für Normung)

1931

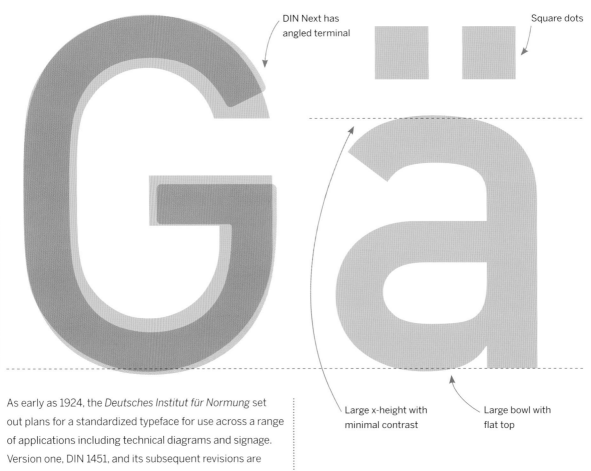

DIN Next has angled terminal

Square dots

DIN 1451 Mittelschrift and DIN Next Regular

Large x-height with minimal contrast

Large bowl with flat top

As early as 1924, the *Deutsches Institut für Normung* set out plans for a standardized typeface for use across a range of applications including technical diagrams and signage. Version one, DIN 1451, and its subsequent revisions are still the dominant public typeface in Germany.

9/12pt DIN Next Regular (Linotype)

LOREM IPSUM DOLOR SIT AMET, CONSECTETUER ADIPISCING ELIT, SED DIAM NONUMMY NIBH EUISMOD tincidunt ut laoreet dolore magna aliquam erat volutpat. Ut wisi enim ad minim veniam, quis nostrud exerci tation ullamcorper suscipit lobortis nisl ut aliquip ex ea commodo consequat. Duis autem vel eum iriure dolor in hendrerit in vulputate velit esse

12/15pt DIN Next Regular (Linotype)

LOREM IPSUM DOLOR SIT AMET, CONSECTETUER ADIPISCING ELIT, SED diam nonummy nibh euismod tincidunt ut laoreet dolore magna aliquam erat volutpat. Ut wisi enim ad minim veniam, quis nostrud exerci tation ullamcorper suscipit lobortis nisl ut aliquip ex ea

DIN, or more precisely DIN 1451 when referring to the original version, is arguably the most German of German Geometric sans serif typefaces. The abbreviation DIN is taken from the Deutsches Institut für Normung, which translates as the German Institute for Standardization—all standards laid down in Germany have their own specific DIN code. The original designer(s) remain anonymous as DIN 1451 was designed by committee, beginning with the 1924 proposals for a typeface that could be used across a wide range of applications, including public signage and printed matter. However, the origins of the design stretch as far back as 1905 and the lettering style used as a standard by the Königlich Preußische Eisenbahn-Verwaltung (Royal Prussian Railway Administration) on railway platforms and rolling stock.

The basic proportions of the characters were drawn to conform to a grid, an advantageous feature that would help to eliminate issues including poor letter spacing if the type was applied by nonprofessional typographers. The first version of the standard was published in 1931, detailing separate models for mechanically engraved lettering, hand-drawn lettering, stenciled type and a version for print.

Contemporary digital interpretations have kept pace with the traditional uses for the typeface. The first digital version was released in 1990 by Linotype and Adobe and consisted of just two weights, DIN Mittelschrift (Medium) and DIN Engschrift (Condensed). A third weight, DIN Breitschrift (Extended) also existed but was never widely used so wasn't carried forward to the digital platform. Despite the limitations of two choices with no italic option, the face became popular among designers looking for a clean, industrial sans serif face for headline and display work. Then in 1994 Albert-Jan Pool, a Dutch type designer who had previously worked at the Hamburg-based typesetting systems manufacturer Scangraphic, and been the manager of type design at the URW type foundry, was commissioned to create a revised version of DIN for FontShop, that would be marketed under their FontFont brand. FF DIN is a 10-weight/20-style family, that includes condensed widths, whereas Lintoype's DIN Next by Akira Kobayashi is an even larger family with a seven-weight/14-style set of standard width fonts plus seven condensed weights. There's also the five-weight FF DIN Round family, designed in 2010, and a DIN Next Rounded equivalent.

DIN Next Regular

DIN Next Rounded Regular

DIN Next and DIN Next Rounded share exactly the same metrics

Times New Roman

| **Country of origin:** United Kingdom | **Classification:** Transitional Serif
| **Designers:** Stanley Morison and Victor Lardent

1932

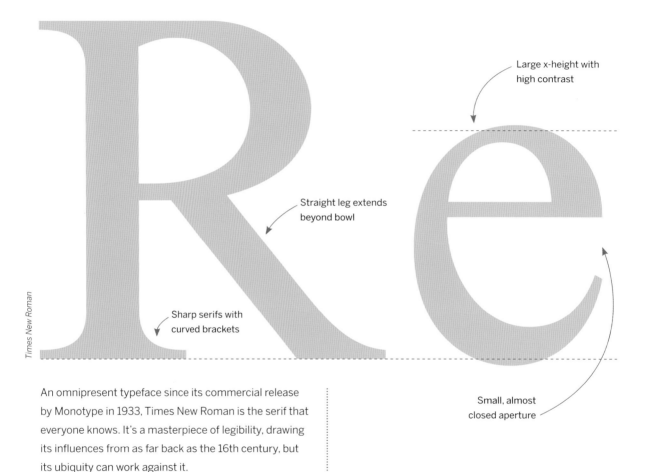

Large x-height with high contrast

Straight leg extends beyond bowl

Sharp serifs with curved brackets

Small, almost closed aperture

Times New Roman

An omnipresent typeface since its commercial release by Monotype in 1933, Times New Roman is the serif that everyone knows. It's a masterpiece of legibility, drawing its influences from as far back as the 16th century, but its ubiquity can work against it.

9/12pt Times New Roman (Monotype)

LOREM IPSUM DOLOR SIT AMET, CONSECTETUER ADIPISCING ELIT, SED diam nonummy nibh euismod tincidunt ut laoreet dolore magna aliquam erat volutpat. Ut wisi enim ad minim veniam, quis nostrud exerci tation ullamcorper suscipit lobortis nisl ut aliquip ex ea commodo consequat. Duis autem vel eum iriure dolor in

12/15pt Times New Roman (Monotype)

LOREM IPSUM DOLOR SIT AMET, CONSECTETUER ADIPISCING elit, sed diam nonummy nibh euismod tincidunt ut laoreet dolore magna aliquam erat volutpat. Ut wisi enim ad minim veniam, quis nostrud exerci tation ullamcorper suscipit lobortis nisl ut

Times New Roman is so well known outside of the design and type community that I've heard people refer to any and all serif faces simply as Times. It's included as part of every computer's operating system and has been the default font for every copy of Microsoft Windows since version 3.1, released in 1992. It's now also the default for Mac OS X (since Apple switched from Linotype's Times Roman) and is the typeface of choice for all U.S. diplomatic documents. Given this level of ubiquity, many professional designers shun its use, which is a bit of a shame, as it is of course a very fine and highly legible typeface with excellent space-saving properties.

The design is attributed to Monotype's Stanley Morison and Victor Lardent, a draftsman employed by *The Times* newspaper. Morison was the typographic advisor to *The Times* from 1929 to 1944 and was convinced that a new typeface was essential to the continued success of a newspaper that had begun to look dated and somewhat illegible. Inspiration for the new face came from Plantin, Robert Granjon's 16th-century Old Style serif revived by Frank Hinman Pierpont for Monotype in 1913. Morison and Lardent sharpened up the design, creating a Transitional serif with finer details and a little more contrast. There exists some controversy about whether Morison really is the designer; it's been proposed that in 1903 an unused version of Times New Roman drawn by a Boston yacht designer named Starling Burgess was submitted to the Lanston Monotype offices in the U.S. and had somehow found its way to Morison's drawing board, but the evidence doesn't stack up enough to be conclusive.

So what's the difference between Times Roman and Times New Roman? Times Roman is the name used by Linotype, and by any companies that license the face from them. Times New Roman is the Monotype name, but the faces are practically the same design because Monotype licensed it to Linotype in the days when *The Times* was composed on Linotype equipment. Linotype couldn't use the same name for their commercial version of the face but were granted the trademark for Times Roman in 1945. There are small differences in some characters, and the metrics vary slightly, but the proportions are very close so differences only become evident at larger point sizes.

You need look no further than Monotype's digitized version today for all your Times New Roman needs as it's true to the original and contains all the available weights and styles. However, if you own the Linotype version instead there's no genuine reason to purchase the Monotype release.

Times New Roman (Monotype)

Times Roman

The free version of Times Roman bundled with operating systems may lack typographic niceties such as ligatures

Albertus

| **Country of origin:** United Kingdom | **Classification:** Glyphic
| **Designer:** Berthold Wolpe

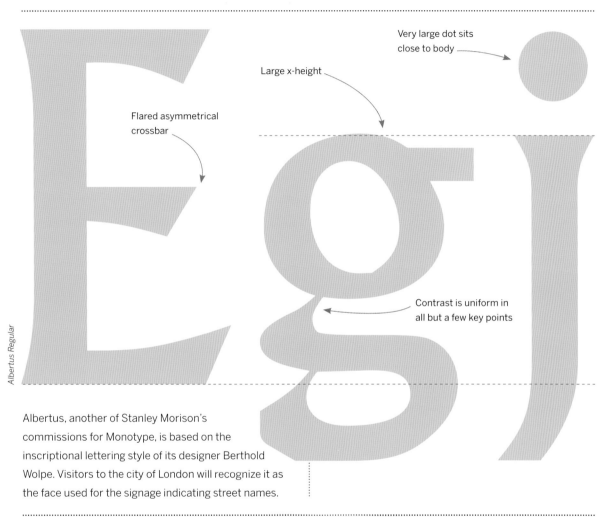

Very large dot sits close to body

Large x-height

Flared asymmetrical crossbar

Contrast is uniform in all but a few key points

Albertus Regular

Albertus, another of Stanley Morison's commissions for Monotype, is based on the inscriptional lettering style of its designer Berthold Wolpe. Visitors to the city of London will recognize it as the face used for the signage indicating street names.

18pt Albertus Regular (Monotype)

AGJMRSegk

72pt Albertus Regular (Monotype)

36pt Albertus Regular (Monotype)

AGJMRSegk

AGJMRSegk

Albertus is the first of several typefaces to be designed by Berthold Wolpe, born in Offenbach am Main near Frankfurt, Germany. Wolpe was a student of the great calligrapher and type designer Rudolf Koch; Koch spent much of his career at the Klingspor Type Foundry in Offenbach and taught at the city's technical institute. It was here that Wolpe learned the lettering and engraving skills that would later inform his design for Albertus, named after the 13th-century German philosopher and theologian Albertus Magnus.

Wolpe met Monotype's Stanley Morison during a visit to England in 1932 and was commissioned to design Albertus after Morison had seen and admired lettering he'd cut in bronze. Albertus is based directly on the style of Wolpe's engraved characters, a fact clearly evident in the glyphic styling of the flared strokes and chiseled shaping. Rather than cut impressions of each character, Wolpe instead removed the background to create raised characters, cutting the outlines first then removing the inner shapes of the counters. By 1935, when the titling weight was first released by Monotype, the rise of National Socialism in Germany had persuaded Wolpe to move permanently to England, where he designed further display weights for Albertus between 1938 and 1940: Light, Roman and Bold. An italic style with a distinctly narrow width accompanies the roman weight. Personally I find it a bit of an odd fit and have never used it— perhaps it was drawn to appease the demands of a foundry catering to the more modern customer? Wolpe's best-known typeface became one of the most successful 20th-century display faces, appearing on British coins, city of London street signs, and as the typeface of choice for many movie title sequences.

Wolpe stayed in England for the rest of his life, spending most of his career working as a designer for the English publisher Faber & Faber. He also taught at Camberwell College of Art and the Royal College of Art in London, receiving an OBE (Order of the British Empire) in 1983. Monotype's digitized version, also available as Albertus MT from Linotype and Adobe, is a good interpretation but the titling weight appears to have never made it to the digital format.

AGRdkl3

Albertus Regular

AGRdkl3

The slightly curious italic style of Albertus is considerably narrower than the roman, more so than the average italic style

Albertus Italic

Rockwell

| **Country of origin:** United States | **Classification:** Geometric Slab
| **Designer:** Monotype

1933–1934

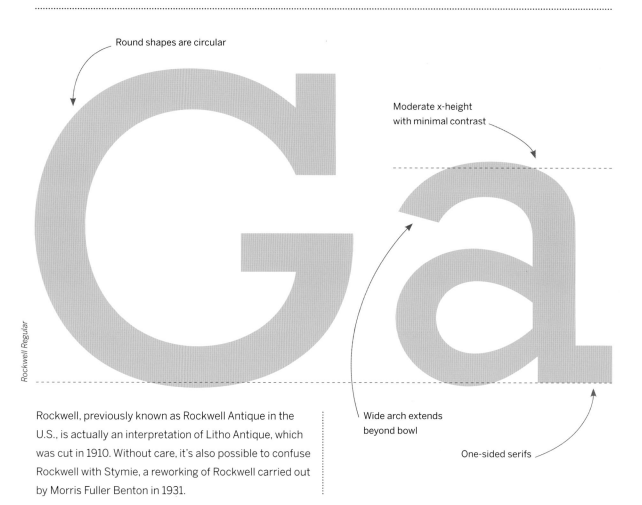

Round shapes are circular

Moderate x-height with minimal contrast

Rockwell Regular

Wide arch extends beyond bowl

One-sided serifs

Rockwell, previously known as Rockwell Antique in the U.S., is actually an interpretation of Litho Antique, which was cut in 1910. Without care, it's also possible to confuse Rockwell with Stymie, a reworking of Rockwell carried out by Morris Fuller Benton in 1931.

9/12pt Rockwell Regular (Monotype)

LOREM IPSUM DOLOR SIT AMET, CONSECTETUER ADIPISCING ELIT, SED DIAM NONUMMY NIBH euismod tincidunt ut laoreet dolore magna aliquam erat volutpat. Ut wisi enim ad minim veniam, quis nostrud exerci tation ullamcorper suscipit lobortis nisl ut aliquip ex ea commodo consequat. Duis autem vel eum iriure dolor in

12/15pt Rockwell Regular (Monotype)

LOREM IPSUM DOLOR SIT AMET, CONSECTETUER ADIPISCING ELIT, sed diam nonummy nibh euismod tincidunt ut laoreet dolore magna aliquam erat volutpat. Ut wisi enim ad minim veniam, quis nostrud exerci tation ullamcorper suscipit lobortis

Before we begin to discuss Rockwell we should mention Litho Antique, a face cut by William Schraubstädter for the Inland Type Foundry of St. Louis and issued in 1910, because it provides the basis for Rockwell. American Type Founders purchased Inland in 1911, issuing their first revival of Litho Antique in the 1920s before releasing a second in 1931, with new weights designed by Morris Fuller Benton, which they renamed Rockwell Antique. The trail becomes a little confused at this point, because in the same year Benton decided a few more design tweaks were needed and redrew Rockwell Antique once again, refining some characters and changing the name to Stymie Bold. Around the same time similar Geometric slabs, or Egyptians, were experiencing a surge in popularity in Europe and Monotype, under the supervision of Frank Hinman Pierpont at Monotype's Salfords works, produced their own version of Rockwell based on the earlier 1931 ATF release of Rockwell Antique. The confusion results from the fact that Monotype mistakenly named their typeface Stymie Bold rather than Rockwell, thus creating two versions of a typeface with the same name but different designs. The situation was

eventually rectified and Monotype released a correct version of Stymie Bold in 1936, but to this day the two faces are often confused with one another.

Rockwell was conceived partly as a competitor to the already popular Memphis, released a few years earlier by the Stempel Type Foundry in Frankfurt. Although both typefaces are Geometric slabs, Rockwell has a more antique feel given its origins as an interpretation of an older face. Characters like the double-story "a" and the round dots above the "i" and "j" feel less constructed, making it a better choice for projects that require a more historic flavor.

The original release of the correctly named Rockwell family grew to contain four weights from Light through to Extra Bold, plus two condensed weights, a Regular and a Bold. Monotype's digitized family, also published on license by Adobe, contains the same range of weights but the standard widths gain an italic style of oblique romans.

OGOQij

Rockwell Regular

Round characters like the "C" and "G" follow the form of the "O," with only a small amount of deviation. The round dots on the "i" and "j" give the face a more historical feel compared to other Geometric slabs

Peignot

| **Country of origin:** France | **Classification:** Display/Peignotian
| **Designer:** A.M. Cassandre

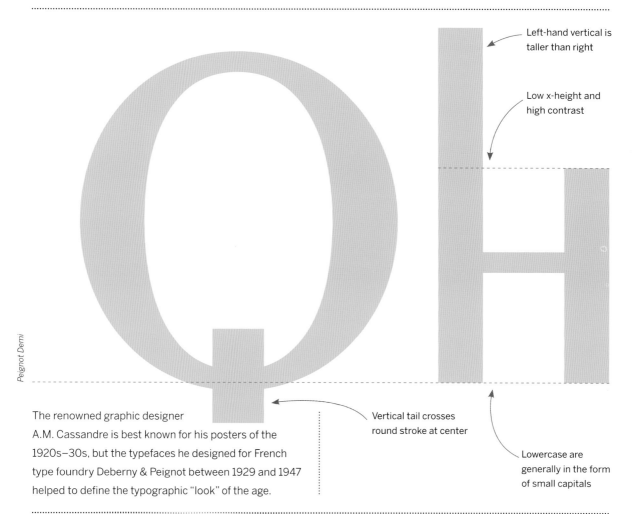

Peignot Demi

1937

Left-hand vertical is taller than right

Low x-height and high contrast

Vertical tail crosses round stroke at center

Lowercase are generally in the form of small capitals

The renowned graphic designer A.M. Cassandre is best known for his posters of the 1920s–30s, but the typefaces he designed for French type foundry Deberny & Peignot between 1929 and 1947 helped to define the typographic "look" of the age.

9/12pt Peignot Light (Linotype)

LOREM IPSUM DOLOR SIT AMET, CONSECTETUER ADIPISCING ELIT, SED DIAM NONUMMY NIBH EUISMOD tincidunt ut laoreet dolore magna aliquam erat volutpat. Ut wisi enim ad minim veniam, quis nostrud exerci tation ullamcorper suscipit lobortis nisl ut aliquip ex ea commodo consequat. Duis autem vel eum iriure dolor in hendrerit in vulputate velit esse molestie consequat, vel illum dolore eu feugiat nulla facilisis at

12/15pt Peignot Light (Linotype)

LOREM IPSUM DOLOR SIT AMET, CONSECTETUER ADIPISCING ELIT, SED diam nonummy nibh euismod tincidunt ut laoreet dolore magna aliquam erat volutpat. Ut wisi enim ad minim veniam, quis nostrud exerci tation ullamcorper suscipit lobortis nisl ut aliquip ex ea commodo consequat. Duis autem vel eum

If there were ever a typeface to symbolize France in the 1930s, this is it. Peignot was designed by the great poster designer and graphic artist Adolphe Mouron Cassandre in 1937 for the Parisian type foundry Deberny & Peignot, as a commission from the owner, Charles Peignot. Although he was better known for his influential posters, Cassandre designed several typefaces for D&P, including Bifur in 1929 and Acier Noir in 1936, but Peignot is arguably the best known and most enduring.

Peignot benefited from a dramatic launch when it was chosen as the official typeface for the 1937 Paris World's Fair. It was applied to everything from exhibition stands to the towers of the Palais de Chaillot, sited at the Trocadéro and opposite the Eiffel Tower. Cassandre was insistent about the face's suitability for text, even though its outward appearance labels it as a decorative display face. It's an unusual concept with all lowercase characters except the "b," "d" and "f" drawn as small caps, and the "h" is particularly curious with its left-hand vertical stroke rising to the same height as the ascenders. Somewhat surprisingly, the origins of the typeface stem from medieval calligraphy.

Cassandre designed Peignot as a kind of experiment—he wanted to push the boundaries of traditional roman letterforms to create a new kind of stylized text face that would retain its legibility despite the unusual forms of the lowercase. Medieval half-uncial calligraphy freely mixed upper- and lowercase letterforms with elongated ascenders and descenders, so why not map those qualities onto a structured sans serif form echoing the contemporary typefaces of the day. Peignot suffered a dip in popularity during the 1950s when the International Typographic Style was at its height, but prevails as a go-to face when an art deco flavor is required.

This hybrid mix makes it almost impossible to fit Peignot within any of the regular classifications; it's not a Humanist sans, it's not a Geometric sans, it's not a Display, but rather a mixture of all these. Fortunately, Luc Devroye has coined the phrase "Peignotian" to categorize typefaces like Peignot, and it works for me. The digital version published by Linotype contains three weights: Light, Demi, which corresponds to the original Regular weight, and Bold. The titling weight is currently not available as a digital font.

Peignot Demi

Peignot's lowercase character set is a curious mix of small caps that rise to the x-height and lowercase letterforms

Caledonia

| **Country of origin:** United States | **Classification:** Rational Serif
| **Designer:** William Addison Dwiggins

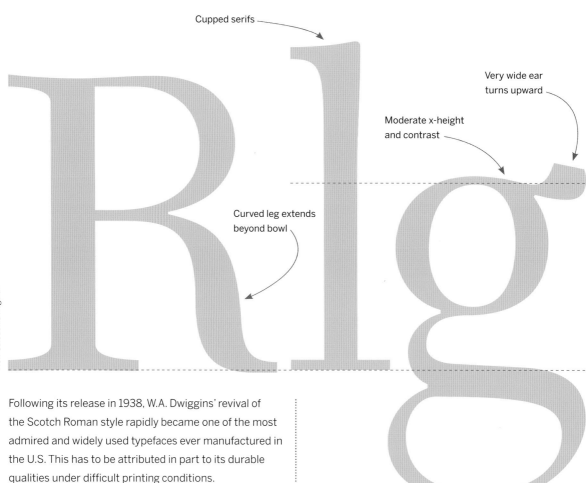

Cupped serifs

Very wide ear turns upward

Moderate x-height and contrast

Curved leg extends beyond bowl

New Caledonia Regular

Following its release in 1938, W.A. Dwiggins' revival of the Scotch Roman style rapidly became one of the most admired and widely used typefaces ever manufactured in the U.S. This has to be attributed in part to its durable qualities under difficult printing conditions.

9/12pt New Caledonia Regular (Linotype)

LOREM IPSUM DOLOR SIT AMET, CONSECTETUER ADIPISCING ELIT, SED DIAM nonummy nibh euismod tincidunt ut laoreet dolore magna aliquam erat volutpat. Ut wisi enim ad minim veniam, quis nostrud exerci tation ullamcorper suscipit lobortis nisl ut aliquip ex ea commodo consequat. Duis autem vel eum iriure dolor in hendrerit in vulputate

12/15pt New Caledonia Regular (Linotype)

LOREM IPSUM DOLOR SIT AMET, CONSECTETUER ADIPISCING ELIT, sed diam nonummy nibh euismod tincidunt ut laoreet dolore magna aliquam erat volutpat. Ut wisi enim ad minim veniam, quis nostrud exerci tation ullamcorper suscipit lobortis nisl ut

Caledonia is arguably the best of the typefaces designed by William Addison Dwiggins for Mergenthaler Linotype in 1938—historically it's certainly been the most successful. At the age of 19, Dwiggins attended the Frank Holme School of Illustration in Chicago where he was taught lettering by Frederic W. Goudy, but he didn't design his first typeface until his late 40s. An observation regarding the paucity of sans serif typefaces made in *Layout and Advertising*, a manual written by Dwiggins and published in 1928, prompted Harry Gage of Linotype to invite him to design a typeface himself. He came up with Metro, an interesting but not wholly successful sans that evidently did well enough to prompt further commissions, and his relationship with Linotype prevailed until his death 27 years later. Alongside his type design work Dwiggins worked as a graphic designer, enjoying a long association with the publisher Alfred A. Knopf. He also ran his own marionette theater, making his own puppets and writing the plays.

The inspiration for Caledonia was drawn from two sources; Dwiggins was very fond of the faces cut by Alexander Wilson's Glasgow foundry and at the Edinburgh foundry of William Miller during the early 19th century, a style known as Scotch Roman. It's this connection that provides the name Caledonia, the Latin name used by the

Romans for Scotland. He was also a fan of the slightly later English faces cut by William Martin for William Bulmer of the Shakespeare Press. Caledonia takes elements from both styles without looking overtly like either; Dwiggins injected a great deal of personality into the design and the characters feel lively and quite calligraphic. The Regular weight and its italic counterpart were joined 2 years after the original release by a Bold and a Bold Italic, and there was at one time a Condensed Bold designed specifically for use in newspaper headlines. The face was designed to work specifically for machine composition using the Linotype system, which most newspaper publishers preferred, and was all the more successful for it, but a version was manufactured as foundry type and marketed in Germany as Cornelia.

Linotype released an updated version of Caledonia in 1979, naming it New Caledonia, and the digital version published by Adobe and Linotype is based on this design. The family was increased to four weights ranging from Regular through Semi Bold and Bold to Black. There are also true small caps and Old Style figure options available for the Regular and Bold weights.

New Caledonia Regular

Scotch Roman Regular　　The influence of Scotch Roman over New Caledonia is clear when they're viewed together

Palatino

| **Country of origin:** Germany | **Classification:** Old Style Serif
| **Designer:** Hermann Zapf

1948–1950

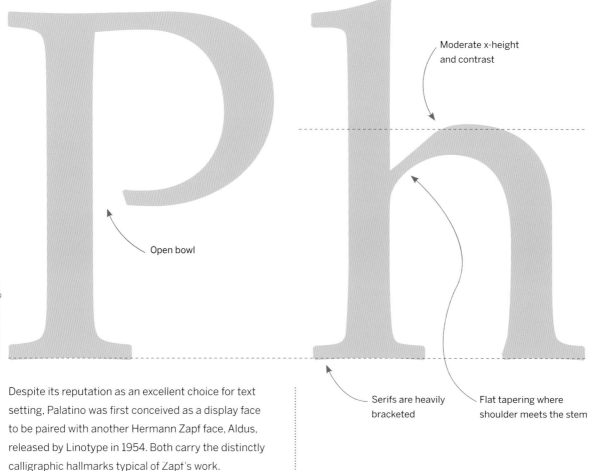

Palatino Nova Regular

Moderate x-height and contrast

Open bowl

Serifs are heavily bracketed

Flat tapering where shoulder meets the stem

Despite its reputation as an excellent choice for text setting, Palatino was first conceived as a display face to be paired with another Hermann Zapf face, Aldus, released by Linotype in 1954. Both carry the distinctly calligraphic hallmarks typical of Zapf's work.

9/12pt Palatino Nova Regular (Linotype)

LOREM IPSUM DOLOR SIT AMET, CONSECTETUER ADIPISCING ELIT, SED DIAM nonummy nibh euismod tincidunt ut laoreet dolore magna aliquam erat volutpat. Ut wisi enim ad minim veniam, quis nostrud exerci tation ullamcorper suscipit lobortis nisl ut aliquip ex ea commodo consequat. Duis autem vel eum iriure

12/15pt Palatino Nova Regular (Linotype)

LOREM IPSUM DOLOR SIT AMET, CONSECTETUER ADIPISCING ELIT, sed diam nonummy nibh euismod tincidunt ut laoreet dolore magna aliquam erat volutpat. Ut wisi enim ad minim veniam, quis nostrud exerci tation ullamcorper suscipit lobortis

Palatino was designed for Linotype between 1948 and 1950 by the noted calligrapher, designer and teacher Hermann Zapf. Its name refers to the Renaissance writing master Giovanni Battista Palatino but isn't based on his work in any way. The calligraphic flavor of the face is derived from Zapf's own lettering skills. It's arguably his best-known typeface, not solely because of the design but because of its ubiquity. It's long been a top choice for setting the text of good-quality books despite the fact that it was first conceived as a display face; Aldus was designed by Zapf and released in 1954 as a companion face for smaller text setting. It's also been bundled as part of the Mac operating system for many years, so is consequently a familiar face to nondesigners.

The first Palatino was cut by August Rosenberger at Stempel's Frankfurt foundry; the first three weights were a roman with an accompanying italic, plus a Bold roman, and these were released as both foundry type and as Linotype matrices in 1950. From the very start there were differences between versions of this changeable face. The foundry italic was narrower than the Linotype machine version and there were different optical sizes above and below 12 point. For some reason there were also differences between the European and American versions, the latter being introduced in 1954. Then in 1963 Zapf adapted the design once again to suit the new phototypesetting technology, and to their detriment early digital versions were based on designs from this period.

There are a lot of digitized Palatino families around, some of which are better than others. Given the number of predigital versions produced, trying to match one of the currently available PostScript or OpenType families with the design of the original foundry type was a challenging exercise. However, Linotype's 2005 release Palatino Nova (overseen once again by Zapf himself with Monotype Type Director Akira Kobayashi) irons out many of the imperfections that crept in during previous revisions and attempts to return as closely as possible to the original ideas behind Palatino. Alongside the four weights and eight styles there are two new titling weights, which have been adapted from faces designed by Zapf in the early 1950s, plus a number of new alternative characters. You're reading text set in Palatino Nova Regular now; it's the principal font used for the running text throughout this book.

Palatino Nova Regular

A wealth of alternative characters, such as the ampersand with a calligraphic bar, reflect Zapf's style. Aldus Nova is also available as a finer cut suitable for display setting

Palatino Nova Regular and Aldus Nova Book (gray tint)

Melior

| **Country of origin:** Germany | **Classification:** Rational Serif
| **Designer:** Hermann Zapf

1952

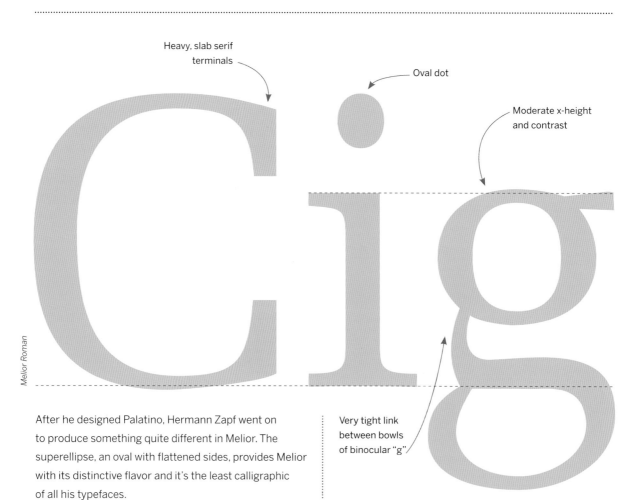

Heavy, slab serif terminals

Oval dot

Moderate x-height and contrast

Very tight link between bowls of binocular "g"

Melior Roman

After he designed Palatino, Hermann Zapf went on to produce something quite different in Melior. The superellipse, an oval with flattened sides, provides Melior with its distinctive flavor and it's the least calligraphic of all his typefaces.

9/12pt Melior Roman (Linotype)

LOREM IPSUM DOLOR SIT AMET, CONSECTETUER ADIPISCING ELIT, SED DIAM nonummy nibh euismod tincidunt ut laoreet dolore magna aliquam erat volutpat. Ut wisi enim ad minim veniam, quis nostrud exerci tation ullamcorper suscipit lobortis nisl ut aliquip ex ea commodo consequat. Duis autem vel eum iriure

12/15pt Melior Roman (Linotype)

LOREM IPSUM DOLOR SIT AMET, CONSECTETUER ADIPISCING ELIT, sed diam nonummy nibh euismod tincidunt ut laoreet dolore magna aliquam erat volutpat. Ut wisi enim ad minim veniam, quis nostrud exerci tation ullamcorper suscipit lobortis

Hermann Zapf was at work on the design for Melior at around the same time as Palatino, discussed on the previous spread. Once again the typeface was cut at Stempel for Linotype and even by today's standards its design is fairly unique. It remains one of the few serif faces to be based on a form called the superellipse, an oval with sides that are almost flat. The shape is far more common in Grotesque sans serifs and in square form Geometrics such as Eurostile; for the right kind of project, Melior can make a good seriffed partner for sans serifs that meet a similar criteria of form.

Melior is sometimes referred to as an Ionic, this being an alternative category name for a Clarendon, but it's classed here as a Rational serif because of its vertical stress, moderately high contrast, and constructed form. It was conceived specifically as a high performance typeface for newspapers that could function under the most difficult of printing conditions and Zapf was able to study the technical requirements of a range of printing techniques including letterpress, offset lithography and gravure during a trip to Linotype's U.S. offices in 1951. Melior proved popular and managed to survive the phototypesetting era intact; its rounded terminals and heavy drooped serifs lend themselves to the relatively unfocused phototype technology without experiencing a significant loss of detail.

Linotype's digital version, also available from Adobe, still offers the same two weights, Roman and Bold, although there is now also a Bold italic style, and the OpenType version has added over a hundred new glyphs to the full character set. It may seem surprising that such an influential face hasn't been expanded into a larger family with additional weights like so many others, but bear in mind that its design is very much of its time and doesn't necessarily lend itself to a broad range of applications. It remains an excellent choice for projects that need to reference the mid 20th century.

The superellipse is also known as a Lamé curve, after the 19th-century French mathematician Gabriel Lamé. The shape is far more common to Grotesque sans serif faces and square-form Geometrics, but Zapf used it to uniquely striking effect with Melior

Melior Roman

Mistral

| **Country of origin:** France | **Classification:** Casual Script
| **Designer:** Roger Excoffon

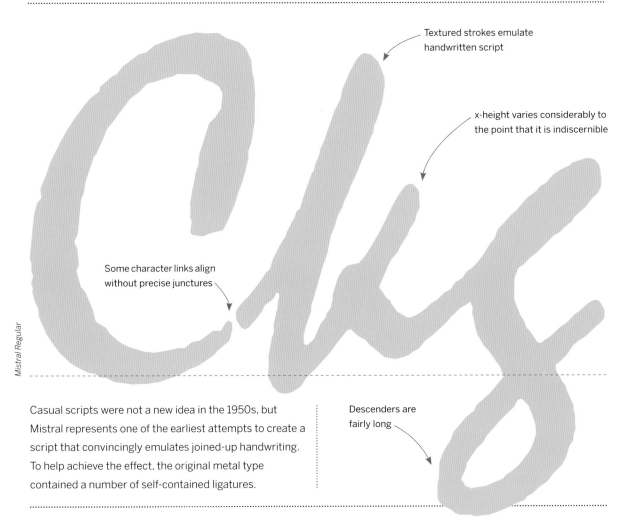

Textured strokes emulate handwritten script

x-height varies considerably to the point that it is indiscernible

Some character links align without precise junctures

Mistral Regular

Casual scripts were not a new idea in the 1950s, but Mistral represents one of the earliest attempts to create a script that convincingly emulates joined-up handwriting. To help achieve the effect, the original metal type contained a number of self-contained ligatures.

Descenders are fairly long

18pt Mistral Regular (Fonderie Olive)

RGamsty48

36pt Mistral Regular (Fonderie Olive)

RGamsty48

72pt Mistral Regular (Fonderie Olive)

RGamsty48

112   The Evolution of Type

The genius of Mistral, conceived by French designer Roger Excoffon for Fonderie Olive in 1953, is key to its inclusion in this book. By no means was Mistral the first casual script to attempt the emulation of joined-up text, but at that point in time it was the most successful. To understand the cleverness of Excoffon's achievement it's necessary to take the opportunity to explain an important difference between the way Monotype and Linotype machines composed type.

Creating convincingly fluid script setting in metal was challenging because of the need for kerning, or the spacing between each typeset character. This must vary constantly to produce good setting and it's particularly crucial for setting any kind of script. To get around the problem, characters could project beyond the edges of the metal bodies of foundry type to overlap the shoulder of its neighbor—these extensions were called kerns. Ligatures such as fi, ffi, fl and so on were also used extensively to alleviate the problem. The Monotype machine used individually cast pieces of type so kerning wasn't a problem, but the Linotype assembled a line of matrices before casting a single slug of metal (a line o' type) and could not kern. If you compare old Monotype and Linotype typeface samplers you can see how some Linotype characters like the "f" or "y," particularly in their italic styles, have details pulled back into the width of the body to accommodate the restriction imposed by the technology. These issues have, of course, been corrected in modern digital releases but at the time ligature glyphs were the only option for the Linotype system.

By design, Excoffon somehow managed to create a combined set of individual characters and ligatures that worked on both machines. He was one of the first designers to introduce alternates for standard glyphs to create the random sense that the setting was handwritten, and he cleverly varied the baseline to further enhance the effect. Today the genius of the original design is, of course, taken care of by OpenType technology's automatic glyph substitution.

There are a couple of digital versions of Mistral available today. The offering from Linotype and Adobe sticks to the single weight designed by Excoffon and personally I would recommend this option. There's also a version adapted by Phill Grimshaw and published by ITC that adds a Light weight with a small caps style but for me the extra weight doesn't feel like Excoffon's Mistral. If a lighter script is required it might be better to look at an alternative choice of font, but that's just a personal viewpoint.

Although it's no match for contemporary OpenType scripts, Mistral is nonetheless an impressive achievement for its time

Mistral Regular

Trump Mediaeval

| **Country of origin:** Germany | **Classification:** Old Style Serif
| **Designer:** Georg Trump

1954

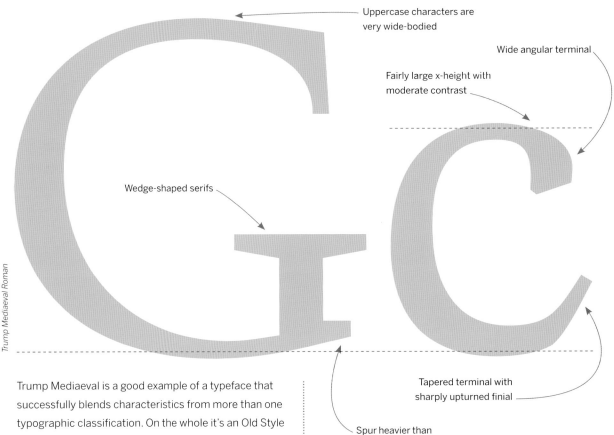

Trump Mediaeval Roman

Uppercase characters are very wide-bodied

Wide angular terminal

Fairly large x-height with moderate contrast

Wedge-shaped serifs

Tapered terminal with sharply upturned finial

Spur heavier than round stroke

Trump Mediaeval is a good example of a typeface that successfully blends characteristics from more than one typographic classification. On the whole it's an Old Style serif and is classed as such, but there are also traces of Humanist serif present in the letter shapes and details.

9/12pt Trump Mediaeval Roman (Linotype)

LOREM IPSUM DOLOR SIT AMET, CONSECTETUER ADIPISCING ELIT, SED diam nonummy nibh euismod tincidunt ut laoreet dolore magna aliquam erat volutpat. Ut wisi enim ad minim veniam, quis nostrud exerci tation ullamcorper suscipit lobortis nisl ut aliquip ex ea commodo consequat. Duis autem vel eum

12/15pt Trump Mediaeval Roman (Linotype)

LOREM IPSUM DOLOR SIT AMET, CONSECTETUER ADIPISCING elit, sed diam nonummy nibh euismod tincidunt ut laoreet dolore magna aliquam erat volutpat. Ut wisi enim ad minim veniam, quis nostrud exerci tation ullamcorper suscipit

Trump Mediaeval was designed by Georg Trump for the Weber Type Foundry, which was based in Stuttgart, Germany, until its closure in 1970. Trump studied at Stuttgart's Staatliche Kuntsgewerbeschule (State School of Arts and Crafts) where he was taught by Ernst Schneidler, and he later became a teacher himself, lecturing alongside Jan Tschichold at the Meisterschule für Deutchlands Buchdrucker (Master School for German Printers) in Munich following an invitation from Paul Renner, the designer of Futura. He became director of the school after both Tschichold and Renner were dismissed under pressure from the Nazis because of their subversive views.

Trump Mediaeval was initially released by Weber as foundry type for hand-setting before Linotype began to distribute the face for mechanical composition shortly afterward. Its name is a little confusing as the "mediaeval" appendage could be taken to mean the face takes its origins from blackletter type. This is obviously not the case and can be explained by the fact that the term was used in Germany as an adjective to indicate roman faces that were particularly dark in color. It has much more in common with the late-15th-century Humanist (or Venetian) serifs designed by the likes of

Nicolas Jenson, but Trump achieved something with his typeface that feels more modern by bringing in elements reminiscent of an Old Style. There's a sharpness to the serifs and an overall angularity that sets it apart from other Old Styles, particularly when compared to Palatino, which was arguably its nearest competitor at the time of its release. One could mistake it for a Contemporary serif, a classification introduced postdigital to cover serifs that take their influence from a range of historical sources. The italic is particularly successful—it's an oblique roman with just a couple of cursive touches for the "a" and the "f," and the ampersand is a thing of beauty.

Linotype's digital release, also available from Adobe, sadly lacks some of the original characters and weights. It includes Roman and Bold weights, both of which have an italic style, and there are separate fonts for small caps and Old Style figures. However, there are no swash capitals or alternate characters accompanying the Italic, and the Extra Bold and Bold Condensed weights have never been digitized. The titling weight Trump Gravur is also missing from the Linotype family but is available as a single font published by ARTypes.

Trump Mediaeval's italic is an oblique roman with (unusually) just a couple of cursive characters

Trump Mediaeval Roman and Italic

Folio

| **Country of origin:** Germany | **Classification:** Grotesque Sans
| **Designers:** Konrad F. Bauer and Walter Baum

1957–1962

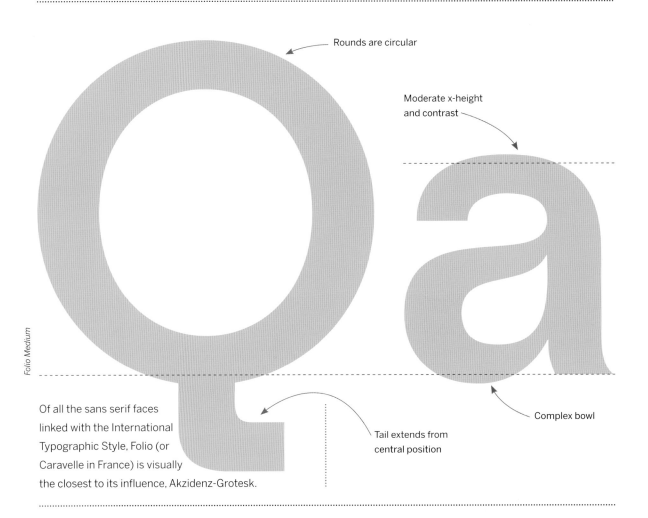

Rounds are circular

Moderate x-height and contrast

Folio Medium

Complex bowl

Tail extends from central position

Of all the sans serif faces linked with the International Typographic Style, Folio (or Caravelle in France) is visually the closest to its influence, Akzidenz-Grotesk.

9/12pt Folio Medium (Bauer Types S.A.)

LOREM IPSUM DOLOR SIT AMET, CONSECTETUER ADIPISCING ELIT, SED DIAM nonummy nibh euismod tincidunt ut laoreet dolore magna aliquam erat volutpat. Ut wisi enim ad minim veniam, quis nostrud exerci tation ullamcorper suscipit lobortis nisl ut aliquip ex ea commodo consequat. Duis autem vel eum iriure dolor in

12/15pt Folio Medium (Bauer Types S.A.)

LOREM IPSUM DOLOR SIT AMET, CONSECTETUER ADIPISCING ELIT, sed diam nonummy nibh euismod tincidunt ut laoreet dolore magna aliquam erat volutpat. Ut wisi enim ad minim veniam, quis nostrud exerci tation ullamcorper suscipit lobortis nisl

Konrad F. Bauer and Walter Baum designed all of their typefaces as a team while working together at the Bauer Type Foundry in Frankfurt. Bauer was head of the foundry's art department and Baum headed up the graphics studio (it's unclear how these departments differed) and the pair can lay claim to being the designers of the first Grotesque slab (or Clarendon) with an accompanying italic style, known variously as Fortune, Volta and—in the U.S.—Fortuna. There are several versions of Volta currently available in the digital format, and we now also have some excellent contemporary Grotesque slabs with proper italic styles such as Hoefler & Co.'s Sentinel.

Folio is a member of the hallowed group of Neo-Grotesque sans serif faces that have come to represent the International Typographic Style, the others being Univers and Neue Haas Grotesk/Helvetica. Like these better-known faces, which were released around the same time, Folio was heavily influenced by the design of Akzidenz-Grotesk. In fact, its design is somewhat closer to the turn-of-the-century sans serif than either Univers or Neue Haas Grotesk, both of which have a visibly larger x-height.

Perhaps the larger range of weights and styles offered by these similar new typeface families contributed to Folio experiencing only moderate European success on its release; perhaps the lack of italic styles made a commercial difference. However, it did well enough in the U.S. because Bauer licensed it to the Intertype Corporation for use on their line-casting machines, and the foundry still maintained a good distribution network for its hand-set foundry type during the 1950s period. After managing with only three basic weights for around 5 years, Extra Bold and Bold Condensed weights were added in 1962, and the family was also licensed to Fonderie Typographique Française and marketed in France as Caravelle.

The digital version of Folio survives reasonably intact, with Light, Medium, Bold, Extra Bold, and Bold Condensed weights that are close to the original design. Curiously, there appears to have been a Medium extended weight in existence at some point, perhaps it was added by Intertype, but it hasn't been digitized.

Folio Medium

Akzidenz Grotesk Medium

Univers

| **Country of origin:** France | **Classification:** Neo-Grotesque Sans
| **Designer:** Adrian Frutiger

1957

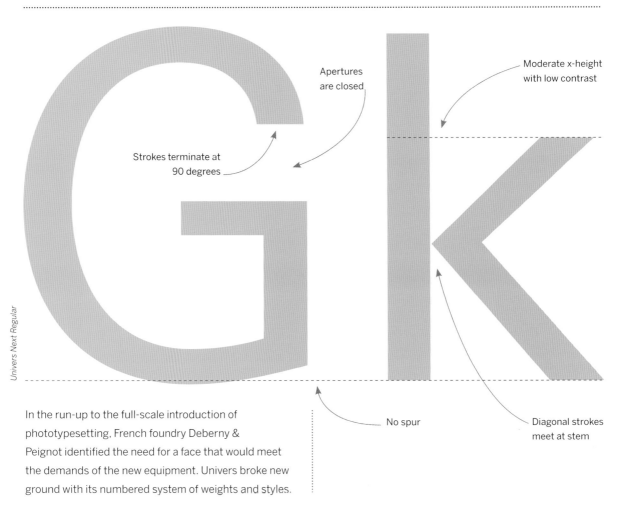

Univers Next Regular

Moderate x-height with low contrast

Apertures are closed

Strokes terminate at 90 degrees

No spur

Diagonal strokes meet at stem

In the run-up to the full-scale introduction of phototypesetting, French foundry Deberny & Peignot identified the need for a face that would meet the demands of the new equipment. Univers broke new ground with its numbered system of weights and styles.

9/12pt Univers Next Regular (Linotype)

LOREM IPSUM DOLOR SIT AMET, CONSECTETUER ADIPISCING ELIT, SED DIAM nonummy nibh euismod tincidunt ut laoreet dolore magna aliquam erat volutpat. Ut wisi enim ad minim veniam, quis nostrud exerci tation ullamcorper suscipit lobortis nisl ut aliquip ex ea commodo consequat. Duis autem vel eum iriure

12/15pt Univers Next Regular (Linotype)

LOREM IPSUM DOLOR SIT AMET, CONSECTETUER ADIPISCING ELIT, sed diam nonummy nibh euismod tincidunt ut laoreet dolore magna aliquam erat volutpat. Ut wisi enim ad minim veniam, quis nostrud exerci tation ullamcorper suscipit lobortis

Univers can thank the phototypesetting technology that emerged during the 1950s for its start. The face was designed by Adrian Frutiger in 1957 following a brief from the French foundry Deberny & Peignot. Frutiger had been employed at the foundry since the early 1950s, and had designed a few "test" faces before creating the successful Transitional serif face Meridien in 1955. D&P wanted to offer a new sans serif in their collection that could work with the Lumitype machines, soon to become the most popular phototypesetting system used throughout France. Letterpress was still used widely at the time, as was hot metal, so Univers became the first member of the select group of faces designed for simultaneous use as foundry type for hand-setting, for hot metal machine composition on the Monotype system, and for photosetting.

Instead of following the usual method of adapting an existing type design, Frutiger persuaded the foundry to allow him to use work he had begun as a student at the Zurich art school as a basis for the new typeface. Early trials were successful and Frutiger developed a range of weights and styles that he categorized not by the normal system of Roman, Bold and so on but by numerical classification. He started with the Regular Roman weight, which he designated as Univers 55, then drew a further 20 different styles split into six weights and four widths.

Romans were assigned odd numbers, italics took the even numbers, and the first digit of each number indicates the weight of the strokes with 3 the lightest and 8 the heaviest. The four widths are indicated by the second digit of each number, with 3 the widest and 9 the most condensed. It's a very simple and effective system, but Monotype ignored it for their version and reverted to calling the fonts standard names. Therefore Univers 56 would be Univers Roman Italic, and so on.

Today there are a few digital options available from the usual sources, the most familiar of which is probably Linotype's standard offering, that includes all the weights of the original face. Given that there were different adaptations of the face designed for different technologies from the outset, earlier digitized versions varied. Linotype's version, completed in 1997 by foundry staff overseen by Frutiger, was a completely redrawn version of the typeface first designed for photocomposition. The metrics were reassessed to create a more even color for text and the thick-to-thin stroke ratios were refined. In 2010 this process was taken even further, cleaning up any lingering phototype compromises to create Univers Next, which is the most faithful design in comparison with Frutiger's original drawings and part of Linotype's Platinum Collection.

4555657585
4757675363793

Univers

Neue Haas Grotesk/ Helvetica

| **Country of origin:** Switzerland (Germany) | **Classification:** Neo-Grotesque Sans
| **Designers:** Max Miedinger and Eduard Hoffmann

1957

Neue Helvetica bowl occupies upper half of body

Neue Haas Grotesk has slightly larger bowl, increasing cap height

Moderate x-height and very low contrast

Leg connects to arm

Neue Haas Grotesk Text 55 Roman and Neue Helvetica 55 Roman

Mildly curved leg

The famous typeface Helvetica (it has its own movie) was known as Neue Haas Grotesk for the first few years of its existence, becoming Helvetica in 1961 during its production at the Stempel type foundry. Its enormous popularity makes it the most recognizable *Swiss* typeface.

Single-story "g" with compact lower stroke

9/12pt Neue Haas Grotesk 55 Roman (Linotype)

LOREM IPSUM DOLOR SIT AMET, CONSECTETUER ADIPISCING ELIT, SED DIAM nonummy nibh euismod tincidunt ut laoreet dolore magna aliquam erat volutpat. Ut wisi enim ad minim veniam, quis nostrud exerci tation ullamcorper suscipit lobortis nisl ut aliquip ex ea commodo consequat. Duis autem vel eum iriure

12/15pt Neue Haas Grotesk 55 Roman (Linotype)

LOREM IPSUM DOLOR SIT AMET, CONSECTETUER ADIPISCING ELIT, sed diam nonummy nibh euismod tincidunt ut laoreet dolore magna aliquam erat volutpat. Ut wisi enim ad minim veniam, quis nostrud exerci tation ullamcorper suscipit lobortis

Between 1957 and 1961 Helvetica had a different name—Neue Haas Grotesk. Designed by Max Miedinger with art direction from Eduard Hoffmann for the Haas Type Foundry in Münchenstein, Switzerland, the project was conceived as an attempt to improve on Akzidenz-Grotesk. Their Neo-Grotesque sans was planned as a competitor for other popular German and British sans serifs launched in the 1950s, and was a big hit for the foundry thanks to the emergent postwar success of the International Typographic Style.

In 1961 Stempel, the main supplier of matrices for Linotype machines, were asked to produce a version of the typeface that would work correctly on their system. It's at this point that the name changes to Helvetica, a derivation of Helvetia which is the Latin name for Switzerland, and is also when Miedinger's original design starts to become diluted. Linotype machines required the matrices of different weights to be the same width, so the proportions of bolder weights had to be made narrower. This technical requirement, unnecessary for the Monotype system, which cast separate sorts, was responsible for the unraveling of many a carefully considered typeface design over the years, unless, of course, the face was designed specifically for the Linotype system. As new technology began to replace hot metal, Helvetica underwent a further set of redraws when it transitioned from metal to phototypesetting, moving the face even further away from the original concept. For some years the Helvetica family suffered a range of mismatched weights and styles.

So how many digital versions of Helvetica are out there? A good number, no doubt, with many unauthorized copies available to download, but sticking to the commercial offerings we have Linotype's Helvetica and Neue Helvetica. The latter is a 1983 version redrawn and digitized by Stempel in a generally successful attempt to iron out the lack of coordination between existing weights and styles. It adopted a numerical naming system similar to that used by Adrian Frutiger for his Univers family. Better still, we now have Neue Haas Grotesk, a faithful revival of the original design described by Christian Schwartz as a "restoration project," with three text weights and eight display weights, all of which have an accompanying italic style. It was first commissioned in 2004 for a redesign of *The Guardian* newspaper, but not used; the project was finally completed in 2010 for Richard Turley of *Bloomsberg Businessweek* before its commercial release. And how many typefaces can claim to have starred in their own movie? The feature-length film *Helvetica*, produced and directed by Gary Hustwit in 2007, confirmed Helvetica's position as the number one sans serif typeface.

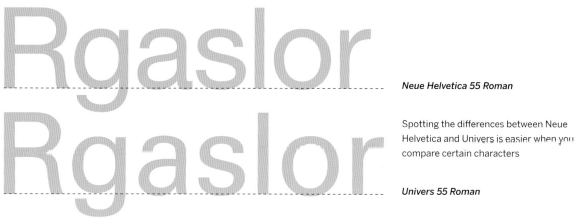

Neue Helvetica 55 Roman

Spotting the differences between Neue Helvetica and Univers is easier when you compare certain characters

Univers 55 Roman

Transport

| **Country of origin:** United Kingdom | **Classification:** Geometric Sans
| **Designers:** Margaret Calvert and Jock Kinneir

1957–1963

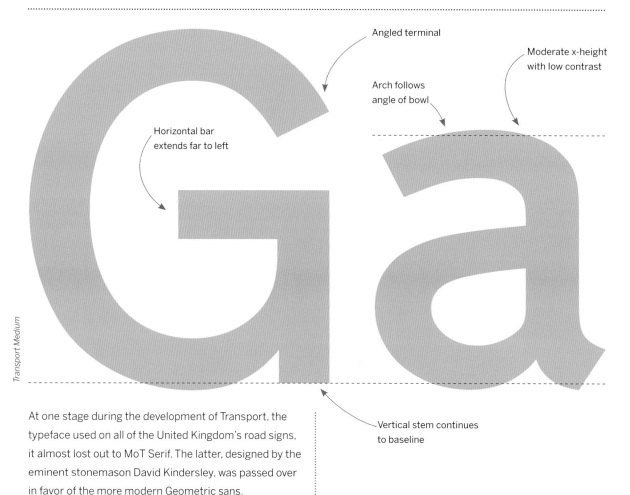

Angled terminal

Moderate x-height with low contrast

Arch follows angle of bowl

Horizontal bar extends far to left

Vertical stem continues to baseline

Transport Medium

At one stage during the development of Transport, the typeface used on all of the United Kingdom's road signs, it almost lost out to MoT Serif. The latter, designed by the eminent stonemason David Kindersley, was passed over in favor of the more modern Geometric sans.

18pt Transport Medium (URW++)

Rgaslor

36pt Transport Medium (URW++)

Rgaslor

72pt Transport Medium (URW++)

Rgaslor

During its development, Transport was the cause of a serious public argument, but it did prove one thing beyond a doubt—it's easier to read lowercase letters when they're flashing past at 70 miles per hour. The designers Jock Kinneir and Margaret Calvert began their professional partnership after Kinneir invited Calvert to collaborate on a signage project for London's newly renovated Gatwick Airport. Existing typefaces were tested and rejected so Kinneir designed his own, a face drawing its influences from Edward Johnston's designs for the London Underground. The success of the project drew in more signage work and the pair were subsequently asked by Colin Anderson, the chairman of the committee appointed to oversee the design of signs for the new M1 motorway between London and Yorkshire, to act as consultants.

The initial brief contained an affirmation that the committee liked the look of the German typeface DIN, but Kinneir and Calvert chose to ignore this, seeing the engineered face as unrefined and inappropriate for the English landscape. They did, however, draw a good deal of inspiration from Akzidenz-Grotesk, and their subsequent design (a Geometric sans with Grotesque leanings) was named Transport. It was during this stage of the design process that they realized a mixture of uppercase and lowercase characters were easier to read at speed. The design was deemed a success and the adoption of the American white-on-blue color scheme completed their work.

But what about that argument? It all began when the typographer Herbert Spencer published pieces in *The Guardian* and *The Times Literary Supplement* bemoaning the disparity of design across the signage appearing in London and on ordinary roads throughout Britain. Kinneir proposed using Transport with a color treatment using white-on-green with yellow numerals for A-roads and black on white for all other routes. This was quickly accepted, but the famous stonemason and lettering artist David Kindersley (an apprentice of Eric Gill) had worked on an alternative face called MoT Serif and wasn't happy that his work had been overlooked. An angry public exchange ensued with letters published in the press, but ultimately, and after a series of tests, Kinneir and Calvert's sans serif won out against the visually pleasing but less "scientific" serif face. Transport is still used on road signs throughout much of mainland Europe.

The digital version available from Hamburg's URW++ type foundry is the most correct in terms of sticking to Calvert and Kinneir's original design, with a Medium and a Bold weight. There's also Transport New from independent foundry K-Type, a redraw that adds a lighter weight and a number of additional glyphs while refining a number of characters, but the URW++ seems to me to be the more authentic of the two.

Transport Medium Transport is less engineered than DIN, but there are perhaps more similarities than one might think

DIN 1451 Mittelschrift

THE TECH THAT TIME FORGOT

Despite its retrospectively poor reputation, it would be unfair to stigmatize phototypesetting completely as it filled the gap between metal and digital type, and was the first system to combine typesetting and computers with any degree of success. Nonetheless, there are many design professionals familiar with the older technology who would prefer to quietly forget all about it.

Experiments with photosetting began as early as the 1930s, but the first generation of commercial machines emerged during the late 1950s. In their original form, the "cold type" machines functioned a little like the mechanical hot metal casters manufactured by Monotype; they used the combination of a keyboard, a punched paper tape, and compressed air to control the movement of a matrix case and additionally a shutter to mask unwanted characters. Instead of metal matrices, small photographic negatives of each separate character in a font were arrayed in the interchangeable matrix case and exposed on to either photographic film or a roll of

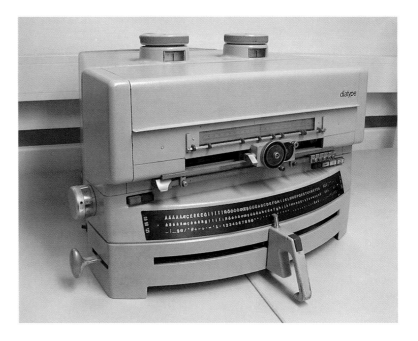

Berthold's semi-automatic Diatype, an early machine designed for setting headlines which was manufactured between 1952 and 1960.

photosensitive paper, that could then be processed and used for film composition or paste-up. Earlier machines such as Berthold's semi-automatic Diatype, manufactured between 1952 and 1960, were designed primarily for setting headlines and could only set a single column of text, but later improvements enabled complete pages with multiple columns of text to be output directly to film. The development of equipment with the ability to project characters directly onto a cathode ray tube (CRT) screen removed much of the mechanization from the process, enabling the production of cheaper and more compact machines, which in turn facilitated the expansion of typesetting technology to smaller companies with limited space. Long-established type foundries and professional compositors suddenly found themselves up against new competition and had to learn to adapt quickly. By the mid 1960s, phototypesetting was already beginning to take over from hot metal, and it grew to dominate the market until the desktop publishing revolution transformed (or in fact destroyed) the typesetting industry a mere 30 years later.

A possible reason for the take-up of phototypesetting, aside from the convenience and relative running costs, was the degree of control the designer had over the final setting. Kerning (or character spacing) could be specified with far greater flexibility because the physical limitation created by the body-widths of metal type was no longer an issue. Very tight character spacing, at the time a popular technique used to help increase the point size of headline text over short measures to achieve more impact, typically characterizes typesetting from the period. Also, line spacing (still referred to as leading even today) could be closed up by specifying a negative value, for example 12-point text on 10-point leading, allowing more lines per column if space was at a premium. As the technology evolved, it also became possible to manipulate letterforms to create faux condensed or expanded type (not a good thing) or to completely distort letterforms to create unusual typographic effects. Designers were naturally keen to push the new technology to its limits to see how far they could go, and unfortunately too far was often the case. Letterforms designed with great care over long periods of time were systematically spoiled by the well-intended but ill-informed exploitation of the latest techniques on offer.

But what did this mean for the typefaces themselves? Purists rightly claim that the quality (or perhaps integrity is a more fitting word to use in this context) of phototypesetting never hit the same level as that achieved by good hot metal setting, although the last generation of Lasercomp machines manufactured by Monotype in the late 1970s and early 1980s was certainly an improvement over earlier machines. Aside from any bad layout decisions made by designers, the physical reproduction of letterforms was often below par. To create setting at different point sizes, the operator used a lens to magnify or reduce characters using a single matrix, which inevitably led to an overall drop in quality. In the days of hot metal, to ensure optical consistency between point sizes the punches or mechanically routed matrices for smaller point sizes were cut with slightly heavier strokes to ensure type didn't break up when printed. Therefore, if you were to somehow enlarge a printed 6-point hot metal character to 18 point it would appear too bold, but using a single matrix for all sizes of photocomposition also does exactly this. To help

compensate for this, the big type foundries such as Monotype produced three different sizes of matrices for each typeface with appropriate adjustments to the stroke widths, designated as the A, B, and C matrices. However, many typesetters didn't bother to switch to the correct matrix "A" for smaller type or "C" for larger sizes, and simply used matrix "B" for everything. In practice, this meant that type was often set with a visual weight that didn't harmonize visually with the original design of the font.

Despite these shortfalls, phototypesetting gradually edged out hot metal as the principal method for setting type and, as mentioned earlier in this book, the growing dominance of offset lithography over letterpress printing also played its part in this shift. Interestingly, it was still possible to order hot metal setting from a few companies during the early 1980s but one had to shop around, and thanks to a resurgence in popularity for the unique feel of hot metal setting there is now a growing number of specialist printing firms that maintain old Linotype and Monotype machines for commercial typesetting. The technology behind phototypesetting has, however, disappeared completely.

Hermann Zapf

In an odd twist of fate, the rise of National Socialism in 1930s Germany steered one of our greatest 20th-century calligraphers and type designers towards his profession. Born in Nuremberg in 1918, Hermann Zapf was headed for a career in electrical engineering before his father, a trade union official at a large factory, was sacked as a political undesirable by his employers when the Nazis came to power. This meant Zapf was unable to embark on the further education he'd planned, and instead took an apprenticeship as a retoucher at a printing firm, Karl Ulrich & Co. In 1935, he visited an exhibition of the work of type designer Rudolf Koch (see page 54) and Zapf was immediately drawn to the idea of becoming a calligrapher. Zapf obtained copies of Koch's book *Das Schreiben als Kunstfertigkeit* (The Skill of Calligraphy) and Edward Johnston's publication *Writing & Illuminating & Lettering*, taught himself the basic skills, and the rest as they say is history.

Zapf was soon commissioned by the Stempel foundry and began designing typefaces for them in 1938; his first face was a blackletter named Gilgengart. World War II saw Zapf conscripted into the army as a cartographer and he spent time as a French prisoner of war before returning to Germany. During the course of the war, much of Stempel's stock of type had been destroyed by the extensive bombing of Frankfurt, and Zapf was the principal designer tasked with building their collection back up with fresh new designs. Ironically, the tradition of blackletter faces that had prevailed in Germany before the war had switched to roman letterforms after the Nazis condemned blackletter in 1941; their reasoning that it was of Jewish origin has been cited for this turnaround, but it was also a practical decision based on the fact that blackletter type was unreadable to people outside Germany. Zapf began work on a new roman face in 1946, basing his design on Renaissance letterforms, and by 1948 the typeface you're reading now, Palatino, was completed. Stempel faces were effectively Linotype commissions, as the foundry enjoyed an almost exclusive relationship with the typesetting giant, manufacturing Linotype matrices for use throughout most of Europe, and Palatino was immediately adapted for machine composition. A few years later, Zapf designed a slightly lighter version for setting at smaller point sizes and named it Aldus.

Around the same time as his work on Palatino, Zapf drew another highly original face, Melior, which was designed to function across a variety of difficult printing conditions including letterpress, offset lithography and gravure. His additional output during the period from 1948 to 1958 was prolific; he designed dozens of faces during this 10-year period, an effort culminating in what is perhaps his most original and innovative roman face, Optima. It's a Humanist Sans quite unlike any other with its Glyphic qualities; to quote Zapf himself it's a "serifless roman." Zapf resigned his post at Stempel in 1956 to spend more time working on his other great love, book design, but has continued to design type ever since, amassing a total of over 200 faces. He has also overseen the transition of many of his faces to the digital platform, introducing improvements along the way, and at the time of writing remains active at the age of 96.

Adrian Frutiger

Adrian Frutiger's two monumental sans serif faces, the Neo-Grotesque Univers and the Humanist Frutiger, are the two faces that this great 20th-century type designer will always be remembered for, but his big break came a little earlier than the late 1950s courtesy of a certain Charles Peignot. The famous French type founder picked up on the talents of the young Swiss designer when he saw a 1952 design Frutiger had produced for a brochure entitled *History of Letters*. Peignot was looking for a designer capable of helping Deberny & Peignot transition successfully into the age of phototypesetting as they were closely associated with the new Lumitype machines which were set to become the most popular typesetting system used in France at that time. After supervising the adaptation of a number of classic faces for phototypesetting in the early 1950s, and after designing several faces including the highly regarded Meridien, Frutiger was asked to design a new sans serif for the D&P list. Frutiger persuaded Peignot to allow him to develop an idea he'd started as a student at the Zurich school of arts, and in 1957 Univers was completed. It was the first typeface to be designed for simultaneous use as foundry type for hand-setting, for hot metal machine composition on the Monotype system, and for photosetting. The design of all 21 of the weights and styles of the Univers family were completed before any commercial production commenced, an unusual occurrence by any standard, and the success of the face upheld Peignot's faith in Frutiger's concept.

Univers was hugely influential and other type foundries were quick to follow the orderly numbered system which Frutiger devised for his type family. The contemporary Neue Haas Grotesk (later Helvetica) uses Akzidenz-Grotesk as its source of inspiration and its 1957 release initially used conventional naming, but later releases notably adopted a similar system to order the weights. Frutiger received many commissions on the back of his work on Univers and he gained something of a reputation for designing highly legible faces after an adapted version of Univers was used for the signage at Orly airport near Paris. Other major designs produced during the 1960s and 1970s include Apollo (1964), Serifa (1967), OCR-B (1968) and Iridium (1975), but it's Roissy, the typeface he designed for the signage at the new Charles de Gaulle airport outside Paris, that would reset the bar for legible sans serif faces. The face was renamed Frutiger when Linotype released it commercially in 1976 and its curiously timeless qualities which belie its origins as a signage face for a modern airport help to maintain the face's popularity today, almost 40 years after it first appeared.

Frutiger has been involved in the adaptation of all his faces for the digital platform, which helps to maintain the integrity of the original design concepts; his 2009 Neue Frutiger is a great example of a classic face that has survived technological transition intact.

Optima

| **Country of origin:** Germany | **Classification:** Humanist Sans
| **Designer:** Hermann Zapf

1958

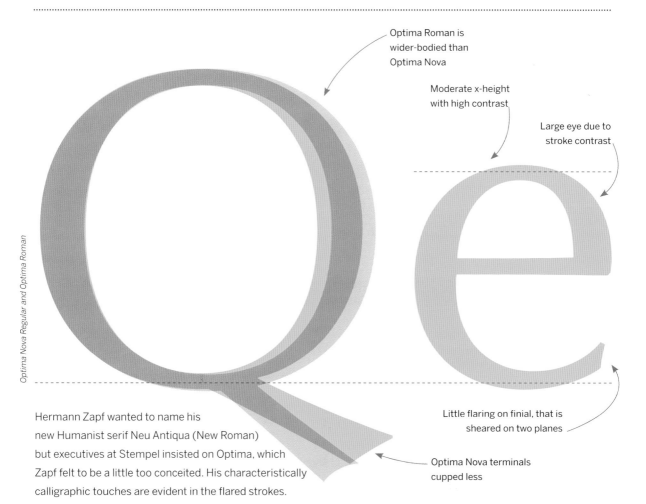

Optima Nova Regular and Optima Roman

Optima Roman is wider-bodied than Optima Nova

Moderate x-height with high contrast

Large eye due to stroke contrast

Little flaring on finial, that is sheared on two planes

Optima Nova terminals cupped less

Hermann Zapf wanted to name his new Humanist serif Neu Antiqua (New Roman) but executives at Stempel insisted on Optima, which Zapf felt to be a little too conceited. His characteristically calligraphic touches are evident in the flared strokes.

9/12pt Optima Nova Regular (Linotype)

LOREM IPSUM DOLOR SIT AMET, CONSECTETUER ADIPISCING ELIT, SED DIAM NONUMMY NIBH euismod tincidunt ut laoreet dolore magna aliquam erat volutpat. Ut wisi enim ad minim veniam, quis nostrud exerci tation ullamcorper suscipit lobortis nisl ut aliquip ex ea commodo consequat. Duis autem vel eum iriure dolor in hendrerit in vulputate

12/15pt Optima Nova Regular (Linotype)

LOREM IPSUM DOLOR SIT AMET, CONSECTETUER ADIPISCING ELIT, SED diam nonummy nibh euismod tincidunt ut laoreet dolore magna aliquam erat volutpat. Ut wisi enim ad minim veniam, quis nostrud exerci tation ullamcorper suscipit lobortis nisl ut aliquip ex ea

In all its beauty, Optima was sent to test those of us who like to try to classify typefaces. Essentially it's a Humanist sans—the characters mimic the proportions of an Old Style serif but those serifs are missing. It's also quite Glyphic with its tapered strokes and delicately flared terminals. Despite these oddities, Optima is a face that can look both serene and businesslike (in a paneled boardroom kind of way) at the same time.

Hermann Zapf began work on the design of Optima in 1952, wanting to create a sans serif face that could answer the criticism from some quarters that the contemporary choices of faces in that particular style lacked character and were difficult to read when set as text. His original name for the face, Neu Antiqua (New Roman), was dropped by Stempel, who manufactured and released it as Optima in three weights of foundry type and Linotype matrices in 1958. Zapf's modesty compelled him to comment to Stempel's marketing staff that the name sounded rather boastful—he was clearly overruled. Zapf's typeface designs all bear testament to his credentials as a calligrapher and Optima is no exception. It's Zapf's calligraphic skills that are instrumental in injecting the Humanist elements to his design; the flaring of the strokes is actually quite subtle but it's just enough to provide a sense that the characters have been drawn rather than constructed. Optima is another face that has been widely copied—there are poor impersonators out there—but this hasn't diminished the regard in which the face is held. Notably, Optima was chosen to letter the names recorded on Washington, DC's Vietnam Veterans Memorial Wall.

The standard digital release from Linotype is perfectly good and includes six weights with italic styles from Roman to Extra Black. However, in 2002 Zapf collaborated with Akira Kobayashi, currently one of Monotype's Type Directors, to create Optima Nova. The original design has been adapted to bring the typeface into the 21st century, reworking the weights into an expanded seven-weight family along with small caps and Old Style figures. There are also five new condensed weights, and a titling weight consisting of uppercase characters. Significantly, the oblique roman italics have been redesigned, introducing some cursive elements to several characters that, in this author's opinion, make this face even more beautiful.

The proportions of Optima Nova's italic weights have been adjusted and several characters are cursive, departing from the oblique roman of older versions

abfg *abfg*

Optima Nova Italic

Optima Italic

Antique Olive

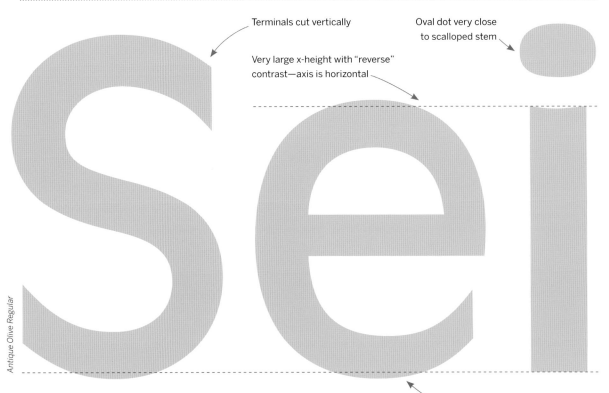

Terminals cut vertically

Oval dot very close to scalloped stem

Very large x-height with "reverse" contrast—axis is horizontal

Antique Olive Regular

The "Antique" of Antique Olive doesn't refer to the maturity of this relatively recent and wonderfully quirky typeface. In France, where the face was designed for the Fonderie Olive type foundry in Marseille, Antique was the traditional term used to describe a sans serif face.

Round glyphs are slightly egg-shaped with narrow end at the baseline

9/12pt Antique Olive Regular (URW++)

LOREM IPSUM DOLOR SIT AMET, CONSECTETUER ADIPISCING ELIT, SED DIAM NONUMMY NIBH EUISMOD tincidunt ut laoreet dolore magna aliquam erat volutpat. Ut wisi enim ad minim veniam, quis nostrud exerci tation ullamcorper suscipit lobortis nisl ut aliquip ex ea commodo consequat. Duis autem vel eum iriure dolor in hendrerit in vulputate

12/15pt Antique Olive Regular (URW++)

LOREM IPSUM DOLOR SIT AMET, CONSECTETUER ADIPISCING ELIT, SED diam nonummy nibh euismod tincidunt ut laoreet dolore magna aliquam erat volutpat. Ut wisi enim ad minim veniam, quis nostrud exerci tation ullamcorper suscipit lobortis nisl ut

Roger Excoffon is perhaps one of the most unfairly appraised typeface designers in recent history. His background as a graphic designer of considerable skill informed the ideas behind his typefaces and for their time (the late 1940s to the late 1960s) they were pitched perfectly, but by the 1980s they had been reduced to the status of "novelty" faces that were only suitable for light-minded projects. Nothing could be further from the truth as faces such as Banco, Choc, Mistral, and Antique Olive are cleverly realized designs that have thankfully regained their stature as important typefaces and have gone on to influence a whole new generation of contemporary designers.

Despite what some people might believe, the name doesn't stem from the fact that the round characters are "olive" shaped. Antique Olive's name (which was Catsilou at first) was formed from the French term equivalent to sans serif (antique) and from the foundry where it was designed and manufactured, the Marseille-based Fonderie Olive. It was designed in part as a characterful alternative to the other well-known Neo-Grotesque sans faces of the time, such as Helvetica and Univers. Marketing for the new face was cleverly pitched; the first weight to be released was the ultra-heavy Antique Olive Nord, where the unusual stress and form of the face was less evident. This massively bold font was popular, especially for use in logos, so when Regular weights followed as additions to the family they weren't immediately rejected as too unusual for practical uses.

There are a couple of viable options when it comes to a digitized version of Antique Olive. Linotype's version, also published by Adobe, looks fine in use and is probably the most widespread in terms of the average font collections, but feels a little "squashed," for want of a better term. However, the metrics of the version published by URW++ seem more comfortable in comparison; it's conjecture on my part but perhaps the Linotype version was digitized from an adapted cut adjusted to fit within widths demanded by the Linotype mechanical compositor. If you like Antique Olive you might also choose to take a look at the Neo-Humanist sans FF Balance, a face designed in 1993 by Evert Bloemsma, that exhibits a similar form with reversed stress and was strongly influenced by Antique Olive's design.

FF Balance is a Neo-Humanist face that features the same reversed stress as Antique Olive

Antique Olive Regular

FF Balance Regular

Amelia

| **Country of origin:** United States | **Classification:** Display
| **Designer:** Stan Davis

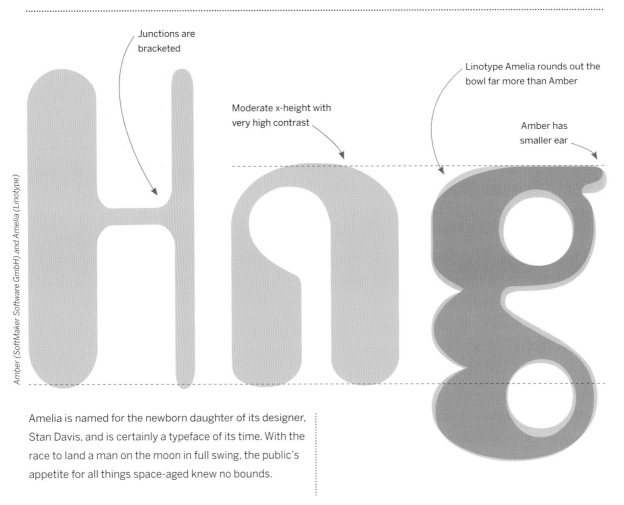

Amber (SoftMaker Software GmbH) and Amelia (Linotype)

Junctions are bracketed

Moderate x-height with very high contrast

Linotype Amelia rounds out the bowl far more than Amber

Amber has smaller ear

Amelia is named for the newborn daughter of its designer, Stan Davis, and is certainly a typeface of its time. With the race to land a man on the moon in full swing, the public's appetite for all things space-aged knew no bounds.

18pt Amber (SoftMaker Software GmbH)

36pt Amber (SoftMaker Software GmbH)

72pt Amber (SoftMaker Software GmbH)

Of all the typefaces featured in this book, Amelia's is one of the more controversial stories. I've included it partly because it carries clear personal memories for me. It was designed around the same time as I was born so, as a child at school, my first impressions of graphic design and typography were based on the style of highly distinctive display faces like Amelia, which were hugely popular during the late 1960s and 1970s. Amelia is arguably most famous for its use as the principal face used for the title sequence of The Beatles' animated film *Yellow Submarine* (1968), and for the Moon Boot logo that appears on the footwear which became highly fashionable during the late 1970s and 1980s. Dozens of typefaces with a "scientific" look appeared during the third quarter of the 20th century—the height of the space race and a period in which new technologies kicked off the digital revolution.

However, the typeface shown on this page isn't truly Amelia. The story begins when Stan Davis designed his original version for an international typeface design competition sponsored by the Visual Graphics Corporation in 1964. He named it after his newborn daughter and the successful and influential face went on to be used in a number of diverse areas of design; the music industry loved it, it became a face symbolic of the 1960s, it graced the covers of numerous science-fiction novels, and was used extensively to represent emerging computer technology. But, like many other typefaces before and since, alternative versions have been created by other large foundries and marketed as Amelia, and Davis has been very vocal about his dislike for them—a perfectly fair view, which all designers are entitled to take. The versions from Linotype and Bitstream—created legally and in good faith according to the foundries (and who am I to dispute this)—do indeed deviate quite noticeably from the original in form; they're not essentially "wrong" but simply different, so are technically not Amelia. The main discrepancies can be found in the rounding of the corners of strokes and other details.

During the writing of this book, I tried on several occasions to obtain a digitized version of the original font via an email address posted within several online articles about the Amelia controversy. Sadly, I failed to elicit a response, so maybe the address is no longer active. However, thanks to research carried out by the mathematician and typeface historian Luc Devroye (luc.devroye.org/fonts.html) the face shown has been identified as the closest available facsimile to Davis' original design. A770-Deco was released by Martin Kotulla's company SoftMaker Software GmbH as freeware, and is based closely on the original design. So, in its absence, I hope it suffices to represent Amelia accurately. Incidentally, the font name used by SoftMaker has more recently been changed to Amber.

Submarine

Amber

Sabon

| **Country of origin:** Germany | **Classification:** Old Style Serif
| **Designer:** Jan Tschichold

1964–1967

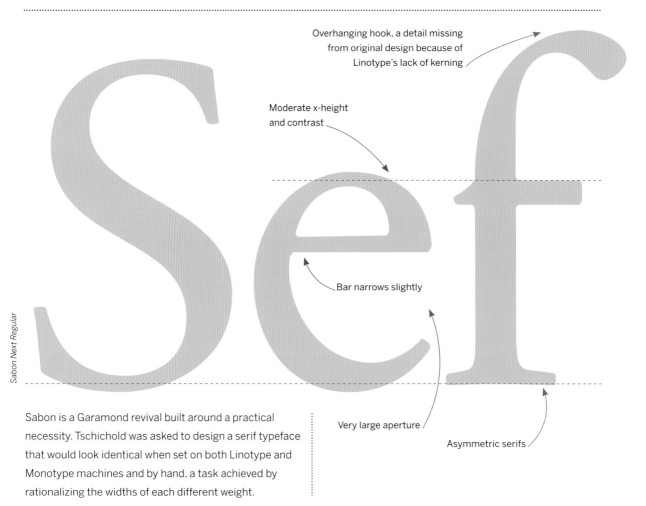

Overhanging hook, a detail missing
from original design because of
Linotype's lack of kerning

Moderate x-height
and contrast

Bar narrows slightly

Sabon Next Regular

Very large aperture

Asymmetric serifs

Sabon is a Garamond revival built around a practical necessity. Tschichold was asked to design a serif typeface that would look identical when set on both Linotype and Monotype machines and by hand, a task achieved by rationalizing the widths of each different weight.

9/12pt Sabon Next Regular (Linotype)

LOREM IPSUM DOLOR SIT AMET, CONSECTETUER ADIPISCING ELIT, SED DIAM nonummy nibh euismod tincidunt ut laoreet dolore magna aliquam erat volutpat. Ut wisi enim ad minim veniam, quis nostrud exerci tation ullamcorper suscipit lobortis nisl ut aliquip ex ea commodo consequat. Duis autem vel eum iriure dolor in hendrerit in vulputate

12/15pt Sabon Next Regular (Linotype)

LOREM IPSUM DOLOR SIT AMET, CONSECTETUER ADIPISCING ELIT, sed diam nonummy nibh euismod tincidunt ut laoreet dolore magna aliquam erat volutpat. Ut wisi enim ad minim veniam, quis nostrud exerci tation ullamcorper suscipit lobortis nisl ut

Sabon was created to meet a challenging brief from an alliance of German printers; they required a new serif typeface that would look the same when set mechanically on either the Linotype or Monotype machines, and when set by hand using foundry type. This demanding design task was undertaken by the gifted calligrapher, book designer and typeface designer Jan Tschichold as a joint commission from Monotype, Linotype and the Stempel Type Foundry in Frankfurt.

Tschichold took his inspiration from a specimen sheet of type thought to be manufactured from original punches cut by Claude Garamond and Robert Granjon; the roman was a Garamond, the italic a Granjon. When Garamond died in 1561, most of his punches were sold to Christopher Plantin's Antwerp-based foundry and printshop, while some found their way to a Frankfurt foundry named Egenolff-Berner with some help from a punch cutter named Jacob Sabon (who provides the name of Tschichold's typeface). On Sabon's death, foundry owner Konrad Berner married his widow, and printed the specimen sheet using the Garamond/Granjon type in 1592. This explains why Sabon is often referred to as a Garamond revival, although strictly speaking it's a fully rethought adaptation.

To fulfill the brief, Tschichold designed Sabon's two weights and their accompanying italic styles so that each would take up exactly the same width. This decision was influenced principally by the Linotype machine that used a "duplex" system of casting; it could set two different weights of a typeface in a single slug as long as the widths of each font matched. Principally a book designer, Tschichold only designed four typefaces and Sabon was the last, but it's considered a highlight of his career and proved to be a huge and enduring success.

Sabon's transition to the digital platform has been as interesting as the story behind its original creation. It was one of the first typefaces to be transferred to the digital platform in the 1980s with versions from Monotype and Linotype, both of which retain the two standard weights of Roman and Bold with italic styles. Linotype's version works perfectly well, but be aware that Monotype's is considerably lighter in color. However, a more compelling offer lies with Sabon Next, a contemporary revival designed by Jean François Porchez for Linotype; it's based on the original drawings that Stempel used to manufacture the foundry type for hand setting. The family has been expanded to six weights with all the usual OpenType extras, plus a display weight for setting above 20 points, and a set of ornaments. There is also a version named Sabon eText designed by Steve Matteson, developed for Monotype as part of their eText Collection specifically for use on eReaders and tablets.

Monotype's version of Sabon (right) is very light when compared to Sabon Next, which is closer to the original foundry type, the best of the original cuts

Gyra Gyra

Sabon Next Regular

Sabon Regular

OCR-A and OCR-B

| **Country of origin:** United States/Switzerland | **Classification:** Geometric Sans
| **Designers:** American Type Founders (OCR-A), Adrian Frutiger (OCR-B)

1966–1968

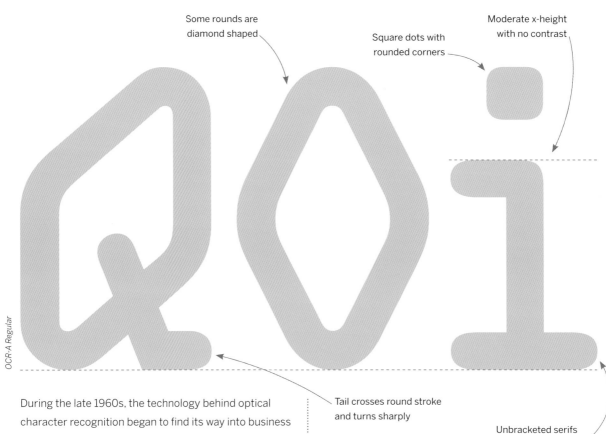

Some rounds are diamond shaped

Square dots with rounded corners

Moderate x-height with no contrast

OCR-A Regular

Tail crosses round stroke and turns sharply

Unbracketed serifs with round ends

During the late 1960s, the technology behind optical character recognition began to find its way into business and banking systems. The simple letterforms of OCR-A and OCR-B were designed specifically for these applications, and the font is monospaced to aid scanning.

18pt OCR-A Regular (Adobe)

CGaegpr18

36pt OCR-A Regular (Adobe)

CGaegpr18

72pt OCR-A Regular (Adobe)

CGaegpr18

When optical character recognition (OCR) first became a practical reality that could be used to process the kind of documents issued by banks and credit card companies, the need for a font that could be read by both computers and people was identified. OCR-A was developed by the American National Standards Institute between 1966 and 1968 using letterforms designed specifically to be read by scanning devices. The font is monospaced, meaning each glyph occupies exactly the same horizontal space when set. This improves the legibility of the font for scanning, as do the contrast-free strokes. Despite the unusual form of some characters the font is still readable, offering obvious advantage over older coded systems.

The original release was produced in its single weight by American Type Founders in 1968, but has been incrementally updated and improved as phototypesetting and digital technology replaced metal. In the same year, the European Computer Manufacturers Association (ECMA) decided that, on its own, OCR-A wasn't suitable for use in Europe, and Adrian Frutiger was commissioned on behalf of Monotype to design an alternative, OCR-B. The decision was based on their view that a more recognizable set of letterforms would encourage the wider implementation of OCR technology, and by 1973 OCR-B was also made a world standard.

OCR-A and OCR-B are commercially available from the usual large font vendors—for example, there are nine or ten versions of each available from MyFonts, with the Linotype and Adobe versions looking closest to the original design. Versions of the fonts can also be downloaded under a permissive free software license from the Comprehensive TeX Archive Network (CTAN). There are also dozens of free "rogue" versions available for download, but they vary considerably and using unlicensed fonts is, of course, a habit to be discouraged, even when there are legitimate free versions available elsewhere. Optical character recognition is so advanced these days that both these faces are more or less obsolete but they can still be useful if one wants to evoke a certain "dated" feel for a financial graphic.

OCR-B

The letterforms of OCR-B are far more straightforward than those of OCR-A

Americana

| **Country of origin:** United States | **Classification:** Rational Serif
| **Designer:** Richard Isbell

1966

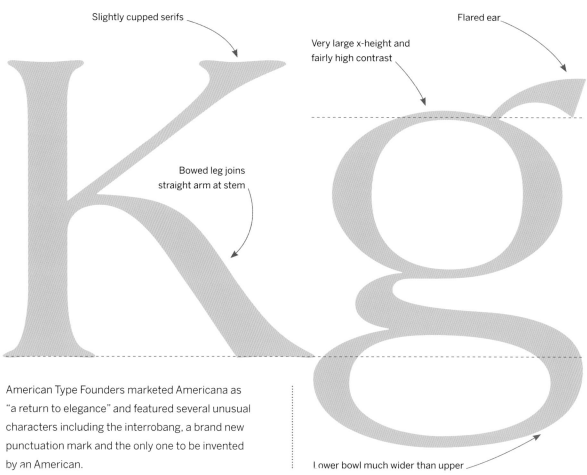

Americana Roman

Slightly cupped serifs

Flared ear

Very large x-height and fairly high contrast

Bowed leg joins straight arm at stem

Lower bowl much wider than upper

American Type Founders marketed Americana as "a return to elegance" and featured several unusual characters including the interrobang, a brand new punctuation mark and the only one to be invented by an American.

9/12pt Americana Roman (Linotype)

LOREM IPSUM DOLOR SIT AMET, CONSECTETUER ADIPISCING ELIT, SED diam nonummy nibh euismod tincidunt ut laoreet dolore magna aliquam erat volutpat. Ut wisi enim ad minim veniam, quis nostrud exerci tation ullamcorper suscipit lobortis nisl ut aliquip ex ea commodo consequat. Duis

12/15pt Americana Roman (Linotype)

LOREM IPSUM DOLOR SIT AMET, CONSECTETUER ADIPISCING elit, sed diam nonummy nibh euismod tincidunt ut laoreet dolore magna aliquam erat volutpat. Ut wisi enim ad minim veniam, quis nostrud exerci tation

Americana was designed in 1966 by Richard Isbell, a designer, illustrator and lettering artist based in Detroit. Given his location, Isbell worked extensively with clients from the automobile industry and there's something about the face (notwithstanding its name) that's reminiscent of the flamboyant styling of a classic mid-century American car. Perhaps it's the sharp serifs or the oversized counters with their enormous x-height?

Americana was first released by American Type Founders and marketed as "the most successful face ATF has introduced in many years; it is the result of an assignment to 'return to elegance,' being Richard Isbell's interpretation of that trend." The appearance of a number of unusual characters in the ATF version makes the face stand out; a short dash aligning with the center of the cap height as well as lowercase hyphens and a center dot were rare. However, the most unusual character of all was the interrobang, an amalgamation of an exclamation mark and a question mark. The glyph was invented in 1962 by a New York advertising executive named Martin K. Speckter, and Isbell chose to include it in the character set of

Americana. The Americana family was completed a few years after the first weights were released with the addition of Americana Extra Bold—the last ever newly designed typeface to be cut by the once mighty American Type Founders. The final ATF catalog was published in 1976 and never updated, apart from added inserts stating which of its faces were no longer available.

Of the digital versions available today, there isn't much to distinguish one from the other apart from the extra glyphs available in OpenType fonts. There are versions created by Linotype, Adobe, URW++ and Bitstream, all with the same two Regular and Bold weights with an italic style for the Regular weight, but sadly the most interesting character of all, the interrobang, is missing from all of them. It's not a frequently used character, but what a shame that it's never been included.

Bring back the interrobang.
It's not possible to create an interrobang
by overlaying the two characters, as the
exclamation mark is too tall

Americana Extra Bold

Serifa

| **Country of origin:** Germany | **Classification:** Geometric Slab
| **Designer:** Adrian Frutiger

1967

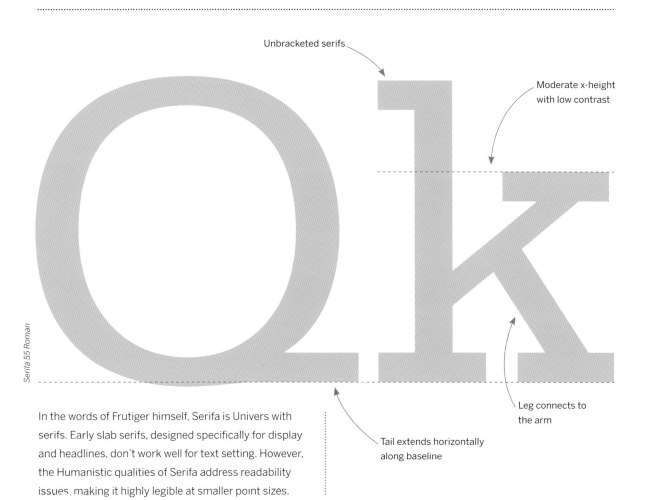

Unbracketed serifs

Moderate x-height
with low contrast

Serifa 55 Roman

Leg connects to
the arm

Tail extends horizontally
along baseline

In the words of Frutiger himself, Serifa is Univers with serifs. Early slab serifs, designed specifically for display and headlines, don't work well for text setting. However, the Humanistic qualities of Serifa address readability issues, making it highly legible at smaller point sizes.

9/12pt Serifa 55 Roman (Bauer Types S.A.)

LOREM IPSUM DOLOR SIT AMET, CONSECTETUER ADIPISCING ELIT, SED DIAM nonummy nibh euismod tincidunt ut laoreet dolore magna aliquam erat volutpat. Ut wisi enim ad minim veniam, quis nostrud exerci tation ullamcorper suscipit lobortis nisl ut aliquip ex ea commodo consequat. Duis autem vel eum

12/15pt Serifa 55 Roman (Bauer Types S.A.)

LOREM IPSUM DOLOR SIT AMET, CONSECTETUER ADIPISCING ELIT, sed diam nonummy nibh euismod tincidunt ut laoreet dolore magna aliquam erat volutpat. Ut wisi enim ad minim veniam, quis nostrud exerci tation ullamcorper suscipit

Serifa, a design begun in 1964 by Adrian Frutiger for Frankfurt's Bauer Type Foundry and released in 1967, is Univers with serifs. Frutiger himself coined this description of his Geometric slab. The unbracketed square serifs make this an Egyptian, if one were to apply traditional terminology, as it follows the style of slab serifs popular in the 19th century and later revived during the early 20th century in faces such as Memphis. Frutiger based Serifa closely on the letterforms of Univers, retaining stroke widths and structure as closely as was practical, although Serifa's characters are naturally drawn a little wider to accommodate the serifs. The close relationship between Univers and Serifa means they make a harmonious team when used together, and it's worth pointing out that for a Geometric serif, Serifa works pretty well when set in smaller point sizes as running text. Legibility is aided by the fact that the small amount of contrast displayed in the strokes of Univers has been carried over to Serifa, giving it a more Humanist feel than most other Geometric slabs.

Frutiger dropped his usual numbering system when naming the weights and styles of Serifa and used a standard naming convention instead. However, he opted to return to numbered weights when in 1977 he designed a follow-up companion face to Serifa. Glypha was designed for Stempel and published by Linotype, and is effectively a condensed version of Serifa. The Glypha family is comprised of five weights from 35 Thin to 75 Black, each with an italic style. Like Serifa, Glypha works quite well at small sizes, with legibility aided by a degree of contrast in the stroke widths.

Serifa is available in digital versions from Linotype, Adobe, URW++, Bitstream, Tilde and Elsner+Flake. The URW++ version is expansive, with five standard width weights plus a Condensed Medium. The Elsner+Flake and Tilde versions are similarly featured, whereas the Adobe family contains only three weights and their italic styles. On examination, there's little to distinguish these different versions from one another; the URW++ offers the extra weight options if you really need the Thin weight but bear in mind that their Medium weight has no italic style.

In comparison, the similarities between Serifa and Univers are clear

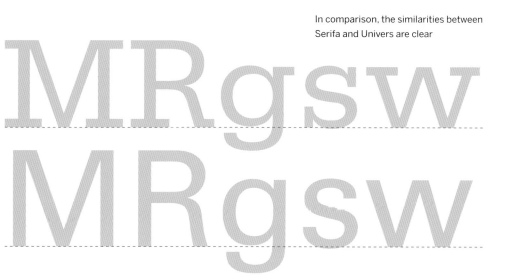

Serifa and Univers

Syntax

| **Country of origin:** Germany | **Classification:** Humanist Sans
| **Designer:** Hans Eduard Meier

1969

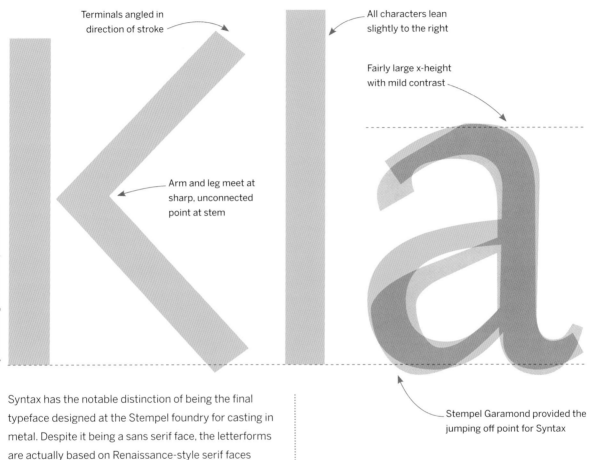

Terminals angled in direction of stroke

All characters lean slightly to the right

Fairly large x-height with mild contrast

Arm and leg meet at sharp, unconnected point at stem

Stempel Garamond provided the jumping off point for Syntax

Syntax Next Regular and Stempel Garamond

Syntax has the notable distinction of being the final typeface designed at the Stempel foundry for casting in metal. Despite it being a sans serif face, the letterforms are actually based on Renaissance-style serif faces such as Garamond and Bembo.

9/12pt Syntax Next Regular (Linotype)

LOREM IPSUM DOLOR SIT AMET, CONSECTETUER ADIPISCING ELIT, SED DIAM NONUMMY NIBH euismod tincidunt ut laoreet dolore magna aliquam erat volutpat. Ut wisi enim ad minim veniam, quis nostrud exerci tation ullamcorper suscipit lobortis nisl ut aliquip ex ea commodo consequat. Duis autem vel eum iriure dolor in hendrerit in vulputate

12/15pt Syntax Next Regular (Linotype)

LOREM IPSUM DOLOR SIT AMET, CONSECTETUER ADIPISCING ELIT, sed diam nonummy nibh euismod tincidunt ut laoreet dolore magna aliquam erat volutpat. Ut wisi enim ad minim veniam, quis nostrud exerci tation ullamcorper suscipit lobortis nisl

Syntax has the distinction of being the last ever typeface to be cast as foundry type by the Stempel Type Foundry in Frankfurt, with some sources claiming it's the last to be cast for hand-setting anywhere. This is no longer strictly true, following more recent projects such as the joint venture between the P22 Type Foundry and the late Jim Rimmer to create Stern, the first ever simultaneous release of a face in the digital format and as foundry type. All the same, Syntax represents a milestone in typeface production in its own right.

Hans Eduard Meier began working on his design for Syntax as far back as 1954, but it wasn't until 1969 that the first weights were cut and cast at Stempel. It's a Humanist sans but could almost be thought of as the first Neo-Humanist sans—for me, it wavers between the two classifications with its calligraphic forms, minimal contrast and large x-height. Meier based his original drawings for the face on Stempel Garamond and, although he clearly hasn't just chopped off the serifs, the difference in structure and proportion when comparing the two isn't that far off. One of the most interesting things about Syntax is the forward-leaning axis of the roman; it's only around one half of a degree, so barely perceptible; but this slight lean to the right injects a sense of dynamic energy, that is unusual for a sans serif.

Linotype's digital Syntax family, also published by Adobe, is a good adaptation of the original face with Roman, Bold, Black and Ultra Black weights. The roman has an italic style but other weights do not, and anything heavier than Bold seems to lose the personality of the face; the angled terminals become horizontal and the forward slope is less discernible. However, we also have Syntax Next, an expanded version begun by Hans Meier and Linotype in 1995 and released in 2000. Designed using the original drawings, characters have retained their original foundry type quality, ironing out any of the alterations needed to accommodate Linotype or phototypesetting systems. The family has also been expanded to six weights, all with italic styles, and the usual OpenType niceties of Old Style figures, small caps and so on have been included. The first five weights are all good, retaining the angled terminals, leaving only the Black weight, which in my opinion is too heavy for the design, but it's a small gripe against this excellent digital revival.

Syntax Next Regular

ITC Avant Garde Gothic

| **Country of origin:** United States | **Classification:** Geometric Sans
| **Designers:** Herb Lubalin and Tom Carnase

1970

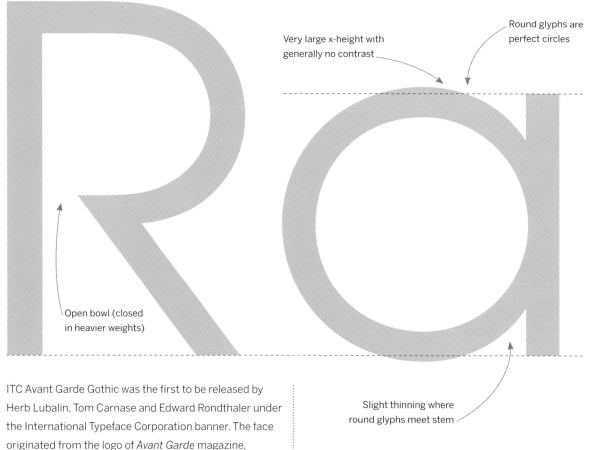

Very large x-height with generally no contrast

Round glyphs are perfect circles

Open bowl (closed in heavier weights)

ITC Avant Garde Gothic Book

Slight thinning where round glyphs meet stem

ITC Avant Garde Gothic was the first to be released by Herb Lubalin, Tom Carnase and Edward Rondthaler under the International Typeface Corporation banner. The face originated from the logo of *Avant Garde* magazine, designed by Lubalin and lettered by Carnase.

9/12pt ITC Avant Garde Gothic Book

LOREM IPSUM DOLOR SIT AMET, CONSECTETUER ADIPISCING ELIT, SED DIAM NONUMMY NIBH euismod tincidunt ut laoreet dolore magna aliquam erat volutpat. Ut wisi enim ad minim veniam, quis nostrud exerci tation ullamcorper suscipit lobortis nisl ut aliquip ex ea commodo consequat. Duis autem vel eum iriure dolor in

12/15pt ITC Avant Garde Gothic Book

LOREM IPSUM DOLOR SIT AMET, CONSECTETUER ADIPISCING ELIT, sed diam nonummy nibh euismod tincidunt ut laoreet dolore magna aliquam erat volutpat. Ut wisi enim ad minim veniam, quis nostrud exerci tation ullamcorper suscipit

The International Typeface Corporation (ITC) was formed in 1970 by the designers Herb Lubalin and Aaron Burns, and Ed Rondthaler of the New York typesetting firm Photo-Lettering Inc. It's the first type foundry to have existed without ever issuing metal type, given its formation at the height of the phototypesetting boom, and operated by licensing its faces to third-party publishers and typesetting companies. The firm's typefaces were promoted via their quarterly *U&lc* magazine, designed by Lubalin until his death in 1981, and the arrival of the magazine on art directors' desks became a much anticipated event.

On its release in 1970, ITC Avant Garde became ITC's first original typeface. The design is based on the hand-lettered logo of *Avant Garde* magazine, published between January 1968 and July 1971 and designed at Lubalin's design firm. The concept for the logo came from Lubalin with lettering by his design partner Tom Carnase. In its original form the type family consisted of separate weights for headline and text setting and was only intended for use in the magazine, but it was released commercially by ITC due to public demand. In 1974 the family was supplemented with condensed weights designed by Ed Benguiat, and obliques were added in 1977. ITC Avant Garde Gothic is notorious for the misuse it has endured over the years; the "leaning" characters and multitude of ligatures encourage extremely tight letter spacing and this trait has often been abused by designers. Benguiat famously quipped that, "The only place Avant Garde looks good is in the words 'Avant Garde.'" Perhaps he has a point but its popularity, particularly among advertising art directors needing to set punchy headlines in limited space, marks it out as one of the key typefaces of the early 1970s.

There are a couple of digital versions of ITC Avant Garde Gothic to consider. The ITC Avant Garde Gothic Pro version, which is now owned by Monotype following a series of acquisitions that saw the ITC cease operations as an independent company, is a five-weight family with italic styles for each and includes a full set of alternative uppercase and lowercase characters and ligatures. However, the italics are uncorrected oblique romans and are less than perfect. Elsner+Flake publish a version of the face with corrected obliques, that look much better, particularly in the case of the rounded letterforms, which benefit the most. Be aware that in E+F's OpenType version the extra ligatures that are such a big part of this face are not integrated into the single weights; they're available as an alternative font for the roman weights but not the obliques.

ITC Avant Garde Gothic is famous for its huge range of discretionary ligatures

CALFANTMN

ITC Avant Garde Gothic Book

Frutiger

| **Country of origin:** France | **Classification:** Humanist Sans
| **Designer:** Adrian Frutiger

1974–1976

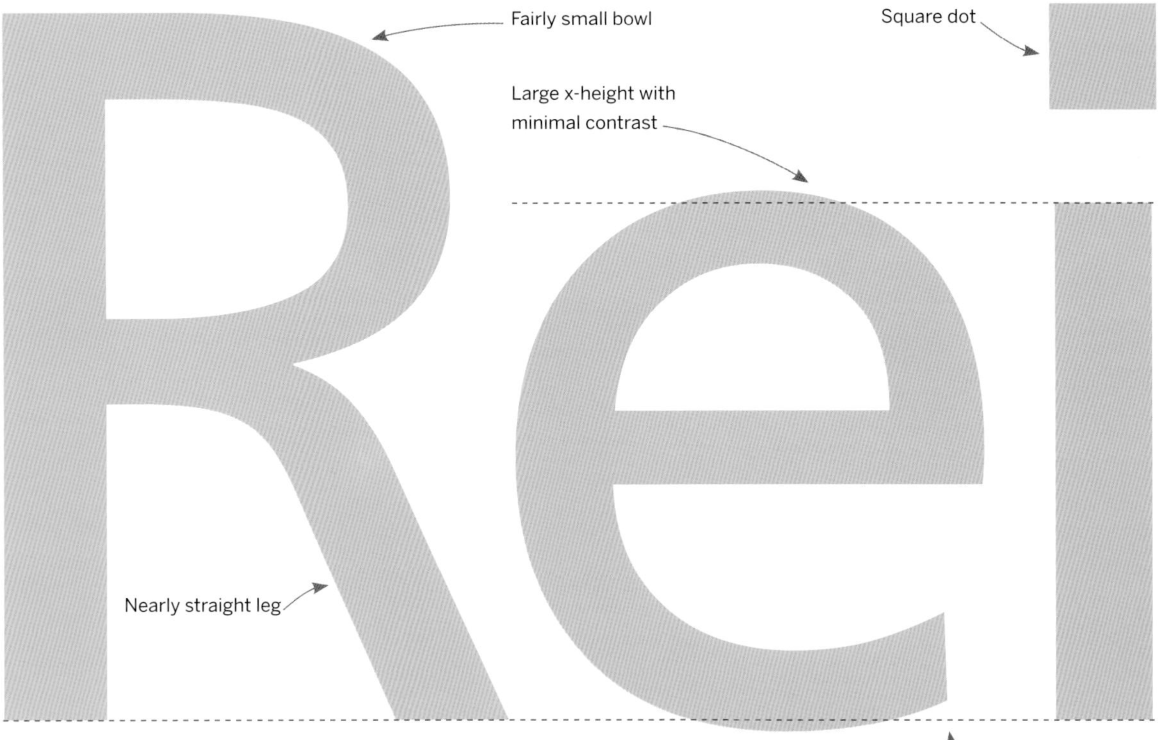

Fairly small bowl

Square dot

Large x-height with minimal contrast

Frutiger Neue Regular

Nearly straight leg

Re i

Strokes point outward with vertically sheared terminals

Adrian Frutiger designed the typeface that was originally named Roissy as a commission from France's new Charles de Gaulle International Airport. The brief called for signage to be legible up close and at distance, and from different angles when either walking or driving.

9/12pt Frutiger Neue Regular (Linotype)

LOREM IPSUM DOLOR SIT AMET, CONSECTETUER ADIPISCING ELIT, SED DIAM NONUMMY NIBH euismod tincidunt ut laoreet dolore magna aliquam erat volutpat. Ut wisi enim ad minim veniam, quis nostrud exerci tation ullamcorper suscipit lobortis nisl ut aliquip ex ea commodo consequat. Duis autem vel eum iriure dolor in

12/15pt Frutiger Neue Regular (Linotype)

LOREM IPSUM DOLOR SIT AMET, CONSECTETUER ADIPISCING ELIT, SED diam nonummy nibh euismod tincidunt ut laoreet dolore magna aliquam erat volutpat. Ut wisi enim ad minim veniam, quis nostrud exerci tation ullamcorper suscipit lobortis

Terminal One of the new Paris Charles de Gaulle airport, a progressive 10-floor circular hub design surrounded by seven satellite buildings with six gates each, first opened in March 1974. A building of that complexity needed clear signage and in 1968 Adrian Frutiger was commissioned to design a typeface for use throughout the terminal. Frutiger had gained a reputation for applying sound design sense to modern signage systems through his work on the Paris Metro (for which he designed a variant of Univers), but for Charles de Gaulle he felt a brand new face was required. He drew inspiration from Univers, but also looked closely at the Humanist sans serif Gill Sans and at Edward Johnston's typographic work for the London Underground.

Frutiger wanted to design a face that passengers could read at a distance and close up, at speed when rushing to catch a flight, in poor light, and from awkward angles. He even tested unfocused versions of his characters to gauge how far they could be pushed before they became unidentifiable. Despite this considerable typographic challenge, the brief was successfully met and Frutiger has since become the de facto choice in many airport terminals and transport hubs around the world. The face was initially named Roissy, after the location of the airport, but switched to Frutiger after the commercial release by Stempel and Linotype in 1976. Stempel, which by now was moving into the manufacture of phototypesetting equipment, used the text version of the original Roissy typeface and the weights were numbered using the same system Frutiger had applied several years earlier to the Univers family.

There have been several digital versions of Frutiger released by Linotype, but there are two available today of particular interest, Frutiger Next and Neue Frutiger. In 1999, Adrian Frutiger carried out an extensive revision across all the weights of Frutiger, introducing an increase in x-height, taller ascenders and narrower letterspacing. Most significantly, the sloping roman italics were redrawn as true cursive italics with subtler transitions between curves and stems. Frutiger Next was designed to broaden the range of applicable uses for the face, particularly in terms of text setting, and it's still a popular choice. However, for purists the better choice is Neue Frutiger, a 2009 revision produced as a collaboration between Frutiger and Akira Kobayashi, that returns the oblique roman italics and introduces a raft of optical improvements, expanding the family to 10 weights with italic styles. The numbering system used for naming the weights of the original typeface has been dropped from these later digital releases.

Neue Frutiger reintroduces the oblique romans replaced by cursive forms in Frutiger Next

aefg aefg

Neue Frutiger Medium Italic

Frutiger Next Medium Italic

ITC Tiffany

| **Country of origin:** United States | **Classification:** Humanist Serif
| **Designer:** Edward Benguiat

1974

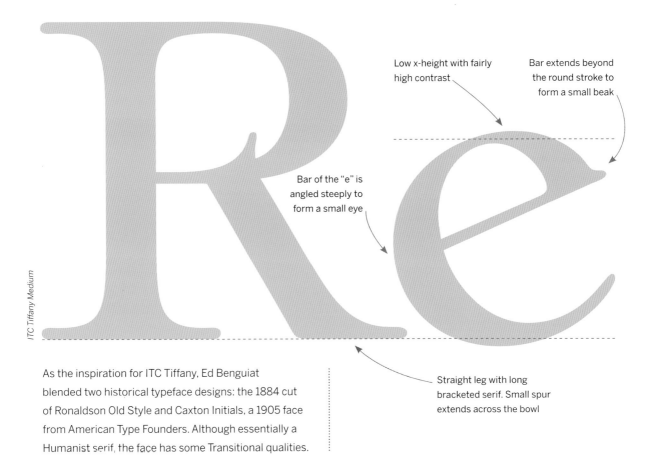

ITC Tiffany Medium

Low x-height with fairly high contrast

Bar extends beyond the round stroke to form a small beak

Bar of the "e" is angled steeply to form a small eye

Straight leg with long bracketed serif. Small spur extends across the bowl

As the inspiration for ITC Tiffany, Ed Benguiat blended two historical typeface designs: the 1884 cut of Ronaldson Old Style and Caxton Initials, a 1905 face from American Type Founders. Although essentially a Humanist serif, the face has some Transitional qualities.

9/12pt ITC Tiffany Medium

LOREM IPSUM DOLOR SIT AMET, CONSECTETUER ADIPISCING ELIT, SED diam nonummy nibh euismod tincidunt ut laoreet dolore magna aliquam erat volutpat. Ut wisi enim ad minim veniam, quis nostrud exerci tation ullamcorper suscipit lobortis nisl ut aliquip ex ea commodo consequat. Duis

12/15pt ITC Tiffany Medium

LOREM IPSUM DOLOR SIT AMET, CONSECTETUER ADIPISCING elit, sed diam nonummy nibh euismod tincidunt ut laoreet dolore magna aliquam erat volutpat. Ut wisi enim ad minim veniam, quis nostrud exerci tation ullamcorper

The designer of ITC Tiffany, Edward Benguiat, was a musician before he switched to illustration and typeface design. He was a well-known jazz percussionist and played with several big names but, to quote Benguiat himself, "One day I went to the musician's union to pay dues and I saw all these old people who were playing bar mitzvahs and Greek weddings. It occurred to me that one day that's going to be me, so I decided to become an illustrator." He played a big part in establishing the International Typeface Corporation as a major player in the world of commercial type design in the 1970s and 1980s, designed a great many ITC typefaces, and was vice-president by the time the ITC was sold to Esselte Ltd. in 1986.

When it was first released in 1974, the four-weight ITC Tiffany family had no italic styles; they weren't added until 1981. It's a blend of two much older faces, Ronaldson Old Style and Caxton Initials. Ronaldson Old Style was cut by the Philadelphia type foundry MacKellar, Smiths & Jordan in 1884 and provides Tiffany with its very prominent serifs. Frederic W. Goudy designed Caxton Initials for American Type Founders 20 years later in 1905 (apparently he didn't like the end result much) and it provides ITC Tiffany with its Lombardic flourish. The 6-year wait for the italic styles may be explained by the fact that they're true italics rather than oblique romans and had to be designed from scratch, which would have been a major investment for the smaller type foundry. The popularity of ITC Tiffany, particularly among advertising art directors, would have justified the effort of adding the new styles. Another issue at the time, which overlapped the earlier digital era, was the *faux* italic. If an italic style wasn't available, less than scrupulous photosetters would distort the roman to create their own, usually with disastrous results. Providing a proper italic style was really the only way to prevent this happening.

With only one digitized version to choose from, it's fortunate that Linotype's ITC Tiffany is an almost intact version of the original. The four weights of Light, Medium, Demi and Heavy are all there along with their italic styles, but there appears to be one or two alternative glyphs missing on comparison with the character set printed in Vol.8, No.2, of ITC's quarterly journal *U&lc*. However, the odd missing ampersand shouldn't put you off using ITC Tiffany to conjure up the perfect 1970s typographic vibe. If you're interested in reading back issues of *U&lc*, they're available to download at the font.com blog (blog.fonts.com/category/u&lc/).

aefgkwz

ITC Tiffany Medium

aefgkwz

ITC Tiffany Medium Italic

ITC Tiffany's true italics dissuade the creation of *faux* italics, which rarely look good

ITC Bauhaus

| **Country of origin:** United States | **Classification:** Display
| **Designers:** Edward Benguiat and Victor Caruso

1975

Rounds are circular

Relatively low x-height
with no contrast

Terminals follow
path of stroke

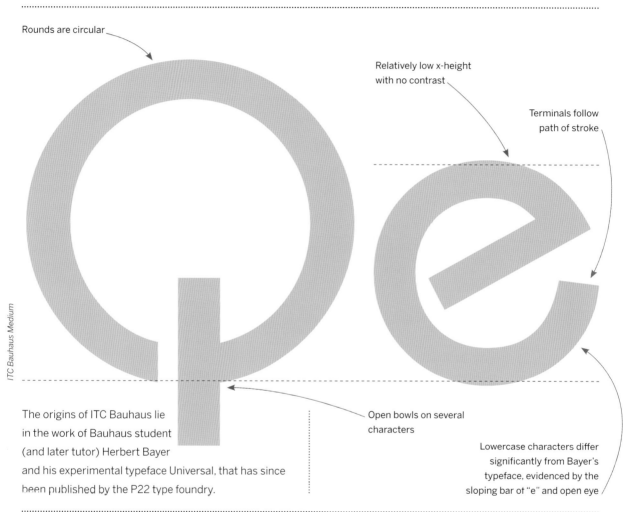

ITC Bauhaus Medium

The origins of ITC Bauhaus lie
in the work of Bauhaus student
(and later tutor) Herbert Bayer
and his experimental typeface Universal, that has since
been published by the P22 type foundry.

Open bowls on several
characters

Lowercase characters differ
significantly from Bayer's
typeface, evidenced by the
sloping bar of "e" and open eye

18pt ITC Bauhaus Demi

36pt ITC Bauhaus Demi

72pt ITC Bauhaus Demi

Before we discuss ITC Bauhaus, we should first talk about Herbert Bayer's experimental typeface Universal, designed while he was a lecturer at the Bauhaus in 1925. Bayer had previously been a student at the Bauhaus in Weimar; he graduated in February 1925 and immediately took up a teaching post at the school's new location in Dessau. Bayer was, of course, a modernist and rejected the prevalent use of blackletter in early-20th-century Germany. He designed his Geometric sans serif as part of a theoretical exploration of contemporary typographic style and argued that, as the spoken word didn't distinguish between uppercase and lowercase, his typeface didn't require both so only created lowercase characters. Bayer saw the typeface as part of a complete writing system (the Bauhaus stopped using uppercase letters in all its publications after 1925) but the face itself was not released commercially at the time. Berthold published a face named Bayer Type in 1935, but it bears no resemblance to Universal; it was a Rational Didone style serif. Today you can purchase an accurate interpretation, P22 Bayer Universal, as part of type foundry P22's Bauhaus set or as an individual font.

ITC Bauhaus was designed by Edward Benguiat and Victor Caruso and is based on Bayer's Universal typeface. Given that there were never any uppercase characters designed for Universal, ITC Bauhaus is very much an interpretation rather than a revival; it's the idea of the Geometric structure that has been carried forward by Benguiat and Caruso. Although it was originally designed at the firm PhotoLettering Inc. as a display face, ITC Bauhaus was marketed as a text face for photocomposition and issued in four text weights ranging from Light to Bold, plus two display weights, Heavy and Heavy Outline. Does it succeed as a text face? It's not particularly legible at smaller point sizes but one must remember that the typographic tastes of the 1970s were very different from today's. To quote Edward Benguiat when speaking at an event in 2011, "I do not think of type as something that should be readable. It should be beautiful. Screw readable."

There are a few digital versions of ITC Bauhaus available today. The best known is published by Linotype in the usual five weights: Light, Medium, DemiBold, Bold and Heavy. A near-identical version published by Adobe contains a few additional alternative glyphs in the OpenType release but essentially the two options are interchangeable. If you happen to come across an old Bitstream release of ITC Bauhaus, I would avoid it as the metrics feel wrong; the round glyphs appear too oval. The letterforms of a version sold by Elsner+Flake look similar to the others but in use the letter spacing seems to be a little tidier, making it a good alternative choice.

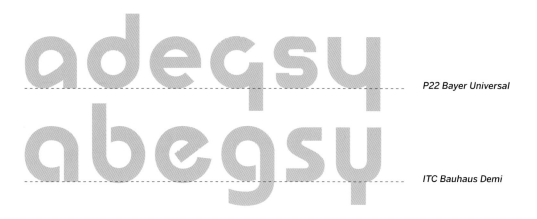

P22 Bayer Universal

ITC Bauhaus Demi

Bell Centennial

| **Country of origin:** United States | **Classification:** Gothic Sans
| **Designer:** Matthew Carter

1975–1978

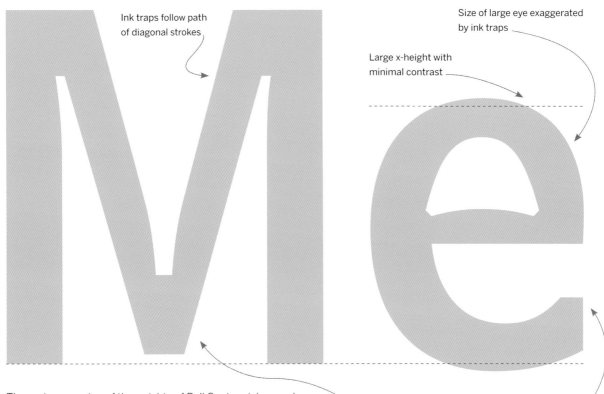

Ink traps follow path
of diagonal strokes

Size of large eye exaggerated
by ink traps

Large x-height with
minimal contrast

Bell Centennial Name & Number

The curious naming of the weights of Bell Centennial stem from its commission by AT&T specifically for use in their telephone book. Space-saving features include the prominent ink traps at the junctions of the strokes, that smooth out when printed at small point sizes.

Ink trap added to
heaviest strokes of
each glyph

Squared terminals

9/12pt Bell Centennial Address (Adobe)

LOREM IPSUM DOLOR SIT AMET, CONSECTETUER ADIPISCING ELIT, SED DIAM NONUMMY NIBH EUISMOD TINCIDUNT UT laoreet dolore magna aliquam erat volutpat. ut wisi enim ad minim veniam, quis nostrud exerci tation ullamcorper suscipit lobortis nisl ut aliquip ex ea commodo consequat. Duis autem vel eum iriure dolor in hendrerit in vulputate velit esse molestie consequat, vel illum dolore eu feugiat nulla facilisis at vero eros

12/15pt Bell Centennial Address (Adobe)

LOREM IPSUM DOLOR SIT AMET, CONSECTETUER ADIPISCING ELIT, SED DIAM nonummy nibh euismod tincidunt ut laoreet dolore magna aliquam erat volutpat. Ut wisi enim ad minim veniam, quis nostrud exerci tation ullamcorper suscipit lobortis nisl ut aliquip ex ea commodo consequat. Duis autem

In 1937, Chauncey H. Griffith developed a new typeface at Linotype, designed primarily for use in the New York City telephone directory. It was named Bell Gothic and at the time was so successful it was quickly adopted as the typeface used to set the text for telephone directories throughout the U.S. Directories and catalogs are generally printed in huge quantities on cheap paper, so serif faces with hairline strokes don't work too well at small point sizes. The sturdiness of Bell Gothic meant it didn't break up as a serif face might, introducing improvements in legibility. Linotype also adapted Bell Gothic for use in newspapers; Furlong contained special characters used to set race-track results, and Market Gothic was designed to set stock-market listings.

The Bell Telephone Company, or AT&T as it had become shortly after its formation, reached its 100th anniversary in July, 1977. To mark the event, the company commissioned a new typeface that would improve on Bell Gothic; the older face had not switched successfully from hot metal to photosetting and results were poor. Bell Centennial was completed by designer Matthew Carter at Linotype in 1978, with its name derived from the timing of the commission. Carter was briefed to design a face that would be highly legible when set as small as 6 point, and he expanded the original two weights into a family of four with names linked specifically to their intended use; Bell Centennial Address, Sub-Caption, Name and Number and Bold Listing. Carter had learned his trade working with metal foundry type and drew all the characters by hand, making liberal use of a technique known as ink trapping to prevent the spread of ink into the tight junctions and counters of the characters when set at very small sizes. The traps aren't apparent until the letters are set at large sizes, when the notches cut into junctions and strokes become visible. This does mean the face looks a little odd when used for larger headline setting, but that hasn't stopped designers doing just that to elicit a response.

The digital choices available today are published by Linotype, Adobe and Bitstream and include the four weights of the original design. There is little reason to choose one over the other, but the extended character sets of the OpenType versions by Linotype and Adobe may sway your decision.

Bell Centennial Address

Bell Centennial Name & Number

Bell Centennial Sub-Caption

Bell Centennial Bold Listing

ITC Galliard

| **Country of origin:** United States | **Classification:** Old Style Serif
| **Designer:** Matthew Carter

1978

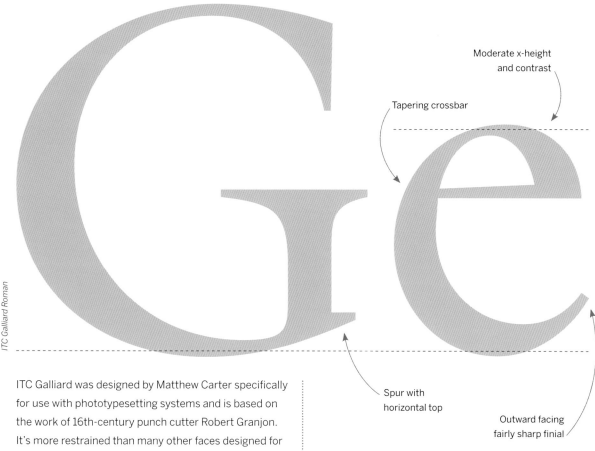

ITC Galliard Roman

Moderate x-height
and contrast

Tapering crossbar

Spur with
horizontal top

Outward facing
fairly sharp finial

ITC Galliard was designed by Matthew Carter specifically for use with phototypesetting systems and is based on the work of 16th-century punch cutter Robert Granjon. It's more restrained than many other faces designed for photosetting, so rather more successful.

9/12pt ITC Galliard Roman

LOREM IPSUM DOLOR SIT AMET, CONSECTETUER ADIPISCING ELIT, SED DIAM nonummy nibh euismod tincidunt ut laoreet dolore magna aliquam erat volutpat. Ut wisi enim ad minim veniam, quis nostrud exerci tation ullamcorper suscipit lobortis nisl ut aliquip ex ea commodo consequat. Duis autem vel eum iriure dolor in hendrerit in

12/15pt ITC Galliard Roman

LOREM IPSUM DOLOR SIT AMET, CONSECTETUER ADIPISCING elit, sed diam nonummy nibh euismod tincidunt ut laoreet dolore magna aliquam erat volutpat. Ut wisi enim ad minim veniam, quis nostrud exerci tation ullamcorper suscipit lobortis nisl ut

ITC Galliard was not always ITC Galliard—the ITC part was added in 1981, a few years after it was designed for Linotype by Matthew Carter. Like many of its predecessors, the face is based on Robert Granjon's 16th-century type. Mike Parker, Linotype's Director of Typographic Development, had visited Antwerp's Plantin-Moretus Museum and was inspired by the examples of Granjon's type he saw there, deciding that a fresh Old Style serif would complement Linotype's existing roster of faces. Granjon is thought to be one of the first punch cutters to assign names rather than simple size references to his type and around 1570 he cut an 8-point font that he called La Galliarde, the name of a popular dance and the source of the name for Carter's typeface. Galliard was developed specifically for use with Linotype's phototypesetting equipment so never existed as metal type, an increasingly common practice from the 1970s onward.

Aaron Burns, the president and cofounder of the International Typeface Corporation, was a huge fan of Linotype's new face and was extremely keen to see it added to the ITC catalog. The pitch he ultimately had to make several times to Linotype reasoned that Galliard would reach many more customers if it were marketed by ITC via their highly regarded *U&lc* magazine. Linotype eventually capitulated in 1981 and licensed Galliard exclusively to ITC. ITC Galliard is an interpretation of the original design that Carter adapted himself, using computer-aided technology to perfect the letterforms. It was indeed successful for ITC and was a popular alternative to the ever present Garamonds of the day, given their shared 16th-century origins.

The digital version of ITC Galliard is published by Monotype as an ITC face, and it's available as an Adobe family. There are four weights with italic styles: Roman, Bold, Black and Ultra. Also, Monotype has created ITC Galliard eText, an adaptation released as part of their eText collection that has been optimized for onscreen viewing.

ITC Galliard Roman

A comparison of ITC Galliard with the Granjon-influenced letterforms of Garamond indicate clear points of reference

Garamond Premier Regular

VAG Rounded

| **Country of origin:** Germany | **Classification:** Geometric Sans
| **Designers:** GGK Advertising Agency

1979

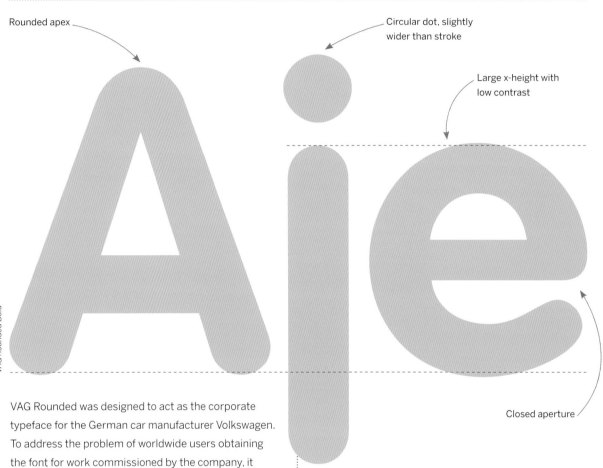

Rounded apex

Circular dot, slightly wider than stroke

Large x-height with low contrast

Closed aperture

VAG Rounded Bold

VAG Rounded was designed to act as the corporate typeface for the German car manufacturer Volkswagen. To address the problem of worldwide users obtaining the font for work commissioned by the company, it was placed in the public domain.

18pt VAG Rounded Bold (Adobe)

RGafsv

36pt VAG Rounded Bold (Adobe)

RGafsv

72pt VAG Rounded Bold (Adobe)

VAG Rounded (or VAG Rundschrift in German) was designed as a corporate typeface for the European automobile manufacturer Volkswagen AG. The meaning of the VAG prefix has been given variously as Volkswagen Audi Group, Volkswagen AG, and as the tongue-in-cheek interpretation Von Adolf Gegründet, which translates as Founded by Adolf. The origins of the face are a little muddy; some sources state that it was conceived in 1979 by Wolf Rogosky and Gerd Hiepler at the advertising agency GGK Düsseldorf, whereas others credit Gerry Barney and the team at the London-based agency Sedley Place. It's possible that both agencies were in part responsible for completing and implementing the design of VAG Rounded, which has been augmented and updated several times in the intervening years.

The need for a single corporate face arose following the 1964 acquisition by Volkswagen of Auto Union GmbH, which subsequently rebranded as Audi. Volkswagen's big plan involved the merger of the dealerships of both brands into one that could go on to sell additional brand acquisitions, and a common identity was required. Prior to VAG Rounded, Volkswagen used Futura whereas Audi used Times—the faces couldn't have been more different—and it was decided that the new face should bridge the gap between a sans serif and a

serif. The concept of a Geometric sans serif with rounded terminals emerged and VAG Rounded was first drawn by hand then completed using a PDP-8, the first successful commercial minicomputer. Volkswagen used the face for all corporate applications until its next rebranding in the late 1980s, releasing it into the public domain to facilitate easy distribution to its agents around the world. Adobe also released a version of VAG Rounded in 1989 with a further update made available in 1995. It remains a popular face that often crops up online, given its propensity for clear on-screen legibility, and it's often used for labeling purposes. I've used Macs for many years and since 2007 VAG Rounded is probably one of the typefaces I look at more than any other—it's the font used on all of Apple's keyboards.

There are a number of commercial offerings to choose from today if you don't have access to a good-quality version from a legitimate free source. Linotype and Adobe publish the standard four-weight family, Bitstream and Elsner+Flake sell single weights, and URW++ have a two-weight family with oblique roman italics. For me this is a typeface that only works as a roman, perhaps because it was designed that way, and the Linotype/Adobe family is the better option.

VAG Rounded Thin

VAG is the typeface used on all of Apple's current range of keyboards

Character map (code points and glyphs):

003D	003E	003F	0040	0041	0042	0043	0044	0045	0046	0047	0048	0049	004A	004B	004C	004D	004E	004F	0050	0051	0052	0053	0054
=	>	?	@	A	B	C	D	E	F	G	H	I	J	K	L	M	N	O	P	Q	R	S	T

005A	005B	005C	005D	005E	005F	0060	0061	0062	0063	0064	0065	0066	0067	0068	0069	006A	006B	006C	006D	006E	006F	0070	0071
Z	[	\	]	^	_	`	a	b	c	d	e	f	g	h	i	j	k	l	m	n	o	p	q

0077	0078	0079	007A	007B	007C	007D	007E	---	00C4	00C5	00C7	00C9	00D1	00D6	00DC	00E1	00E0	00E2	00E4	00E3	00E5	00E7	00E9
w	x	y	z	{	|	}	~		Ä	Å	Ç	É	Ñ	Ö	Ü	á	à	â	ä	ã	å	ç	é

00EE	00EF	00F1	00F3	00F2	00F4	00F6	00F5	00FA	00F9	00FB	00FC	2020	0080	00A2	00A3	00A7	2022	00B6	00DF	00AE	00A9	2122	00B4
î	ï	ñ	ó	ò	ô	ö	õ	ú	ù	û	ü	†	°	¢	£	§	•	¶	ß	®	©	™	´

00B1	2264	2265	00A5	00B5	2202	2211	220F	03C0	222B	00AA	00BA	03A9	00E6	00F8	00BF	00A1	00AC	221A	0192	2248	2206	00AB	00BB
±	≤	≥	¥	µ	∂	∑	∏	π	∫	ª	º	Ω	æ	ø	¿	¡	¬	√	ƒ	≈	∆	«	»

0152	0153	2013	2014	201C	201D	2018	2019	00F7	25CA	00FF	0178	2044	20AC	2039	203A	FB01	FB02	2021	00B7	201A	201E	2030	00C2
Œ	œ	–	—	"	"	'	'	÷	◊	ÿ	Ÿ	⁄	€	‹	›	fi	fl	‡	·	‚	„	‰	Â

00CE	00CF	00CC	00D3	00D4	F8FF	00D2	00DA	00DB	00D9	0131	02C6	02DC	00AF	02D8	02D9	02DA	00B8	02DD	02DB	02C7	---	---	---
Î	Ï	Ì	Ó	Ô		Ò	Ú	Û	Ù	ı	ˆ	˜	¯	˘	˙	˚	¸	˝	˛	ˇ			ff

~	..	-	˘	°	"	·	,	'	!	$	%	&	0	1	2	3	4	5	6	7	8	9	?

F	G	H	I	J	K	L	M	N	O	P	Q	R	S	T	U	V	W	X	Y	Z	À	Á	Â

Ã	Ą	Æ	Ǽ	Ć	Ĉ	Č	Ċ	Ç	Ď	Đ	Đ	È	É	Ê	Ě	Ë	Ē	Ĕ	Ė	Ę	Ĝ	Ğ	Ġ

Ĭ	Î	Ĩ	Ï	Ī	İ	Į	Ĵ	Ķ	Ĺ	Ľ	Ļ	Ł	Ŀ	Ń	Ň	Ñ	Ņ	Ò	Ó	Ô	Õ	Ö	Ō

Ŕ	Ř	Ŗ	Ś	Ŝ	Š	Ş	Ş	Ť	Ţ	Ŧ	Þ	Ù	Ú	Û	Ũ	Ü	Ū	Ŭ	Ů	Ű	Ų	Ŵ	Ŵ

Ỳ	Ź	Ž	Ż	IJ	SS	Ŋ	`	´	^	ˇ	~	..	-	˘	°	"	·	i	¿	€	¢	£	ƒ

1	2	3	4	5	6	7	8	9	0	1	2	3	4	5	6	7	8	9	0	€	$	¢	£

1st	TH	3rd	2nd	&	*	(fist)	(apple)	'N	0	1	2	3	4	5	6	7	8	9	0	1	2	3	4

0	1	2	3	4	5	6	7	8	9	0	1	2	3	4	5	6	7	8	9	€	$	¢	£

b	c	d	e	g	l	m	o	r	s	t	4TH	1ST	th	3RD	2ND	ſ	ct	ft	et	fft	fh	fj	ſp

																	00A4	00A6	00AD	00B2	00B3
¢	†	‡	†	‡	—	–	-	·	¶	§	fi	fl	✠	✲	✾	✠	✤	✿	¤	¦	-	²	³

00D7	00DD	00DE	00F0	00FD	00FE	0100	0101	0102	0103	0104	0105	0106	0107	0108	0109	010A	010B	010C	010D	010E	010F	0110	0111
×	Ý	Þ	ð	ý	þ	Ā	ā	Ă	ă	Ą	ą	Ć	ć	Ĉ	ĉ	Ċ	ċ	Č	č	Ď	ď	Đ	đ

0117	0118	0119	011A	011B	011C	011D	011E	011F	0120	0121	0122	0123	0124	0125	0126	0127	0128	0129	012A	012B	012C	012D	012E
ė	Ę	ę	Ě	ě	Ĝ	ĝ	Ğ	ğ	Ġ	ġ	Ģ	ģ	Ĥ	ĥ	Ħ	ħ	Ĩ	ĩ	Ī	ī	Ĭ	ĭ	Į

0135	0136	0137	0138	0139	013A	013B	013C	013D	013E	013F	0140	0141	0142	0143	0144	0145	0146	0147	0148	0149	014A	014B	014C
ĵ	Ķ	ķ	ĸ	Ĺ	ĺ	Ļ	ļ	Ľ	ľ	Ŀ	ŀ	Ł	ł	Ń	ń	Ņ	ņ	Ň	ň	ŉ	Ŋ	ŋ	Ō

0154	0155	0156	0157	0158	0159	015A	015B	015C	015D	015E	015F	0160	0161	0162	0163	0164	0165	0166	0167	0168	0169	016A	016B
Ŕ	ŕ	Ŗ	ŗ	Ř	ř	Ś	ś	Ŝ	ŝ	Ş	ş	Š	š	Ţ	ţ	Ť	ť	Ŧ	ŧ	Ũ	ũ	Ū	ū

0171	0172	0173	0174	0175	0176	0177	0179	017A	017B	017C	017D	017E	01FA	01FB	01FC	01FD	01FE	01FF	0218	0219	021A	021B	0237
ű	Ų	ų	Ŵ	ŵ	Ŷ	ŷ	Ź	ź	Ż	ż	Ž	ž	Ǻ	ǻ	Ǽ	ǽ	Ǿ	ǿ	Ș	ș	Ț	ț	ȷ

1E82	1E83	1E84	1E85	1EF2	1EF3	2010	2015	203D	2070	2071	2074	2075	2076	2077	2078	2079	207A	207B	207C	207D	207E	207F	2080
Ẃ	ẃ	Ẅ	ẅ	Ỳ	ỳ	‐	―	‽															

PIXEL PERFECT

Back in the late 1980s, the managing director of the London-based graphic design consultancy where I had landed my first job announced that we were going to design and artwork a brochure for a regular client using the small gray box that he had recently purchased at considerable expense. We were dubious at first, thinking it would only be a matter of days before we reverted back to ordering galleys from our regular typesetting firm, but we were wrong. Thanks to the perseverance of a colleague who was designated the main "operator," the Apple Macintosh SE got the job done. We were obviously very impressed, couldn't wait to get hold of a few more Macs so we could all have a go, and the rest is history—the fate of the typesetting industry was sealed.

By the time I first set my own eyes on the genuine article, Apple computers had already been around for quite a few years. The company was founded in 1976 by Steve Jobs, Steve Wozniak and Ronald Wayne, and the first models were certainly not intended for use as design tools. However, in 1979 Apple formed a connection with Xerox as part of a share-option deal and Jobs and several other Apple employees, were given access to the company's Palo Alto Research Center, where they encountered the Xerox Alto personal computer. The Alto was never a true commercial product (although around 2,000 units were manufactured) but crucially it was the first personal computer (PC) to use a graphical user interface (UI) and a point-and-click mouse—bitmapped graphics allowed basic rendering of type onscreen and the screen image matched printed output. Jobs and his colleagues were immediately convinced that this was the way to go and their experience provided the basis for the design of the early Macintosh UI and machines, beginning with the Apple Lisa in 1983.

Notwithstanding the importance of the Macintosh as a key player in kickstarting the desktop publishing revolution, on its own it would never have made the impact it eventually did. Along with the ability to handle images, it was vital that fonts could be displayed accurately onscreen and output to a printer as "what you see is what you get" or WYSIWYG characters. As we know, the earliest bitmapped fonts weren't anywhere near the quality of the typesetting we can produce today but they were, all the same, a massive leap forwards and in their time inspired a particular graphic style for grungy-looking pixellated typesetting. At first, Apple designed their own typefaces to avoid the cost of licensing fonts from a third party, but these were never going to fully satisfy the market and possibly helped contribute to Apple's less than spectacular early sales figures. Furthermore, software that would enable graphic designers to set type and create layouts in a digital environment that mimicked the traditional artworking process was badly needed. The products of two other companies, Adobe and Aldus, combined with the Macintosh platform, provided everything that was needed to enable designers to take control of their own typesetting and artworking needs.

Adobe was formed in 1982 by a group of former Xerox employees who wanted to develop their ideas for a page description language that they called PostScript. Essentially, PostScript is a computer language capable of creating vector graphics which, unlike bitmaps, are fully scalable mathematically described geometric shapes. Bitmap fonts that previously could only be used at a specific size without significant loss of quality could now be drawn as smooth outlines and set at whatever size the designer wished, with the only limitation being the maximum size allowed by the software in use. Without this development the desktop publishing revolution wouldn't have been possible, making PostScript arguably the most important development for typesetting since the invention of the Linotype and Monotype machines in the late 1880s.

Early in 1984, an ex-newspaper editor by the name of Paul Brainerd had been working for a company that manufactured the industrial-sized and enormously expensive computer workstations that were used by the publishing industry at that time. Brainerd was convinced that it would be possible to do the same job as these large machines on a much smaller personal computer if the right software solutions were available. He was made redundant when the company was bought out by Kodak (look what happened to them) and used the opportunity to start up a new company to realize his vision and develop publishing

software for PCs. The company was called Aldus, named for the 15th-century Italian printer and publisher Aldus Manutius (see page 22), and the software, released in its original version in 1985, was Pagemaker. Pagemaker was the first software package capable of replicating the familiar design and artwork environment on a screen. Text could be set in columns below a headline with integrated images, just like a regular piece of paste-up, and in many ways this was the beauty of this early pioneering software. The only obstacle to gaining complete competence was getting over the initial reservations about using a computer. It seems crazy to think this nowadays when 4-year-old children sit happily tapping away on their parents' iPad but 30 years ago PCs were an expensive luxury that few people could afford to own and use at home, and technophobia was rife. Pagemaker turned everything on its head and within a few years there were Macintosh workstations appearing in every design consultancy.

Apple's contribution during these early days of desktop publishing were not limited solely to the computers themselves. The company's Laserwriter, introduced around the same time as Pagemaker in 1985, was one of the first mass market desktop-sized printers that included a built-in PostScript interpreter, making it capable of outputting sharp text and graphics, albeit in mono and at a rather slow eight pages per minute. Indeed, the knowledge that Apple was developing the Laserwriter played its part in spurring Paul Brainerd on with his development of Pagemaker, as the two products made perfect partners. Amazingly, the Laserwriter was more than double the price of the Macs available at that time; interesting when one considers how cost-effective laserwriters can be today.

So that covers the early hardware and software that enabled us to begin to enjoy the flexibility and convenience we have with our current workstations, be they a Mac or a PC running Windows, but what about the fonts themselves? Once again we have Adobe to thank for the technology that gave us PostScript Type 1 fonts, alongside the Apple/Microsoft collaboration that developed the TrueType format, leading to the Adobe/Microsoft development of the current OpenType format.

PostScript Type 1 fonts (there were various numbered formats all the way up to Type 42 but we'll stick to the basic format here) used separate font files to render the characters onscreen and as a printed image. The printer font component contained the important data that described the precise outline of each character or glyph in a font, and the screen font was a hinted and anti-aliased bitmap that enabled the font to be displayed with varying degrees of accuracy on the screen, depending on the size it was set at. To help resolve the problematic rendering of fonts onscreen, and to respond to the competition created by TrueType fonts (see below), Adobe also developed a neat program called Adobe Type Manager that rendered fonts onscreen by scaling information contained in the printer font files, making it an essential tool for professional designers and typesetters working in the digital format.

TrueType was developed as an alternative to Adobe's PostScript font format and came with the added advantage of only requiring a single font file for each style of type in a family—no bitmap components were required to render the font on a screen. The format first appeared in 1991 and much of the technology remains as part of the font-handling components of Apple's OS X system software. In my own experience, Adobe's format tended to prevail over TrueType as a part of a professional consultancy's collection of fonts, perhaps because Adobe's work as an early developer of digital fonts produced a larger selection from which to choose. More importantly, there were also well-documented issues where non-PostScript TrueType fonts refused to print when sent to imagesetters using a PostScript-reliant RIP (Raster Image Processor)—a big problem in a professional workflow. However, both formats are now effectively outdated following the advent of OpenType and most new fonts are now marketed in the OpenType format.

OpenType was built off the original framework of the TrueType format, but adds a great deal to the mix. Significantly, a single OpenType font file can contain up to 65,536 glyphs whereas the older Adobe PostScript Type 1 file format could only manage 256. Does anyone remember when PostScript fonts came with an "Expert Set," that contained extra glyphs such as Old Style numbers, fractions, or non-standard ligatures that couldn't fit into one font file? This is no longer necessary as all those extra glyphs can now be accommodated. OpenType fonts are also cross-compatible so they can be installed on both Macs and Windows PCs. Finally, the advance features of OpenType provide type designers with the opportunity to include data that can substitute alternative glyphs into text, depending on the order of characters in a word. This advantage is particularly evident when using a contemporary script font, which is likely to include many alternative glyphs in order to achieve perfect linkages between characters.

From Pagemaker, through QuarkXPress and on to Adobe's Creative Cloud applications such as InDesign and Illustrator, digital font technology has managed to keep pace and is now able to replicate the finest qualities of hot metal typesetting using optically sized fonts and advanced typographic features. Thankfully, there are also many inspiring type foundries and individual designers that continue to create both the exciting new typefaces and the brilliantly realized revivals of classic metal faces that have been inaccessible to present-day designers for so many years.

Robert Slimbach

Robert Slimbach is an accidental type designer. Born in Evanston, Illinois, in 1956, Slimbach attended college at the University of California on an athletics scholarship, but his subsequent career was destined to propel him along an entirely different route. His father worked as a photoengraver and printer, which may well have influenced his decision to become involved in the running of a small silk-screen printshop after completing his studies. Much of the work he produced at this time involved hand-lettering and this is an interesting aspect of his development as a type designer—it highlights the fact that successful practitioners so often start with a grounding in calligraphy, which enables them to fully understand how letterforms are constructed. I recall a much valued lesson from my own time at art school when our typography lecturer instilled in us that, if you can't draw a character, you may never fully understand the bigger typographic picture. He was absolutely right and it's one of the most important things I learned way back when.

In 1983, Slimbach joined the typesetting firm Autologic to help supplement his income and during his time with the company he learned a great deal about the classic approach to typeface design. Following his time with Autologic he worked as a freelancer, creating two typefaces for the International Typeface Corporation, ITC Slimbach and ITC Giovanni. Another well-known type designer, Sumner Stone, knew Slimbach from his time at Autologic and invited him to join Adobe in 1987. The move would prove to be a decisive moment in Slimbach's developing career and his first designs for Adobe were Utopia, a versatile Transitional serif, and the much-lauded Adobe Garamond which, along with its more recent release as Garamond Premier, is widely regarded as the best digital interpretation of the original 16th-century face. A year later, in 1990, Slimbach designed Minion, an Old Style serif which has since become a modern classic; it's a hardworking go-to serif that in some ways fills the same space that, although not directly interpreting a Caslon or a Sabon, provides designers with a typeface that simply works. A couple of years later the Humanist sans, Myriad, which was designed as a collaboration with Carol Twombly, did for sans serifs what Minion had previously done for serifs. Many more faces that have rightly earned their place in the Adobe Originals program have followed since then—a personal favorite of mine is the wonderfully calligraphic Humanist serif Brioso released in 2003—and Slimbach continues to work with Adobe at the time of writing.

Zuzana Licko

Zuzana Licko (which is pronounced *Litch-ko*) was born in Bratislava in the former Republic of Czechoslovakia in 1961. Her family emigrated to the U.S. when she was a child and she went on to study architecture, photography and computer programming before achieving her degree in graphic communications from the University of California. Licko's exposure to computers began relatively early as her father worked as a biomathematician—she would often help him with his data processing, something that would stand her in good stead a few years later.

While studying at college Licko took a calligraphy class, finding it physically difficult because she's left-handed and had to work with her right, but the experience would prove to be influential to her later career decisions. It was also at college that she met her husband, Rudy VanderLans, a Dutch designer who had studied at the Royal Academy of Art in the Hague before relocating to California to study photography. In 1984, and feeling somewhat directionless after accepting a variety of design-related jobs, they acquired a Macintosh computer and, as quoted in an interview that appeared in No.43, Vol.11, of *Eye* magazine, "… everything started to fall into place." The exploratory process of learning to use the Mac forced them to question much of what they'd been taught about graphic design and in the same year they decided to form Emigre, one of the most creative partnerships to emerge during the 1980s.

Emigre is a design studio, digital type foundry and magazine publisher, and has generated its

fair share of controversy over the years. This is largely due to Licko's highly experimental early type designs, which weren't initially to everyone's tastes, but her work was hugely important and Emigre is rightly credited as the first company to distribute original fonts designed on and made for a computer. Licko's first brace of bitmap fonts, Emperor, Emigre and Oakland, were designed using public-domain software and were never intended to be inaccurate representations of existing fonts, output poorly on a low resolution printer. These fonts were original concepts that were designed specifically to work with the technology of the day and this is perhaps one of the most interesting aspects of Licko's progression as a type designer; her concepts echo the way digital technology developed throughout the 1980s and 1990s. By 1986 she'd designed Citizen, a smoother bitmap that represented the improvements in laser printing technology. Base Nine and Base Twelve were designed for the Emigre website in 1995 when it was still very difficult to achieve good typographic results online and evolved into faces that could be used for print projects. Licko has since designed some fine typefaces of a more traditional nature; for example, Filosofia is a cheerful Rational Didone and Mrs Eaves is a very individual Transitional serif. It has to be said that, regardless of the conceptual approach taken, Licko's faces are always vocal and full of character.

Tobias Frere-Jones

Tobias Frere-Jones was born in New York, in 1970, and continues to live and work there. His interest in typography and letterforms began at an early age and, while still a high school student, he received a communication from the renowned type designer Ed Benguiat offering him lessons at the class he taught at the School of Visual Arts—Benguiat's eye had been caught by Frere-Jones' entry to a design competition. He went on to study graphic design at Rhode Island School of Design and, after graduation in 1992, joined the staff at Font Bureau in Boston where he was involved in creating some of the foundry's most popular fonts, including Interstate and Benton Sans, with Cyrus Highsmith. Benton Sans is the principal sans serif face used throughout this book.

Frere-Jones remained with Font Bureau for 7 years before establishing his creative partnership with Jonathan Hoefler in New York in 1999. Many of the typefaces designed individually by Frere-Jones and collaboratively with Hoefler and the Hoefler & Frere-Jones staff have since become (if this isn't too strong a word to apply to a typeface) legendary. The list of clients he has designed for reads rather like a "Who's Who" of the business and publishing world, with the most famous of all arguably being Gotham, after it was used extensively in Barack Obama's 2008 Presidential campaign. Historical points of reference have always been key to Frere-Jones' design process, which may help to explain why his faces always feel simultaneously well grounded in the typographic tradition yet contemporary and fresh.

In January 2014 the design world was shocked by the news that Hoefler & Frere-Jones had acrimoniously split. Disagreement over the ownership of the design of several fonts had caused the rift and, as the *New York Times* headline declared, "The Beatles of the Type World are Breaking Up." The dispute was thankfully resolved by the end of October 2014 and the terms have remained confidential, but the upside of this meant both individuals were once again able to move forward with their own projects and could continue to provide us with excellent and ground-breaking typefaces. As well as his ongoing work as a type designer, Frere-Jones teaches typeface design at the Yale School of Art alongside fellow designer Matthew Carter.

NB: Typefaces featured in this book designed by Frere-Jones during his time with Hoefler & Frere-Jones, which are still sold by Hoefler & Co., are credited to the latter company, but Frere-Jones' involvement in the original design is mentioned where applicable in the accompanying text.

Christian Schwartz

Christian Schwartz has managed to squeeze a lot into his career, considering that he's still under 40 years of age. Schwartz was born in New Hampshire in 1977 and is a graduate of the Communication Design program at Pennsylvania's Carnegie Mellon University. Amazingly, his first commercial typeface, a Geometric display face named Flywheel, was published when he was just 14 years old. Following his graduation he was offered a three-month spell at MetaDesign in Berlin where he met Erik Spiekermann—the two have frequently collaborated on a variety of type design projects ever since—where he worked on typefaces for Volkswagen as well as more general graphic design projects. Returning to the U.S. he landed a position at Font Bureau in Boston and stayed for 2 years, working with David Berlow and Tobias Frere-Jones among others. Schwartz then relocated to New York, harboring a desire to work as a magazine art director, and freelanced for a few weeks at the studio run by Roger Black (co-founder, with Berlow, of Font Bureau) before realizing that magazine work might not be quite the right direction to take. Black subsequently asked Schwartz to take on a series of lettering and type design projects instead and his future career took shape.

In 2001, Schwartz formed his first company, Orange Italic, with product designer Dino Sanchez, before establishing Schwartzco Inc., a platform which enabled him to design for a number of well-known foundries including Village, FontFont and Emigre. A particularly successful 2002 collaboration with Delaware's prolific digital type foundry House Industries produced the extensive Neutraface family, and a re-release of the three-font Luxury family. Other notable faces, released through Font Bureau, include the Transitional serif Farnham and the Neo-Humanist sans Amplitude.

Since 2005, Schwartz has worked in partnership with London-based designer Paul Barnes under the name Commercial Type. Their first collaboration was a high-end commission from Mark Porter, at that time the creative director at *The Guardian* newspaper, for a new typeface system to use as part of a major redesign. Their work earned them a much coveted Black Pencil award from the British design industry organization D&AD. Other clients include *Esquire* magazine, the Empire State Building, *The New York Times* and Condé Nast. In recognition of his achievements in typeface design, Schwartz was presented with the highly prestigious Prix Charles Peignot by the Association Typographique Internationale (ATypI), an award given every 4 years to a designer under the age of 35 who has made "an outstanding contribution to the field of type design."

Swift (Neue Swift)

| **Country of origin:** The Netherlands | **Classification:** Contemporary Serif
| **Designer:** Gerard Unger

1985–2009

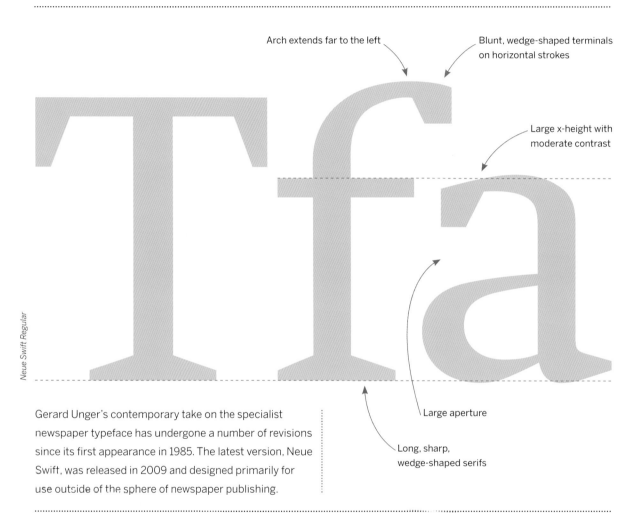

Arch extends far to the left

Blunt, wedge-shaped terminals on horizontal strokes

Large x-height with moderate contrast

Large aperture

Long, sharp, wedge-shaped serifs

Neue Swift Regular

Gerard Unger's contemporary take on the specialist newspaper typeface has undergone a number of revisions since its first appearance in 1985. The latest version, Neue Swift, was released in 2009 and designed primarily for use outside of the sphere of newspaper publishing.

9/12pt Neue Swift Regular (Linotype)

LOREM IPSUM DOLOR SIT AMET, CONSECTETUER ADIPISCING ELIT, SED DIAM NONUMMY NIBH euismod tincidunt ut laoreet dolore magna aliquam erat volutpat. Ut wisi enim ad minim veniam, quis nostrud exerci tation ullamcorper suscipit lobortis nisl ut aliquip ex ea commodo consequat. Duis autem vel eum iriure dolor in hendrerit in

12/15pt Neue Swift Regular (Linotype)

LOREM IPSUM DOLOR SIT AMET, CONSECTETUER ADIPISCING ELIT, SED diam nonummy nibh euismod tincidunt ut laoreet dolore magna aliquam erat volutpat. Ut wisi enim ad minim veniam, quis nostrud exerci tation ullamcorper suscipit lobortis

The Dutch typeface designer Gerard Unger learned his trade as a student at the Gerrit Rietveld Academie in Amsterdam and as an assistant to the renowned graphic designer Wim Crouwel, before beginning a lengthy association with Rudolf Hell, the German company behind the Digiset phototypesetting machine. Unger's earlier typefaces for Hell, such as Demos (1975) and Praxis (1977), were designed to cope with the rigors of the phototypesetting system; the Digiset used a cathode ray tube (CRT) to rasterize characters and the results could be fairly coarse, especially by today's standards.

Swift is named after the fleetingly graceful bird of the same name, and not after the author Jonathan Swift as is sometimes stated. Another of Unger's later typefaces, Gulliver (1993), is named after Swift's eponymous hero and is possibly the source of the confusion. The earliest version of Swift, designed in 1985 for Hell, represents the continuation of Unger's efforts to design a new typeface better suited to dealing with the difficult printing environment of newspaper publishing using high-speed web presses and low-quality paper stock. Classed as a Contemporary serif, Swift has a substantial form; its serifs are chunky and wedge-shaped, junctions between strokes and curves are sturdy, and it has a large x-height to aid legibility at smaller point sizes. Taking his inspiration from the style of 17th-century Dutch serifs cut by the likes of Cristoffel van Dijck, Unger first designed a visually similar face named Hollander in 1983, before following it up a couple of years later with Swift, a reworking of Hollander with particular attention paid to the shapes of serifs and terminals. By 1995 the entire family had been updated and rereleased as Swift 2.0 with 24 separate fonts including small caps and Old Style figures, and had become as popular a choice for magazine and book publishing as it had been for its intended use as a newspaper face. Swift was Unger's final typeface design for Hell prior to his move to Bitstream.

Today, the best digital option is Unger's second update of Swift for Linotype, Neue Swift, released in 2009. Swift 2.0 can still be purchased from the usual online vendors but Neue Swift's expanded character set and OpenType format pretty much renders the earlier release obsolete. The family now contains five standard weights with an italic style each, plus a Black Condensed weight with an accompanying italic; the OpenType format absorbs the small caps and Old Style figures.

Swift takes its inspiration from 17th-century Old Style letterforms

Monotype's Van Dijck is the digital version of a face first released in metal in 1935

Neue Swift Regular

Van Dijck Regular

Rotis

| **Country of origin:** Germany | **Classification:** Neo-Humanist Serif
| **Designer:** Otl Aicher

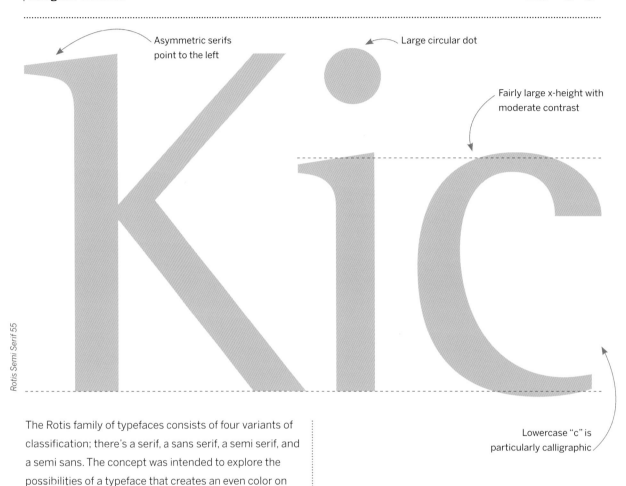

Asymmetric serifs point to the left

Large circular dot

Fairly large x-height with moderate contrast

Rotis Semi Serif 55

Lowercase "c" is particularly calligraphic

The Rotis family of typefaces consists of four variants of classification; there's a serif, a sans serif, a semi serif, and a semi sans. The concept was intended to explore the possibilities of a typeface that creates an even color on the page when set in differing styles.

9/12pt Rotis Semi Serif 55 (Monotype)

LOREM IPSUM DOLOR SIT AMET, CONSECTETUER ADIPISCING ELIT, SED DIAM NONUMMY NIBH euismod tincidunt ut laoreet dolore magna aliquam erat volutpat. Ut wisi enim ad minim veniam, quis nostrud exerci tation ullamcorper suscipit lobortis nisl ut aliquip ex ea commodo consequat. Duis autem vel eum iriure dolor in hendrerit in vulputate velit esse molestie

12/15pt Rotis Semi Serif 55 (Monotype)

LOREM IPSUM DOLOR SIT AMET, CONSECTETUER ADIPISCING ELIT, SED diam nonummy nibh euismod tincidunt ut laoreet dolore magna aliquam erat volutpat. Ut wisi enim ad minim veniam, quis nostrud exerci tation ullamcorper suscipit lobortis nisl ut aliquip ex ea

Together, the Rotis family of fonts form a hybrid consisting of a serif and a sans serif, with a semi sans and a semi serif sitting somewhere between the two. It's a face that draws a particularly emotional response from a number of well-known typographers who really don't like it at all, so why include it in this book? Well, a lot of graphic designers do like it a lot, so there's a clear divide that adds to the story of this contentious face. It was conceived by Otl Aicher, the man behind the extremely successful pictograms designed for the 1972 Olympic Games in Munich that set a new benchmark for information design. Aicher, primarily a graphic designer rather than a typeface specialist, had designed one face prior to tackling the Rotis project. The public transport system in Munich and the signage at Munich Airport used Traffic, designed by Aicher in 1969 a few years before he produced his work for the Olympics.

The concept behind Rotis sets out to explore how a typeface family with both serifs and sans serifs could be designed so each corresponding style, when used together, would create the same typographic color on the page. So, if one block of text was set in Rotis Sans Serif 55 Regular and an adjacent block was set in Rotis Semi Sans 55 Regular, they would display the same level of gray tone. The face was very popular on its release, with many graphic designers lauding its legibility and usefulness. However, a number of well-known typeface designers, including Erik Spiekermann and Gerard Unger, have gone on record as saying they feel Rotis is a reasonable concept that simply hasn't been executed properly. The gist of their argument is that the theory behind Rotis is fair and well meant, but theory doesn't necessarily make a good typeface. This is a personal point of view, of course, and seems to have had a negligible effect on the typeface's overall success.

There are Monotype, Linotype and Adobe versions of Rotis, with little to distinguish one from the other besides the naming of the available styles. Some use a numbering system similar to that devised by Adrian Frutiger for Univers, with the first digit indicating weight and the second indicating style, whereas others are conventionally named for their weights. It's a little confusing switching from one to the other, which doesn't help to quieten the detractors. Additionally, Rotis Sans has been given an overhaul by Alice Savoie and Robin Nicholas for Linotype and released as Rotis II Sans; it has three additional weights of Light, Semi Bold and Black, taking the family to a total of seven weights or 14 styles.

Rotis Semi Serif, Semi Sans and Sans Serif

Out of all the different styles of Rotis that make up the complete set, Rotis Semi Serif is arguably the most interesting, in terms of its individual letterforms

Trajan

| **Country of origin:** United States | **Classification:** Glyphic
| **Designer:** Carol Twombly

1989

Very large x-height with moderate contrast

Brush strokes from original source provide subtle modeling of serifs

Thin serifs with subtle curve

"Q" is a signature character with its very long tail

Trajan Regular

Trajan was one of the first display faces designed exclusively for the new Adobe Originals program, making it somewhat of a digital pioneer. It's based on the carved letterforms forming an inscription at the base of Trajan's Column, a triumphal monument located in Rome, Italy.

18pt Trajan Regular (Adobe)

QUAEROS

72pt Trajan Regular (Adobe)

QUAEROS

36pt Trajan Regular (Adobe)

QUAEROS

Trajan, along with Charlemagne and Lithos, was one of the first display faces created for the Adobe Originals program. It was designed by Carol Twombly in 1989 and is based on letterforms of the *capitalis monumentalis* or Roman square capitals as they appear in the inscription found at the base of Trajan's Column in Rome, Italy. The triumphal column celebrates the Roman emperor Trajan's victory in the Dacian Wars and was completed in 113 CE. As there are no lowercase characters present in the inscription, the digital interpretation of the face is also fully uppercase.

Twombly's Trajan isn't the first typeface inspired by these inscribed Roman characters. Emil Rudolf Weiss designed Weiss (or Weiss Antiqua) between 1926 and 1931, whereas Goudy Trajan from Frederic W. Goudy appeared in 1930; both these faces take direct inspiration from Trajan's Column. There's also a face designed for Stempel by Warren Chappell in 1939–40 named Trajanus, but it has a far more medieval flavor to it than the other interpretations. Trajan is rightly considered a pioneer typeface, given its status as one of the earliest designed solely for the digital platform,

and in many ways the antiquity of its origin aligns nicely with the fact that, during the late 1980s and early 1990s, designers and typographers were making the move from hand-created to computer-generated graphics. Trajan has acquired a reputation as the go-to typeface for promotional movie posters as well as being a very popular face for movie and television title sequences.

Trajan Pro, released in 2001, is an update containing a full set of optically correct small caps to represent the lowercase characters. In 2012, a further update supplemented the existing two weights with a further four; these were designed by Robert Slimbach and the larger family was reissued as Trajan 3. Although there's nothing wrong with an Extra Light or Black Trajan, these weights don't really reflect the essential qualities of the Roman type that inspired Twombly in the first instance. If it's a true interpretation of the inscriptional style that you're after, stick to using the Regular weight.

Trajan Regular

Weiss Regular

Unlike Trajan, Weiss features lowercase characters despite the lack of specific reference at the base of Trajan's column

ITC Officina Sans

| **Country of origin:** Germany | **Classification:** Neo-Humanist Sans
| **Designers:** Erik Spiekermann and Ole Schäfer

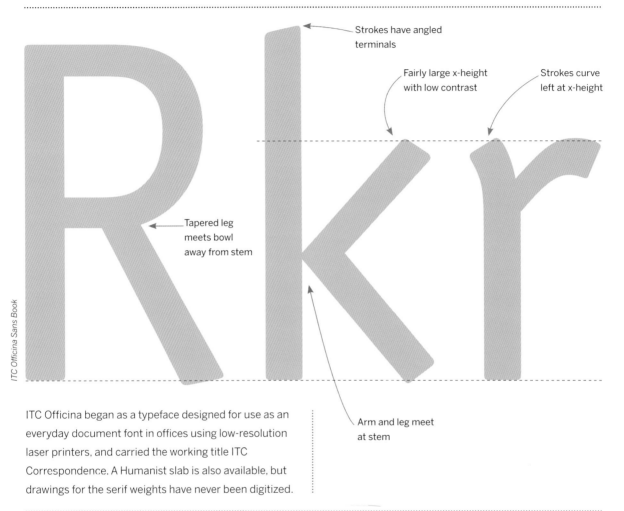

Strokes have angled terminals

Fairly large x-height with low contrast

Strokes curve left at x-height

Tapered leg meets bowl away from stem

Arm and leg meet at stem

ITC Officina Sans Book

ITC Officina began as a typeface designed for use as an everyday document font in offices using low-resolution laser printers, and carried the working title ITC Correspondence. A Humanist slab is also available, but drawings for the serif weights have never been digitized.

9/12pt ITC Officina Sans Book

LOREM IPSUM DOLOR SIT AMET, CONSECTETUER ADIPISCING ELIT, SED DIAM NONUMMY NIBH EUISMOD TINCIDUNT UT laoreet dolore magna aliquam erat volutpat. ut wisi enim ad minim veniam, quis nostrud exerci tation ullamcorper suscipit lobortis nisl ut aliquip ex ea commodo consequat. Duis autem vel eum iriure dolor in hendrerit in vulputate velit esse molestie consequat, vel illum dolore eu feugiat

12/15pt ITC Officina Sans Book

LOREM IPSUM DOLOR SIT AMET, CONSECTETUER ADIPISCING ELIT, SED DIAM nonummy nibh euismod tincidunt ut laoreet dolore magna aliquam erat volutpat. Ut wisi enim ad minim veniam, quis nostrud exerci tation ullamcorper suscipit lobortis nisl ut aliquip ex ea commodo consequat. Duis

Originally called ITC Correspondence, Erik Spiekermann began the first weights of ITC Officina in 1988 and released them a couple of years later. Inspiration comes from the "typewriter" style monospaced fonts Letter Gothic and Courier, and from the work he'd previously carried out when working on a commission from the Deutsche Bundespost (the West German Post Office). That typeface (called PT 55) was ultimately not used by Bundespost but went on to become the large and extremely successful FF Meta family of faces. Spiekermann began with the Book and Bold weights of ITC Officina Sans, his goal being a Neo-Humanist sans serif that would retain its legibility when used to compose business documents printed on low-resolution laser printers. The quality of the output from office printers was a lot lower in the late 1980s than it is today. Type designer Gerard Unger, a friend of Spiekermann's, helped with the early drawings for a seriffed version of the face, but work commitments forced him to withdraw from the project and his take on ITC Officina Serif has never been completed.

Spiekermann worked with the Dutch designer Just van Rossum to complete the two sans serif weights during 1989, and the pair continued the project by adding unbracketed square serifs to the sans, thus creating the Humanist slab ITC Officina Serif. The proportions of both faces are closely linked, with some serif-less characters, such as the "O," an exact match, whereas some widths of ITC Officina Serif have been amended slightly to accommodate the serifs. The digital type foundry URW were responsible for the creation of the font data; this process reflects the way earlier metal typefaces were drawn by independently commissioned typeface designers before manufacture by a type foundry. Spiekermann was reportedly disappointed when the first proofs arrived from ITC as adjustments had been made to his original design for the figures, but a compromise was presumably reached and the face was launched, achieving widespread approval. During the mid 1990s, Ole Schäfer joined Spiekermann's design firm, MetaDesign, and drew the additional weights that now make up the five-weight, 10-style ITC Officina families. In 2001, four display weights were created to accompany ITC Officina Sans, and following their omission from the earlier PostScript versions, Old Style figures and small caps have been added to all OpenType versions.

Some characters, such as the "g," are identical for both the sans serif and serif styles

AFdg AFdg

ITC Officina Sans Book

ITC Officina Serif Book

Template Gothic

| **Country of origin:** United States | **Classification:** Neo-Humanist Sans
| **Designer:** Barry Deck

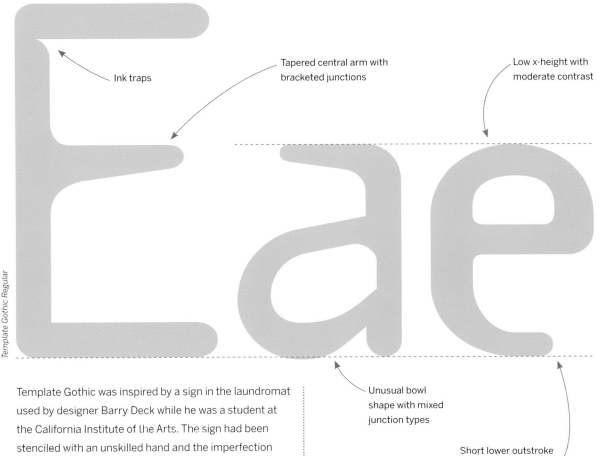

Template Gothic Regular

Ink traps

Tapered central arm with bracketed junctions

Low x-height with moderate contrast

Unusual bowl shape with mixed junction types

Short lower outstroke forms open aperture

Template Gothic was inspired by a sign in the laundromat used by designer Barry Deck while he was a student at the California Institute of the Arts. The sign had been stenciled with an unskilled hand and the imperfection of the work provided a springboard for the design.

9/12pt Template Gothic Regular (Emigre)
LOREM IPSUM DOLOR SIT AMET, CONSECTETUER ADIPISCING ELIT, SED DIAM NONUMMY NIBH EUISMOD tincidunt ut laoreet dolore magna aliquam erat volutpat. Ut wisi enim ad minim veniam, quis nostrud exerci tation ullamcorper suscipit lobortis nisl ut aliquip ex ea commodo consequat. Duis autem vel eum iriure dolor in hendrerit in vulputate velit esse molestie consequat, vel

12/15pt Template Gothic Regular (Emigre)
LOREM IPSUM DOLOR SIT AMET, CONSECTETUER ADIPISCING ELIT, SED diam nonummy nibh euismod tincidunt ut laoreet dolore magna aliquam erat volutpat. Ut wisi enim ad minim veniam, quis nostrud exerci tation ullamcorper suscipit lobortis nisl ut aliquip ex ea

The British writer, design commentator and founder of *Eye* magazine Rick Poynor dubbed Template Gothic "the typeface of the 90s," and it has to be said that the face was used to the point of ubiquity during that decade. It was designed by Barry Deck, a freelance designer who decided to undertake a period of study at the California Institute of the Arts in the late 1980s. The well-known graphic designer and artist Edward Fella was one of his tutors at CalArts and influenced Deck in his fondness for the contemporary trend for deconstructed "grunge" typography. Deck began working on his own typeface designs while attending CalArts and drew the experimental face Template Gothic in 1990.

He was inspired by a hand-stenciled sign on the wall of his local laundromat that had been inexpertly made using a lettering template. The firm eventually replaced it with a professionally produced sign and Deck asked if he could have the original; it was duly handed over, providing him with the basis for the characters designed for Template Gothic. He wanted to create a typeface that looked as though it had been generated as substandard phototypesetting (an all too common problem before digital typesetting arrived) and the tapered, imperfect strokes with their rounded terminals help to create the impression that parts of each character haven't reproduced perfectly. To quote Deck himself, he wanted to reflect "the imperfect language of an imperfect world, inhabited by imperfect beings."

Deck showed his design for Template Gothic to type designer Rudy VanderLans, the co-founder with Zuzana Licko of digital type foundry Emigre (see page 165), during a class visit to VanderLan's studio. It was decided that Emigre should release the face commercially and Template Gothic went on to become one of the most used typefaces of the 1990s. It appeared on numerous promotional posters, picking up a particularly high-profile association with the director Richard Linklater's 1993 coming of age comedy *Dazed and Confused*. VanderLans also used it to set the entirety of the text in issue 19 of *Emigre* magazine, and the face is a part of the Museum of Modern Art's permanent Architecture and Design Collection. There are just two weights, a Regular and a Bold; italic styles have never been drawn, although Deck did design an experimental Regular serif weight in 1992. As far as I'm aware, the serif weight has never been made commercially available.

Template Gothic Regular

The "imperfections" Deck sought to replicate are more pronounced at larger point sizes

FF Scala

| **Country of origin:** The Netherlands | **Classification:** Humanist Serif
| **Designer:** Martin Majoor

1990

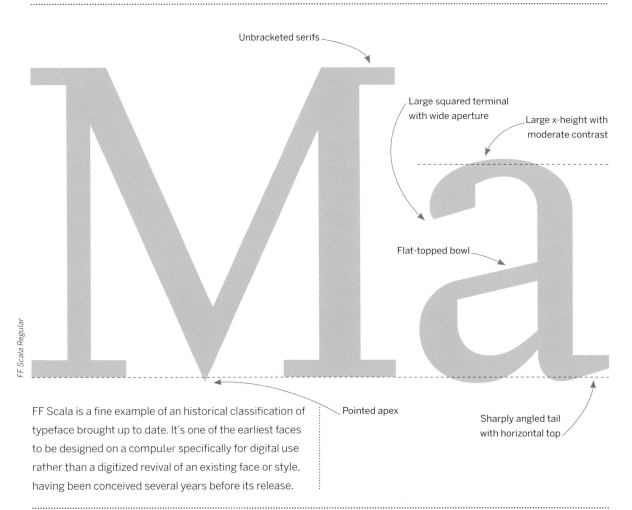

Unbracketed serifs

Large squared terminal with wide aperture

Large x-height with moderate contrast

Flat-topped bowl

FF Scala Regular

Pointed apex

Sharply angled tail with horizontal top

FF Scala is a fine example of an historical classification of typeface brought up to date. It's one of the earliest faces to be designed on a computer specifically for digital use rather than a digitized revival of an existing face or style, having been conceived several years before its release.

9/12pt FF Scala Regular (FontFont)

LOREM IPSUM DOLOR SIT AMET, CONSECTETUER ADIPISCING ELIT, SED DIAM nonummy nibh euismod tincidunt ut laoreet dolore magna aliquam erat volutpat. Ut wisi enim ad minim veniam, quis nostrud exerci tation ullamcorper suscipit lobortis nisl ut aliquip ex ea commodo consequat. Duis autem vel eum iriure dolor in hendrerit in vulputate

12/15pt FF Scala Regular (FontFont)

LOREM IPSUM DOLOR SIT AMET, CONSECTETUER ADIPISCING ELIT, sed diam nonummy nibh euismod tincidunt ut laoreet dolore magna aliquam erat volutpat. Ut wisi enim ad minim veniam, quis nostrud exerci tation ullamcorper suscipit lobortis nisl ut

FF Scala is one of the original, and arguably one of the best, typefaces designed specifically for the digital platform yet acknowledging some of the oldest stylistic principles of typographic form. Dutch typeface designer Martin Majoor began working on the design of FF Scala in the late 1980s, following a commission from Vredenburg concert hall in Utrecht, an historic city in the Netherlands. This explains the name choice, which is taken from the Teatro alla Scala in Milan, Italy. FontShop International, the commercial outlet for the typefaces sold by the digital type foundry FontFont, founded by Erik Spiekermann, Joan Spiekermann, and Neville Brody in 1990, made FF Scala one of their earliest releases.

The face is a polished interpretation (and not a revival) of a 15th-century Humanist serif with some very distinctive additions that make it feel more modern and engineered; a comparison with Eric Gill's ideas for the design of Joanna is reasonable, although Gill's typeface is more Transitional. FF Scala is more angular with sharper, more dynamic detailing and contains a full set of small caps and Old Style numerals. Mention should also be made of FF Scala Sans, a companion face for FF Scala designed by Majoor in 1993. The proportions of the two Scala faces are close but not always exact for corresponding glyphs, and many of the lowercase characters have a common spine. The sans serif also includes all the small cap and Old Style numerals of the serif, an unusual thing for its time that has since become a more common practice.

FF Scala has just two standard weights, Regular and Bold with corresponding italic styles, plus two condensed roman weights; the OpenType version was released as Scala Pro in 2005. This weight range doesn't provide a particularly large choice if a complex typographic hierarchy is needed, but FF Scala excels as a book face and two weights are often all you'll need. Considering that the superfamily is a relatively new idea, Scala's limited range of weights aligns with the historical sources that inspired it.

FF Scala Regular

Joanna Regular

The serifs of Scala and Joanna are distinctly different, in that they're more Transitional, but the constructed qualities (considering Scala is a Humanist serif) are closely related

PMN Caecilia

| **Country of origin:** The Netherlands | **Classification:** Humanist Slab
| **Designer:** Peter Matthias Noordzij

1991

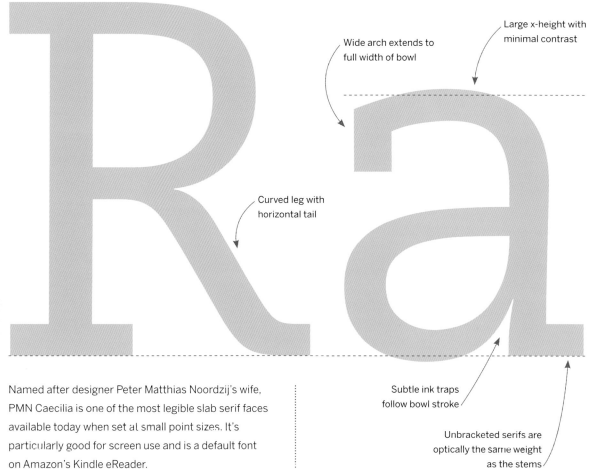

PMN Caecilia 55 Roman

Wide arch extends to
full width of bowl

Large x-height with
minimal contrast

Curved leg with
horizontal tail

Subtle ink traps
follow bowl stroke

Unbracketed serifs are
optically the same weight
as the stems

Named after designer Peter Matthias Noordzij's wife, PMN Caecilia is one of the most legible slab serif faces available today when set at small point sizes. It's particularly good for screen use and is a default font on Amazon's Kindle eReader.

9/12pt PMN Caecilia 55 Roman (Linotype)

LOREM IPSUM DOLOR SIT AMET, CONSECTETUER ADIPISCING ELIT, SED DIAM nonummy nibh euismod tincidunt ut laoreet dolore magna aliquam erat volutpat. Ut wisi enim ad minim veniam, quis nostrud exerci tation ullamcorper suscipit lobortis nisl ut aliquip ex ea commodo consequat. Duis autem

12/15pt PMN Caecilia 55 Roman (Linotype)

LOREM IPSUM DOLOR SIT AMET, CONSECTETUER ADIPISCING ELIT, sed diam nonummy nibh euismod tincidunt ut laoreet dolore magna aliquam erat volutpat. Ut wisi enim ad minim veniam, quis nostrud exerci tation ullamcorper suscipit

Between 1980 and 1985 the Dutch designer Peter Matthias Noordzij studied at the Koninklijke Academie van Beeldende Kunsten (The Royal Academy of Art) in The Hague, Netherlands. His father, Gerrit Noordzij, was the director of the writing and lettering program at the school and taught a number of today's leading Dutch type designers, including Peter Matthias, Luc(as) de Groot and Albert-Jan Pool. Noordzij was a third-year student when he produced the first drawings for his Humanist slab serif PMN Caecilia. The characters are designed to mimic letterforms written with a broad-nibbed pen, hence its classification as a Humanist slab, but PMN Caecilia takes things a little further. Noordzij has taken elements from both Humanist letterforms and low-contrast Geometric slabs, and melded them into what is generally considered to be the first ever Neo-Humanist slab.

Noordzij took his sketches to the ATypI conference in London in 1984, where they grabbed the attention of a number of companies including Monotype and Bitstream, and of Adrian Frutiger, at the time a consultant working for Linotype. A deal to publish the typeface with Linotype was agreed on in 1986 and 4 years later the design was completed; the commercial version of PMN Caecilia was released in 1991. The face had been developed with the working title Academic, but this was changed to represent Noordzij's own initials and for his wife Marie-Cécile.

The strokes display a minimal contrast and the unbracketed serifs are optically the same weight as the stems; these are Geometric slab traits. However, the calligraphic forms push this face into new territory and turn it into a slab serif that is highly legible at small point sizes thanks to its Humanist leanings and its large x-height. And this doesn't just apply to printed text, as the robustness of the square serifs means the face is particularly proficient at remaining legible when used for long passages of text on lower-resolution screens. It's because of this that PMN Caecilia was chosen as one of the default fonts for Amazon's Kindle eReader. The italic weights are also key to the success of the face, being true italics rather than the oblique romans that commonly accompany a Geometric slab.

In the same year that Linotype published PMN Caecilia, Noordzij established the digital arm of Haarlem's historic 18th-century Enschedé Type Foundry.

PMN Caecilia 55 Roman

Rockwell Regular

Directly comparing PMN Caecilia with an overtly Geometric Slab such as Rockwell indicates just how Humanist it really is

FF Meta

| **Country of origin:** Germany | **Classification:** Neo-Humanist Sans
| **Designer:** Erik Spiekermann

1991

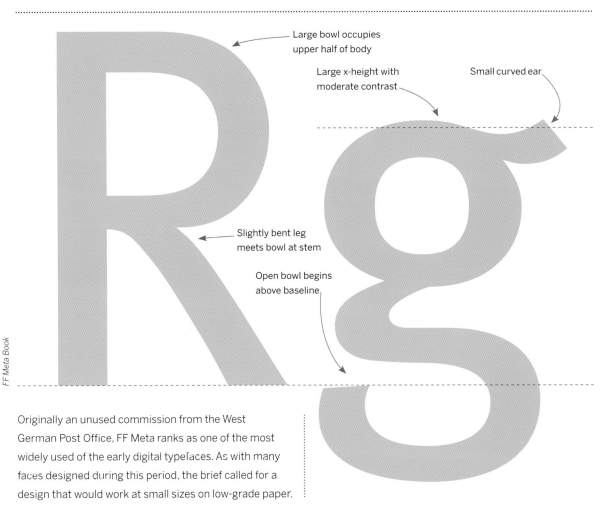

Large bowl occupies
upper half of body

Large x-height with
moderate contrast

Small curved ear

Slightly bent leg
meets bowl at stem

Open bowl begins
above baseline

FF Meta Book

Originally an unused commission from the West
German Post Office, FF Meta ranks as one of the most
widely used of the early digital typefaces. As with many
faces designed during this period, the brief called for a
design that would work at small sizes on low-grade paper.

9/12pt FF Meta Book (FontFont)

LOREM IPSUM DOLOR SIT AMET, CONSECTETUER
ADIPISCING ELIT, SED DIAM NONUMMY NIBH EUISMOD
tincidunt ut laoreet dolore magna aliquam erat
volutpat. Ut wisi enim ad minim veniam, quis nostrud
exerci tation ullamcorper suscipit lobortis nisl ut
aliquip ex ea commodo consequat. Duis autem vel eum
iriure dolor in hendrerit in vulputate velit esse molestie

12/15pt FF Meta Book (FontFont)

LOREM IPSUM DOLOR SIT AMET,
CONSECTETUER ADIPISCING ELIT, SED
diam nonummy nibh euismod tincidunt
ut laoreet dolore magna aliquam erat
volutpat. Ut wisi enim ad minim veniam,
quis nostrud exerci tation ullamcorper
suscipit lobortis nisl ut aliquip ex ea

FF Meta is a superfamily of fonts, designed by Erik Spiekermann that has been the cornerstone of the FontFont library since its release in 1991. FontFont was established in 1990 as an independent type foundry by Spiekermann, his then wife Joan, and British designer Neville Brody around a year after they founded FontShop. Although it still operates as a separate entity, it has been owned by Monotype since its acquisition in July 2014.

FF Meta began as PT55, the concept for a typeface commissioned by the Deutsche Bundespost (the West German Post Office) and designed by Spiekermann in 1985. The brief called for a face that, for reasons of economy, would remain legible when set at small point sizes on low-grade paper stock (a regular challenge for typeface designers over the years). For some reason PT55 was never used, but once FontFont had completed the original weights, renaming the face FF Meta in the process, it proved to be a tremendous commercial success. It became so ubiquitous in the decade following its release that it acquired the moniker "the Helvetica of the 1990s." Like FF Scala before it, FF Meta included a full set of Old Style figures as standard, a factor that undoubtedly helped to bolster its success.

During its 25-year history FF Meta has grown into one of the largest sets of coordinated typeface families in existence, as well as becoming part of the permanent collection of the Museum of Modern Art in New York. The original FF Meta now has eight weights with italic styles ranging from Hairline to Black, plus a condensed width with six weights from Normal to Black. The narrower width once again has accompanying italic styles. In addition to the Neo-Humanist sans face, there is FF Meta Headline, FF Meta Serif and FF Meta Correspondence.

FF Meta Serif is a particularly useful companion face for FF Meta. The design represents a collaborative effort by Spiekermann, Christian Schwartz, and Kris Sowersby and was released in 2007. The addition of the serifs mean its metrics are not absolutely identical, but FF Meta and FF Meta Serif are optically the same so can be used as an integrated sans serif/serif typesetting system.

FF Meta Roman

FF Meta Serif Book

While the metrics of the sans serif and serif styles of Meta are not identical, the letterforms are completely harmonious

HTF Didot

| **Country of origin:** United States | **Classification:** Rational Serif
| **Designer:** Jonathan Hoefler

1991

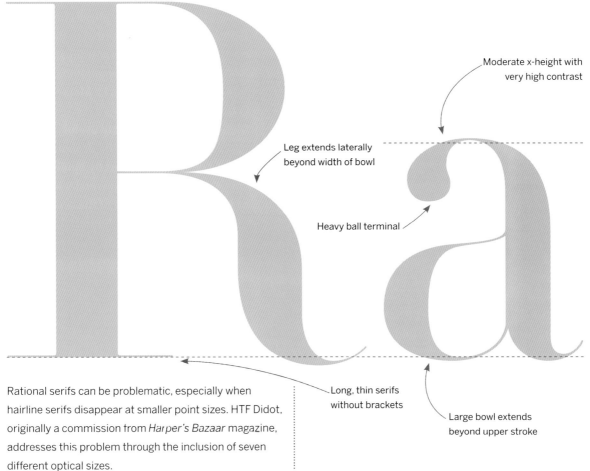

HTF Didot M96 Medium

Moderate x-height with very high contrast

Leg extends laterally beyond width of bowl

Heavy ball terminal

Rational serifs can be problematic, especially when hairline serifs disappear at smaller point sizes. HTF Didot, originally a commission from *Harper's Bazaar* magazine, addresses this problem through the inclusion of seven different optical sizes.

Long, thin serifs without brackets

Large bowl extends beyond upper stroke

18pt HTF Didot M16 Medium (Hoefler & Co.)

36pt HTF Didot M42 Medium (Hoefler & Co.)

Rfegrso

Rfegrso

72pt HTF Didot M64 Medium (Hoefler & Co.)

Rfegrso

For a contemporary revival of the classic Rational serif known as a Modern, look no further than Hoefler & Co.'s HTF Didot, designed by Jonathan Hoefler in 1991. The source of Hoefler's inspiration is derived from the late-18th-century faces designed in France by Firmin Didot, a member of a prominent family of Parisian printers and book publishers with a type foundry established by his grandfather François. Firmin took over punch cutting duties at the foundry in 1783 and a year later cut what is regarded as the first Modern, characterized by very thin hairlines, perfectly flat top serifs, and no bracketing. Didot's faces were more finely featured than those of his famous Italian counterpart Giambattista Bodoni, moving the Rational serif to the furthest point reached in its journey away from the Humanist calligraphic form. It's on Didot's faces, and specifically samples of glyphs from Didot's 1819 *Spécimen des Caractères*, that HTF Didot is based.

It was designed in response to a commission from *Harper's Bazaar* magazine, which underwent a design review in 1991. Editor-in-chief Liz Tilberis and art director Fabien Baron wanted a Didone-style face that could be used over an increased range of point sizes without a loss of quality. The magazine had been using other commercially available versions of Didot for many years—the face was a key element of the magazine's identity—but they were less than perfect when used at sizes other than those they were originally intended for. The problem with Moderns stems from the fact that the hairlines tend to disappear at small point sizes, and appear too heavy at larger point sizes. To combat this problem, Hoefler drew the new face in seven different optical sizes.

When the new *Harper's Bazaar* design launched, the American Society of Magazine Editors called it "one of the most dramatic magazine reinventions in history." The complete HTF Didot family consists of 42 individual fonts; there are three weights, each with an italic style, with each weight supplied in seven optical sizes set at 6, 11, 16, 24, 42, 64 and 96. The italics are true italics; they work very well on their own and at large point sizes as well as when used in conjunction with their roman counterparts, and there is of course the usual collection of extra glyphs expected as part of a contemporary digital typeface, which never actually appeared in any of Firmin Didot's original cuts.

06   11   16   24   42   64   96

HTF Didot Medium

The seven optical sizes of HTF Didot are clearly intended for setting at specific size ranges, but a direct comparison indicates the subtle increase in contrast from 6 to 96

Myriad

| **Country of origin:** United States | **Classification:** Humanist Sans
| **Designers:** Carol Twombly and Robert Slimbach

1992

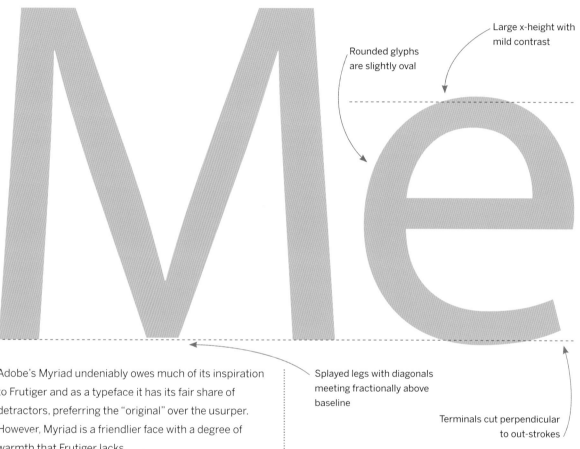

Myriad Regular

Rounded glyphs
are slightly oval

Large x-height with
mild contrast

Splayed legs with diagonals
meeting fractionally above
baseline

Terminals cut perpendicular
to out-strokes

Adobe's Myriad undeniably owes much of its inspiration to Frutiger and as a typeface it has its fair share of detractors, preferring the "original" over the usurper. However, Myriad is a friendlier face with a degree of warmth that Frutiger lacks.

9/12pt Myriad Regular (Adobe)

LOREM IPSUM DOLOR SIT AMET, CONSECTETUER ADIPISCING ELIT, SED DIAM NONUMMY NIBH EUISMOD tincidunt ut laoreet dolore magna aliquam erat volutpat. Ut wisi enim ad minim veniam, quis nostrud exerci tation ullamcorper suscipit lobortis nisl ut aliquip ex ea commodo consequat. Duis autem vel eum iriure dolor in hendrerit in vulputate velit esse molestie

12/15pt Myriad Regular (Adobe)

LOREM IPSUM DOLOR SIT AMET, CONSECTETUER ADIPISCING ELIT, SED diam nonummy nibh euismod tincidunt ut laoreet dolore magna aliquam erat volutpat. Ut wisi enim ad minim veniam, quis nostrud exerci tation ullamcorper suscipit lobortis nisl ut aliquip ex ea

Over the years, Myriad has suffered from its branding as "Adobe's Frutiger," but the reputation is unfair. It's true that there are similarities between the two faces, but Myriad is a more Humanistic and friendly face with its angled terminals and round dots; it's a good choice for projects that need the clarity of a Frutiger but need to feel warmer and more welcoming. It's because of this that Myriad has always been a popular choice for corporate identities—Apple have used it as their principal typeface for many years after switching from Garamond. In terms of historical importance, Myriad earns the distinction of being the first sans serif in the Adobe Originals collection, and as one of the first typefaces designed as a dual-axis Multiple Master font.

Multiple Master fonts, designated by an MM within their name, were an extension to Adobe's Type 1 PostScript font format launched in 1992. Each font file contained data for two or more "masters," turning them into customizable PostScript fonts that allowed the optical adjustment of a typeface's visual characteristics without destroying the letterforms, using what Adobe termed "linear design axes." These axes were able to describe weight, width, optical size and style between a set maximum and minimum range; for example, Myriad's weight axis range was 1 to 830 and its width axis ranged from 1 to 700. Multiple Masters also contained preconfigured "primary font instances" to create a kind of matrix of design styles. For example, Myriad included 15 primary instances; they ranged from Light Condensed (215 LT 300 CN) to Black Semi-extended (830 BL 700 SE), with the numerical elements describing the weights and widths.

On the surface, this sounds ideal; but the format wasn't popular. Desktop publishing applications failed to keep up with the necessary updates to fully support Multiple Master fonts, and type designers were naturally wary about allowing just anyone to decide what their typefaces should look like, preferring to stick to releasing their typefaces in a range of carefully considered weights and widths. Ironically, the format survives through its use by some type designers and via its compatibility with a number of font design applications; a range of individual fonts can be generated using multiple master technology before being optimized as individual font files. However, general support for Multiple Master fonts has virtually disappeared.

Myriad's current OpenType superfamily contains 42 font files covering five weights and four widths with true italic styles that more than make up for the potential loss of flexibility gained via Multiple Master technology. Personally I prefer to leave the precise decisions about weight and width to the type designers themselves, and have no misgivings about Multiple Master's commercial demise.

Myriad Regular

Neue Frutiger Regular

Lexicon

| **Country of origin:** The Netherlands | **Classification:** Humanist Serif/Transitional Serif
| **Designer:** Bram de Does

1992

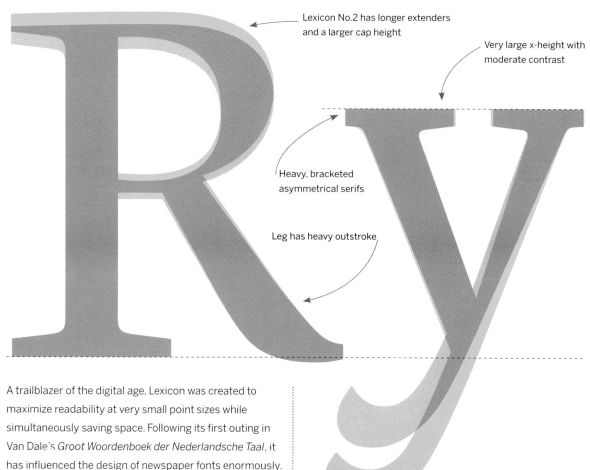

Lexicon No.2 Roman A and Lexicon No.1 Roman A

Lexicon No.2 has longer extenders and a larger cap height

Very large x-height with moderate contrast

Heavy, bracketed asymmetrical serifs

Leg has heavy outstroke

A trailblazer of the digital age, Lexicon was created to maximize readability at very small point sizes while simultaneously saving space. Following its first outing in Van Dale's *Groot Woordenboek der Nederlandsche Taal*, it has influenced the design of newspaper fonts enormously.

9/12pt Lexicon No.1 Roman A (Enschedé)

LOREM IPSUM DOLOR SIT AMET, CONSECTETUER ADIPISCING ELIT, SED DIAM nonummy nibh euismod tincidunt ut laoreet dolore magna aliquam erat volutpat. Ut wisi enim ad minim veniam, quis nostrud exerci tation ullamcorper suscipit lobortis nisl ut aliquip ex ea commodo consequat. Duis autem vel eum iriure

12/15pt Lexicon No.1 Roman A (Enschedé)

LOREM IPSUM DOLOR SIT AMET, CONSECTETUER ADIPISCING ELIT, sed diam nonummy nibh euismod tincidunt ut laoreet dolore magna aliquam erat volutpat. Ut wisi enim ad minim veniam, quis nostrud exerci tation ullamcorper suscipit lobortis nisl

Lexicon was designed as the ultimate space-saving typeface, following a commission from Van Dale's *Het Groot Woordenboek der Nederlandsche Taal (Dictionary of the Dutch Language)*. The Dutch designer and typographer Bram de Does had produced just one other typeface, the Humanist serif Trinité, as a specialist phototypesetting face for Enschedé. This was in 1978 and de Does later declared at the 1983 ATypI conference in Berlin that he would never design another; but he was persuaded to revisit this announcement when Van Dale requested a test version of Trinité for use at 7 point. De Does felt that a complete new face was needed, and a prerelease version of Lexicon was used to set the 1991 edition of Van Dale's dictionary. A year later, in 1992, a commercial version of Lexicon was released by the newly established digital arm of the Enschedé Font Foundry with the help of the designer of PMN Caecilia, Peter Matthias Noordzij, who digitized de Does' drawings using *Ikarus* software. The version currently published by Enschedé is an improved adaptation released in 1995.

Lexicon is a melding of Humanist and Transitional serif; its form is calligraphic with moderate contrast and a fairly consistent angle of stress, but at the same time it feels quite constructed with its narrow forms and very fine junctions where curved strokes meet the stems. The latter helps to combat ink spread that could otherwise create legibility issues, and the Humanist leanings and very large x-height provide exceptional legibility at very small point sizes. However, the cleverness of Lexicon's concept doesn't stop there. The complete family consists of two groups, Lexicon No.1 and Lexicon No.2. The first group features short ascenders and descenders, whereas the second has "normal" length stems. For setting with generous line feed, or leading, Lexicon No.2 should be used but, if space is an issue, leading can be closed up and Lexicon No.1 should be used to compensate for the reduction in line space. The ability to make a retrospective decision to close up, or indeed increase, spacing partway through a project is made possible by the fact that the widths of both groups are identical, so switching from one to the other will never cause any text to reflow.

There are six weights in each group of fonts, each with an accompanying true italic style, using a labeling system where "A" represents the Regular weight and "F" is the boldest. Lexicon has the slightly dubious distinction of often being cited as the world's most expensive typeface, but the space-saving costs it's capable of creating for a large print run of a dictionary or encyclopedia do help to justify the hefty price bracket.

Lexicon No.1

Lexicon's six weights for each of its two groups are designated by letters A to F, with A representing the Regular weight

DTL Fleischmann

| **Country of origin:** The Netherlands | **Classification:** Rational Serif
| **Designer:** Erhard Kaiser

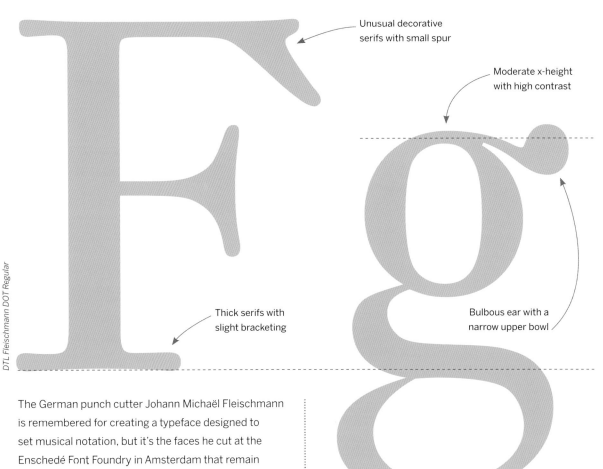

DTL Fleischmann DOT Regular

Unusual decorative serifs with small spur

Moderate x-height with high contrast

Thick serifs with slight bracketing

Bulbous ear with a narrow upper bowl

The German punch cutter Johann Michaël Fleischmann is remembered for creating a typeface designed to set musical notation, but it's the faces he cut at the Enschedé Font Foundry in Amsterdam that remain his greatest legacy.

9/12pt DTL Fleischmann TOT Regular (Dutch Type Library)

LOREM IPSUM DOLOR SIT AMET, CONSECTETUER ADIPISCING ELIT, SED diam nonummy nibh euismod tincidunt ut laoreet dolore magna aliquam erat volutpat. Ut wisi enim ad minim veniam, quis nostrud exerci tation ullamcorper suscipit lobortis nisl ut aliquip ex ea commodo consequat. Duis autem vel eum iriure

12/15pt DTL Fleischmann TOT Regular (Dutch Type Library)

LOREM IPSUM DOLOR SIT AMET, CONSECTETUER adipiscing elit, sed diam nonummy nibh euismod tincidunt ut laoreet dolore magna aliquam erat volutpat. Ut wisi enim ad minim veniam, quis nostrud exerci tation ullamcorper

Alongside his much admired legacy of idiosyncratic but beautiful typefaces cut in the Netherlands during the 18th century, Johann Michaël Fleischmann is remembered for a good idea that turned into an unfortunate commercial failure. He was born in Nuremberg, Germany, but moved to Amsterdam as a young man to pursue a career as a punch cutter. He was employed at a couple of foundries before managing to start his own business in 1732, but struggled financially and his foundry was sold a few years later to the printer Rudolph Wetstein. By 1743 the business once again changed hands and became a part of the famous Enschedé Font Foundry founded by Izaak and Johannes Enschedé in Haarlem. Fleischmann became an employee of Enschedé, staying with them until his death in 1768, and cut many good faces in his time with the firm. Around 1755, Enschedé asked Fleischmann to create a typeface that could be used to reproduce musical notation. Prior to this, song sheets were printed using copper plates engraved by trained musicians. Unfortunately, the face proved too complicated for most musicians to use (with the exception of Leopold Mozart, Wolfgang Amadeus Mozart's father, who published his *Instructions to Play the Violin* using the face in 1766) and financially it was a failure for Enschedé. However,

Fleischmann's rather beautiful Rational serif typefaces were not and it's these that the 1992 revival DTL Fleischmann is based on.

In 1992, Frank E. Blokland of the Dutch Type Library asked the German type designer Erhard Kaiser to create a new typeface based on Fleischmann's work. Kaiser's interpretation is a remarkably true revival of a rather unique face that would otherwise have been consigned to the history books. It manages to capture all of the quirky details that Fleischmann included in his original design; the ornate serifs with their curious extensions on the uppercase "E," "F," "L" and "Z" are particularly prominent and the tail of the "Q" is especially unique in its form. During the course of my research I've read a couple of pieces that question why Kaiser didn't take the opportunity to tighten up the outlines a little, adding some sharper contemporary details in the process, but ultimately I see nothing wrong with trying to create a digital version that captures the original type as closely as possible. The completed family includes options for both text and display setting, all with true italic styles to accompany them, and a pair of useful small cap weights, which are again intended for either text or display setting.

Text and display weights of DTL Fleischmann occupy the same widths, but DOT shows increased contrast

DTL Fleischmann TOT Italic and Regular

DTL Fleischmann TOT and DOT Regular

Mason

| **Country of origin:** United Kingdom | **Classification:** Display
| **Designer:** Jonathan Barnbrook

1992

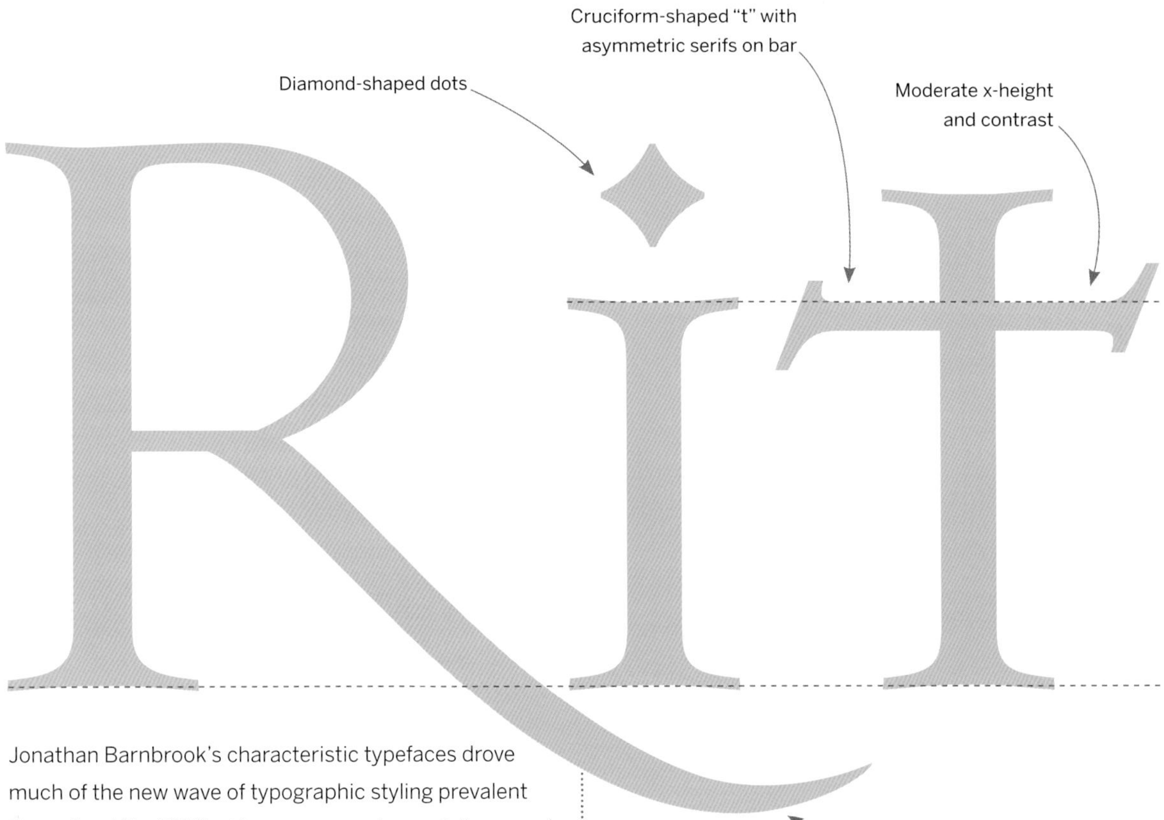

Mason Serif Regular

Diamond-shaped dots

Cruciform-shaped "t" with asymmetric serifs on bar

Moderate x-height and contrast

Long tail dips below baseline

Jonathan Barnbrook's characteristic typefaces drove much of the new wave of typographic styling prevalent throughout the 1990s. Mason was controversially named Manson (after Charles Manson) on its release, but the name was changed after Emigre received complaints.

18pt Mason Serif Regular (Emigre)

ΗΚΕΠΥΖ37

36pt Mason Serif Regular (Emigre)

ΗΚΕΠΥΖ37

72pt Mason Serif Regular (Emigre)

ΗΚΕΠΥΖ37

Jonathan Barnbrook studied at Saint Martin's School of Art and the Royal College of Art in London before founding his own design studio in 1990. He's known as a multi-disciplinarian designer, working as a graphic designer, an industrial designer, and in motion graphics, as well as a typeface designer. He launched his own digital type foundry, VirusFonts, in 1997 but prior to that his earlier faces were released by the Californian foundry Emigre.

Mason was inspired by a range of sources including 19th-century Russian characters, Greek architecture and Renaissance bibles, and started out as Manson; somewhat controversially, Barnbrook decided to name his typeface after the serial killer Charles Manson. He chose the name in an attempt to express the concept of extreme opposite emotions that he'd linked to the feel of the face—love and hate, or beauty and ugliness— but the connection didn't go down at all well in the U.S. Perhaps it was the ecclesiastical feel of the face, a visual attribute that has seen it used to very good effect when a religious tone is required, that caused so many people to get upset by the name's original connotation. Emigre received a large volume of complaints and decided a name change was the only option open to them, but the change arguably helped to promote the face further via the publicity generated. Mason, along with a number of his other faces, helped make Barnbrook one of the highest profile British designers of the 1990s.

The typeface is available in two weights, Regular and Bold, and there are no italic styles. In the same year as Mason's release Barnbrook followed it up with Mason Sans, a sans serif that draws on the work of Edward Johnston and Eric Gill, two designers that Barnbrook cites as personal influences. Like Mason, Mason Sans is available in two weights without italics.

Mason Serif Regular

Mason Sans Regular

Interstate

| **Country of origin:** United Kingdom | **Classification:** Geometric Sans
| **Designer:** Tobias Frere-Jones

1993

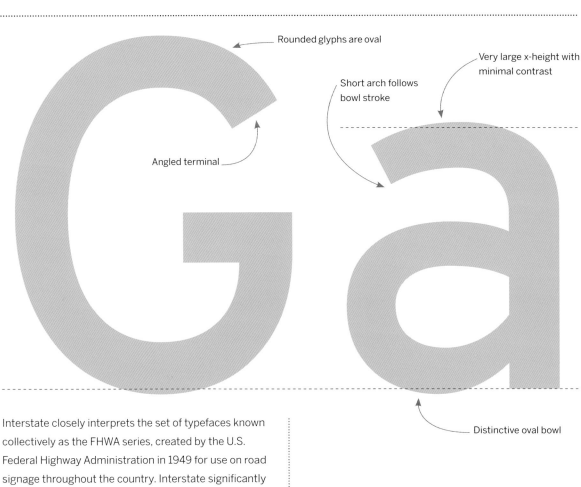

Rounded glyphs are oval

Short arch follows bowl stroke

Very large x-height with minimal contrast

Angled terminal

Distinctive oval bowl

Interstate Regular

Interstate closely interprets the set of typefaces known collectively as the FHWA series, created by the U.S. Federal Highway Administration in 1949 for use on road signage throughout the country. Interstate significantly expands the concept to include legible text weights.

9/12pt Interstate Light (Font Bureau)

LOREM IPSUM DOLOR SIT AMET, CONSECTETUER ADIPISCING ELIT, SED DIAM NONUMMY NIBH euismod tincidunt ut laoreet dolore magna aliquam erat volutpat. Ut wisi enim ad minim veniam, quis nostrud exerci tation ullamcorper suscipit lobortis nisl ut aliquip ex ea commodo consequat. Duis autem vel eum iriure dolor in hendrerit in vulputate

12/15pt Interstate Light (Font Bureau)

LOREM IPSUM DOLOR SIT AMET, CONSECTETUER ADIPISCING ELIT, sed diam nonummy nibh euismod tincidunt ut laoreet dolore magna aliquam erat volutpat. Ut wisi enim ad minim veniam, quis nostrud exerci tation ullamcorper suscipit lobortis

Interstate marks the first appearance in this book of a typeface by the prolific designer Tobias Frere-Jones, who until 2014 was one half of the high-profile digital type foundry Hoefler & Frere-Jones. Frere-Jones had already been involved in the design of more than a dozen typefaces while in the employ of Boston's Font Bureau before embarking on the Interstate project. However, Interstate is one of his earliest faces to maintain a widespread popularity into the 2010s, 20 years after its initial release.

The full range of Interstate's weights and styles were developed between 1993 and 1999 by Frere-Jones and Cyrus Highsmith. It's important to point out that the face is a closely related adaptation of the FHWA series of fonts drawn for the United States Federal Highway Administration in 1949. Frere-Jones took inspiration from the FHWA font, knowing that the structure of the letterforms helped to make it legible at distance and when passing road signs at high speed. That said, Interstate is far from just a signage and display face as it features key refinements that make it suitable for setting at smaller point sizes, and it makes an excellent choice for screen use. It has a large x-height with generously proportioned counters and angled terminals, and for a Geometric sans with low contrast it modulates well when set as running text. Frere-Jones also realized that familiarity plays an important role in the legibility of a typeface, and by referencing letterforms that had been in the daily consciousness of Americans for almost 50 years he would be creating a typeface that people could immediately relate to.

The Interstate family is extensive to say the least, with 40 styles spread across three different widths. Weights range from Hairline to Ultra Black, with italic styles accompanying the normal width weights across the whole range. The condensed width has italics from the Light to Black weights, while the narrowest Compressed width has none. Italics are optically correct oblique romans.

Interstate Hairline

Interstate Ultra Black

Forever synonymous with the FHWA series of typefaces used for road signage in the U.S., Interstate's range of weights is considerable

Giza

| Country of origin: United States **| Classification:** Grotesque Slab
| Designer: David Berlow

1994

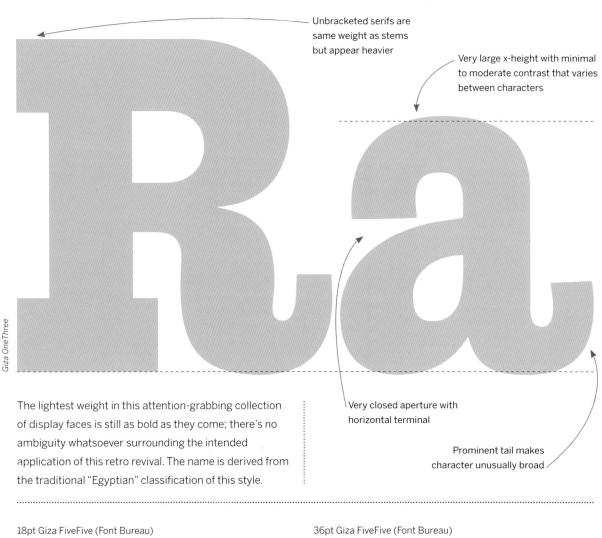

Giza OneThree

Unbracketed serifs are same weight as stems but appear heavier

Very large x-height with minimal to moderate contrast that varies between characters

Very closed aperture with horizontal terminal

Prominent tail makes character unusually broad

The lightest weight in this attention-grabbing collection of display faces is still as bold as they come; there's no ambiguity whatsoever surrounding the intended application of this retro revival. The name is derived from the traditional "Egyptian" classification of this style.

18pt Giza FiveFive (Font Bureau)
QReagrse

36pt Giza FiveFive (Font Bureau)
QReagrse

72pt Giza FiveFive (Font Bureau)
QReagrse

Giza was created by type designer David Berlow, one half of the partnership (along with publication designer and media strategist Roger Black) that founded the important digital type foundry Font Bureau in Boston in 1989. At that time, magazines and newspapers were inexorably shifting from phototypesetting systems to a desktop computer-based production workflow and Font Bureau was launched to provide the fonts for this key area of the publishing industry. We take it for granted that there are now hundreds of good digital fonts to choose from, but in the late 1980s and early 1990s the choice was far more limited. Commissions from the publishing industry have always been, and continue to be, a principal source of new high-quality typefaces.

Giza is named in the tradition of the Egyptian slab serifs that helped inspire it, and it draws a great deal from the slab serif faces cut by Vincent Figgins in the early 19th century. A Figgins specimen book dating from 1845 provided the basis for Berlow's typeface. Giza has a monumental visual impact and captures the feel of the Victorian poster perfectly, but don't try to use it if space is limited as this is a face that needs plenty of room. It's a great example of the way overtly historical typeface styles can be resurrected to perform contemporary roles, and is a timeless design that looks as fresh today as it would have over 150 years ago.

Giza comes in 16 flavors designed around a sequence of weights and widths described in the names of the individual fonts. Giza OneOne is the lightest and narrowest (although none of this family is any lighter than the average Bold) whereas Giza NineFive has the boldest strokes and the greatest width. To navigate the different styles as a progression, I find it easiest to use the second numerical part of each font's name to group the widths, then use the first part to order the weights. It's a fairly idiosyncratic typeface in that sense as widths increase in line with weights (until you get to the nines), so you really need to play around with the face to get a feel for what will work best in any one situation, and play is the right word to use here as this face is basically a heap of fun to work with.

Giza OneOne, ThreeOne, FiveThree, SevenFive and NineOne

Knockout

| **Country of origin:** United States | **Classification:** Grotesque Sans
| **Designer:** Jonathan Hoefler

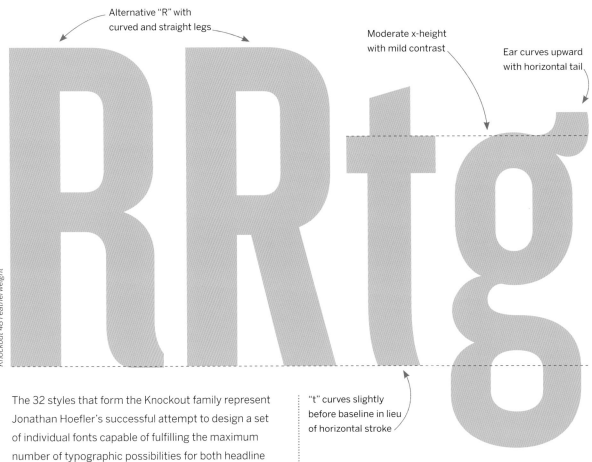

Alternative "R" with curved and straight legs

Moderate x-height with mild contrast

Ear curves upward with horizontal tail

Knockout 48 Featherweight

"t" curves slightly before baseline in lieu of horizontal stroke

The 32 styles that form the Knockout family represent Jonathan Hoefler's successful attempt to design a set of individual fonts capable of fulfilling the maximum number of typographic possibilities for both headline and text setting.

9/12pt Knockout 30 Junior Welterweight (Hoefler & Co.)

LOREM IPSUM DOLOR SIT AMET, CONSECTETUER ADIPISCING ELIT, SED DIAM NONUMMY NIBH EUISMOD TINCIDUNT UT laoreet dolore magna aliquam erat volutpat. ut wisi enim ad minim veniam, quis nostrud exerci tation ullamcorper suscipit lobortis nisl ut aliquip ex ea commodo consequat. Duis autem vel eum iriure dolor in hendrerit in vulputate velit esse molestie consequat, vel illum dolore eu feugiat nulla facilisis at vero eros et

12/15pt Knockout 30 Junior Welterweight (Hoefler & Co.)

LOREM IPSUM DOLOR SIT AMET, CONSECTETUER ADIPISCING ELIT, SED DIAM nonummy nibh euismod tincidunt ut laoreet dolore magna aliquam erat volutpat. Ut wisi enim ad minim veniam, quis nostrud exerci tation ullamcorper suscipit lobortis nisl ut aliquip ex ea commodo consequat. Duis autem vel eum iriure

Sans serif display typefaces from the 19th century were generally carved from wood and were not designed to be brought together in the kind of type families that we're used to seeing today. They were more often designed as a one-off to meet a specific criterion of size, weight, or width, and not always as full character sets, which helps explain why surviving collections of wooden type often contain incomplete alphabets. The concept for the Knockout family was formed with this in mind; Jonathan Hoefler wanted to create an extended family of individually designed fonts that were all slightly different but could also be used together for both display and text setting.

The concept of the type "family" is a relatively new one. Historically speaking, typefaces were created to fulfill either a specific brief or a commercial need with little or no thought given to how one face might combine with another. Italics were designed as stand-alone faces and for many years after their initial appearance at the beginning of the 16th century the idea of designing a paired roman and italic didn't exist. Modernism gave us the type family and, today, being able to select harmonious weights and widths of fonts with matched characteristics is a great help to designers, but we have a tendency to think that this is an essential concern, almost a typographic rule. Not so. Unmatched faces got along with each other perfectly well for hundreds of years and individual typeface designs benefited from the fact that there was no underlying requirement for conformity across a number of weights and styles. This is what we get with Knockout; given the breadth of choice offered here, in many ways the versatility of the collection surpasses that of a more homogeneous family.

The Knockout collection contains 32 individual fonts that cover nine widths and four weights. Styles are assigned titles that would normally be encountered in a boxing ring; the narrowest width is a Flyweight whereas the widest is a Sumo. Weight groups are indicated in a more straightforward way as Junior, Full and Ultimate with no prefix assigned to the equivalent of the Regular weight.

Knockout Junior Flyweight, Bantamweight, Featherweight, Lightweight, Welterweight, Middleweight, Cruiserweight, Heavyweight and Sumo

The widths of Knockout are split into nine groups across four weights, and are naturally named in accordance with the standard boxing weight categories

Knockout Sumo, Full Sumo and Ultimate Sumo

The Thesis Family

| **Country of origin:** Germany | **Classification:** Humanist Sans/Neo-Humanist Sans/Contemporary Serif | **Designer:** Luc(as) de Groot

1994–1999

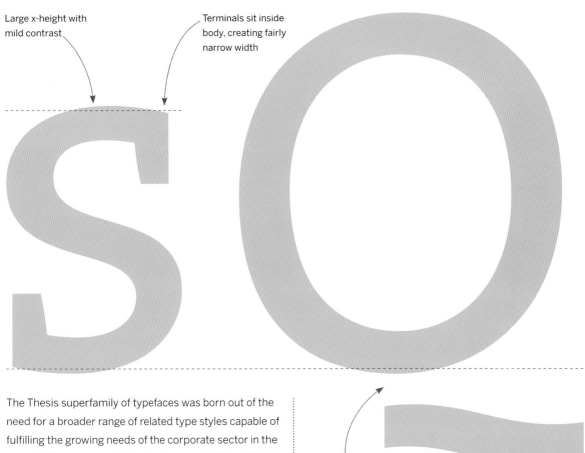

Large x-height with mild contrast

Terminals sit inside body, creating fairly narrow width

TheSerif Plain

Tail doesn't connect with bowl

The Thesis superfamily of typefaces was born out of the need for a broader range of related type styles capable of fulfilling the growing needs of the corporate sector in the early 1990s; compared to today, the availability of digital fonts was considerably more limited.

9/12pt TheSerif Semi Light (FontFabrik)

LOREM IPSUM DOLOR SIT AMET, CONSECTETUER ADIPISCING ELIT, SED DIAM NONUMMY NIBH euismod tincidunt ut laoreet dolore magna aliquam erat volutpat. Ut wisi enim ad minim veniam, quis nostrud exerci tation ullamcorper suscipit lobortis nisl ut aliquip ex ea commodo consequat. Duis autem vel eum iriure dolor in hendrerit in vulputate

12/15pt TheSerif Semi Light (FontFabrik)

LOREM IPSUM DOLOR SIT AMET, CONSECTETUER ADIPISCING ELIT, SED diam nonummy nibh euismod tincidunt ut laoreet dolore magna aliquam erat volutpat. Ut wisi enim ad minim veniam, quis nostrud exerci tation ullamcorper suscipit lobortis

The enormous Thesis superfamily is the work of Dutch type designer Lucas de Groot, or Luc(as) de Groot as he's known professionally. He studied at the Koninklijke Academie van Beeldende Kunsten (The Royal Academy of Art) in The Hague, Netherlands, between 1983 and 1988 alongside several other successful Dutch type designers including Peter Matthias Noordzij and Albert-Jan Pool, and was taught by Gerrit Noordzij. Now based in Berlin, de Groot is the founder of the digital type foundry LucasFonts and the design studio FontFabrik and has designed a number of custom and commercial typefaces, but he's best known for his Thesis project. He's also known for his Interpolation Theory that has influenced the work of many other type designers; an extended explanation of how the theory works can be found at the LucasFonts website.

It's been mentioned already in this book that, in the early 1990s, the list of good digital typefaces available to designers was not as extensive as it is today. De Groot created the Thesis family in answer to this shortfall. Instead of drawing a few weights for early release before following them up with additional weights and styles, de Groot took the relatively unusual step of completing all of the fonts for his extensive family before issuing them commercially in 1994.

From the start, he aimed to provide designers with the widest possible range of fonts with a particular focus on corporate identity. This didn't just mean logos and signage, but rather a provision of fonts that could be used for all aspects of a company's business.

Thesis consists of three main faces, TheSans, TheMix, and TheSerif, with each face consisting of eight weights, all with true italic styles to accompany them. All share similar metrics to encourage optically harmonious setting when the faces are used together. TheMix provided the starting point for the entire Thesis family. It originates from an alphabet designed by de Groot for the Dutch Ministry of Transport, Public Works and Water Management while working at Amsterdam design agency BRS Premsela Vonk. Asymmetric serifs appear on only the lowercase characters, and all serifs are horizontal, helping to create an even rhythm for text setting that aids legibility. TheSerif carries additional serifs on the lowercase and adds them to the uppercase, whereas TheSans (obviously) loses the serifs completely. Since the first release, de Groot has designed an Old Style variant named TheAntiqua, a monospaced version of TheSans, and extra Hairline weights for all styles.

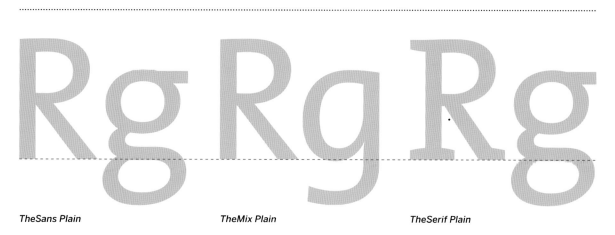

TheSans Plain   TheMix Plain   TheSerif Plain

Verdana

| **Country of origin:** United States | **Classification:** Humanist Sans
| **Designers:** Matthew Carter and Thomas Rickner

1994

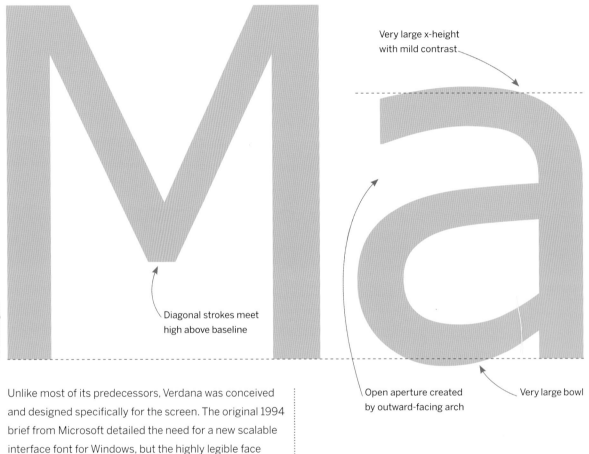

Verdana Regular

Very large x-height
with mild contrast

Diagonal strokes meet
high above baseline

Open aperture created
by outward-facing arch

Very large bowl

Unlike most of its predecessors, Verdana was conceived and designed specifically for the screen. The original 1994 brief from Microsoft detailed the need for a new scalable interface font for Windows, but the highly legible face soon found its way onto many more digital platforms.

9/12pt Verdana Regular (Microsoft)

LOREM IPSUM DOLOR SIT AMET, CONSECTETUER ADIPISCING ELIT, SED DIAM nonummy nibh euismod tincidunt ut laoreet dolore magna aliquam erat volutpat. Ut wisi enim ad minim veniam, quis nostrud exerci tation ullamcorper suscipit lobortis nisl ut aliquip ex ea commodo consequat. Duis

12/15pt Verdana Regular (Microsoft)

LOREM IPSUM DOLOR SIT AMET, CONSECTETUER ADIPISCING elit, sed diam nonummy nibh euismod tincidunt ut laoreet dolore magna aliquam erat volutpat. Ut wisi enim ad minim veniam, quis nostrud exerci tation

The Humanist sans serif typeface Verdana was designed by Matthew Carter and completed by designer and "type engineer" Thomas Rickner, the man responsible for the production of Apple's first TrueType fonts in 1991 and for the hinting of many well-known system fonts including Georgia and Tahoma. Verdana's story begins in 1994 when Virginia Howlett, the head of Microsoft's user interface design team, identified the need for a new screen font for the next release of the Windows operating system (Windows 95), that would help to differentiate it from IBM's OS/2 system. At that time both systems used the same font, MS Sans Serif. The name of the font is derived from the word "verdant," acknowledging the lush surroundings of Microsoft's Redmond headquarters, and Ana, the name of Howlett's daughter.

Matthew Carter was asked to take on the project and adopted a different approach to the standard design process, effectively reversing the procedure. In the early 1990s many user interfaces still used size-specific bitmap fonts but by the mid-1990s desktop UIs utilizing scalable fonts were becoming the norm. Scalable fonts were normally designed with high-resolution printed output in mind, so the designer would draw the outlines first and finalize them prior to the production of the fine-tuned screen fonts.

This tuning of the outlines is known as hinting. However, in the case of Verdana, Carter flipped the process and began with the design of the bitmap shapes in a range of sizes, drawing the outlines afterward. He adopted the approach in the knowledge that it was the way the bitmaps rendered onscreen that was of paramount importance. Once the outlines were completed, Rickner hinted them to exactly match Carter's bitmap patterns, and the internet's "typeface of choice" was ready to go.

The design process overran the release of Windows 95 and Verdana wasn't published until 1996, but it's been included with both the Windows and Mac OS X operating systems ever since, as well as being available as a free download from Microsoft's website. In its day it was the typeface of the web, but today there are many more options available to web designers so Verdana can no longer realistically claim its place as the internet's typeface of choice. However, it's still one of the most widely used faces worldwide and, according to published figures, is installed on around 98 percent of all computers running either Windows or Mac OS systems.

Verdana Regular

Verdana Italic

Benton Sans

| **Country of origin:** United States | **Classification:** Gothic Sans
| **Designers:** Tobias Frere-Jones and Cyrus Highsmith

1995–2008

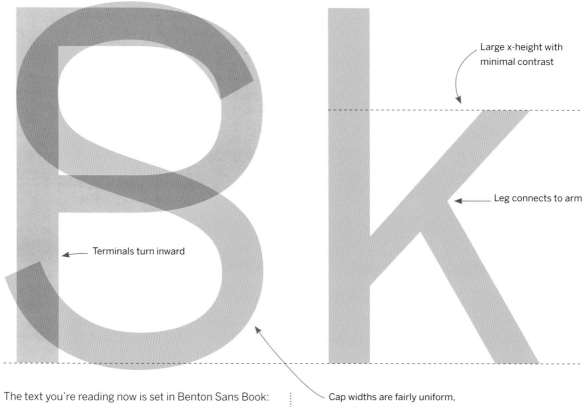

Large x-height with minimal contrast

Leg connects to arm

Terminals turn inward

Benton Sans Regular

Cap widths are fairly uniform, as indicated by the wide "P"

The text you're reading now is set in Benton Sans Book: a contemporary update to News Gothic, designed around 100 years earlier. Typical of modern revivals, the range of weights and styles has been expanded significantly to meet 21st-century standards.

9/12pt Benton Sans Regular (Font Bureau)

LOREM IPSUM DOLOR SIT AMET, CONSECTETUER ADIPISCING ELIT, SED DIAM nonummy nibh euismod tincidunt ut laoreet dolore magna aliquam erat volutpat. Ut wisi enim ad minim veniam, quis nostrud exerci tation ullamcorper suscipit lobortis nisl ut aliquip ex ea commodo consequat. Duis autem vel eum iriure

12/15pt Benton Sans Regular (Font Bureau)

LOREM IPSUM DOLOR SIT AMET, CONSECTETUER ADIPISCING ELIT, sed diam nonummy nibh euismod tincidunt ut laoreet dolore magna aliquam erat volutpat. Ut wisi enim ad minim veniam, quis nostrud exerci tation ullamcorper suscipit lobortis

Benton Sans began as Benton Gothic, a family of fonts begun by Tobias Frere-Jones in 1995 while working at Boston's Font Bureau. The original letterforms were designed in response to commissions from clients including *Martha Stewart Living* for custom corporate fonts and take their inspiration from News Gothic, designed for American Type Founders by Morris Fuller Benton in 1908. Frere-Jones was able to study Benton's original drawings for News Gothic, as well as his designs for Franklin Gothic, which are held at the Smithsonian Institution. Although the face is clearly a close interpretation of News Gothic, it's reasonable to say that Benton Sans is a broader interpretation (not a revival) that draws on both of Benton's sans serifs from this time. This is really how type design (or any design for that matter) truly evolves, using multiple influences and new technology to constantly shift boundaries and expand possibilities.

Benton Gothic comprised seven weights from Thin to Black in two widths and, given that Frere-Jones' design was developed in response to more than one client's requirements, it was decided that the family would benefit from some harmonization before its commercial release. By 2002–03, Font Bureau's Cyrus Highsmith had completed the first stage of the update that would become the Benton Sans family; the name change was appropriate given the adjustments made to the original weights. By 2008 the project was completed, increasing the number of fonts in the expanded family to 128, or 64 in the case of the OpenType version, which absorbs the small caps and alternative characters.

Benton Sans is a prime example of the modern typeface superfamily with eight weights from Thin to Black, all with an italic style, and four widths: Regular, Condensed, Compressed and Extra Compressed. With such a large number of options, it's perfect for building up the typographic hierarchies that are so important for all kinds of publication design. It's also a great choice for building tables as the Compressed and Extra Compressed weights remain legible at smaller point sizes despite their very narrow widths, helped of course by the large x-height. Benton Sans Book is used throughout this book for setting the captions and annotation.

Benton Sans Regular, Condensed Regular, Compressed Regular and Extra Compressed Regular

Base Nine & Twelve

| **Country of origin:** United States | **Classification:** Geometric Sans
| **Designer:** Zuzana Licko

1995

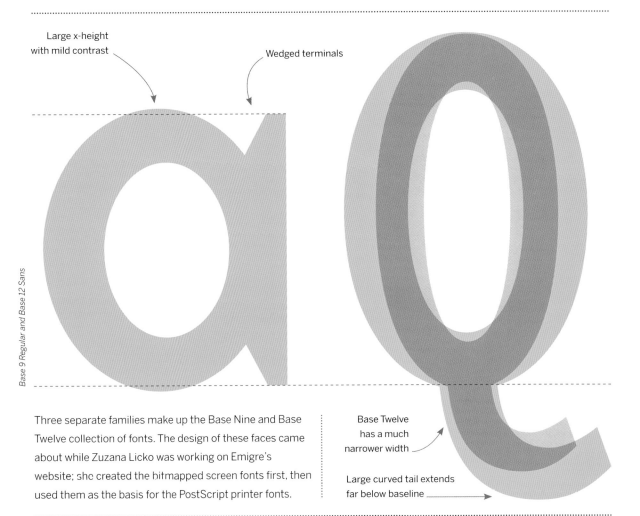

Large x-height with mild contrast

Wedged terminals

Base 9 Regular and Base 12 Sans

Three separate families make up the Base Nine and Base Twelve collection of fonts. The design of these faces came about while Zuzana Licko was working on Emigre's website; she created the hitmapped screen fonts first, then used them as the basis for the PostScript printer fonts.

Base Twelve has a much narrower width

Large curved tail extends far below baseline

9/12pt Base 12 Serif (Emigre)

LOREM IPSUM DOLOR SIT AMET, CONSECTETUER ADIPISCING ELIT, SED DIAM NONUMMY NIBH euismod tincidunt ut laoreet dolore magna aliquam erat volutpat. Ut wisi enim ad minim veniam, quis nostrud exerci tation ullamcorper suscipit lobortis nisl ut aliquip ex ea commodo consequat. Duis autem vel

12/15pt Base 12 Serif (Emigre)

LOREM IPSUM DOLOR SIT AMET, CONSECTETUER ADIPISCING ELIT, sed diam nonummy nibh euismod tincidunt ut laoreet dolore magna aliquam erat volutpat. Ut wisi enim ad minim veniam, quis nostrud exerci tation

Emigre was one of the first digital foundries to take advantage of the new opportunities afforded by electronic and online sales of their typefaces; they used bulletin board software called "Now Serving" to take orders for fonts that could then be emailed to customers before the web began to offer regular online sales solutions. Base Nine and Base Twelve were designed by Zuzana Licko for Emigre in 1995 after identifying a commercial need for a set of bitmap screen fonts that would render cleanly and accurately onscreen, and were accompanied by a companion set of outline printer fonts. Three separate styles were created; a serif and a sans serif were based on a 12-point screen font and named Base Twelve, whereas Base Nine was based on a 9-point screen font.

We talked earlier in the book about Matthew Carter designing bitmaps before outlines when he worked on Verdana, and Base Nine and Twelve were arrived at by a similar process. Licko explains in her online précis of the design process for the faces that "the greatest challenge in harmonizing the legibility of screen fonts with printer fonts is that of spacing." Normally, character widths are determined using the outlines but in this case the bitmaps were used to gauge the widths before outlines were adjusted to fit. The decision to work with a 12-point screen font (for Base Twelve) was based on it being a default size for most applications and web browsers at that time, plus 12-point scales up neatly to the 24- and 36-point bitmap defaults common in the mid 1990s. Base Nine caters for the other common defaults of 9 point and 18 point. In situations where the accurate onscreen display of character shapes and spacing were of paramount importance, using Base Nine and Base Twelve at their predetermined sizes (or multiples thereof) produced cleanly rendered text. Despite the emphasis on screen rendering, the goal to create a set of fonts for print use was also achieved and the faces were extremely popular on their release.

Improvements in the way fonts are rendered onscreen have of course moved things along in the last 20 years, and screen resolutions are much improved, but in 1995 WYSIWYG (what you see is what you get) rendering could be a touch-and-go experience. Base Nine and Base Twelve were certainly trailblazing fonts for their time and have survived intact; all 12 styles can now be purchased in the OpenType format and are great for recalling a 1990s design sensibility.

Base Twelve Sans

Base Twelve Serif

Despite the contemporary styling of the letterforms, Base Twelve Serif follows the convention of using a double-story "g" for the serif weights

FF Dax (FF Daxline)

| **Country of origin:** Germany | **Classification:** Neo-Humanist Sans
| **Designer:** Hans Reichel

1995–2005

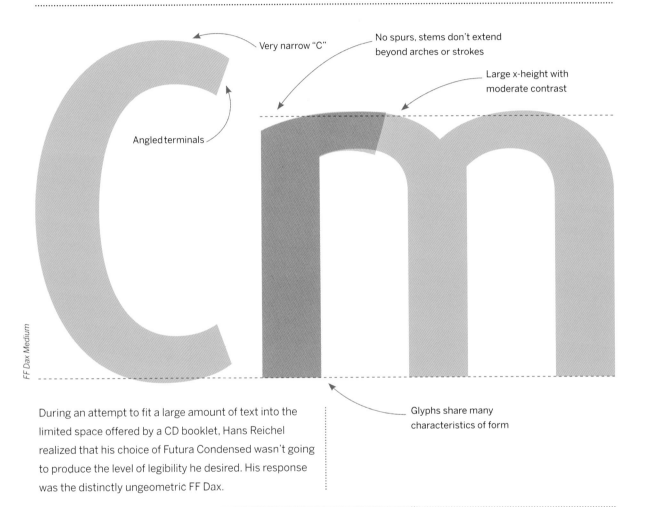

FF Dax Medium

Very narrow "C"

No spurs, stems don't extend beyond arches or strokes

Large x-height with moderate contrast

Angled terminals

Glyphs share many characteristics of form

During an attempt to fit a large amount of text into the limited space offered by a CD booklet, Hans Reichel realized that his choice of Futura Condensed wasn't going to produce the level of legibility he desired. His response was the distinctly ungeometric FF Dax.

9/12pt FF Dax Regular (FontFont)

LOREM IPSUM DOLOR SIT AMET, CONSECTETUER ADIPISCING ELIT, SED DIAM NONUMMY NIBH EUISMOD tincidunt ut laoreet dolore magna aliquam erat volutpat. Ut wisi enim ad minim veniam, quis nostrud exerci tation ullamcorper suscipit lobortis nisl ut aliquip ex ea commodo consequat. Duis autem vel eum iriure dolor in hendrerit in vulputate velit esse molestie

12/15pt FF Dax Regular (FontFont)

LOREM IPSUM DOLOR SIT AMET, CONSECTETUER ADIPISCING ELIT, SED DIAM nonummy nibh euismod tincidunt ut laoreet dolore magna aliquam erat volutpat. Ut wisi enim ad minim veniam, quis nostrud exerci tation ullamcorper suscipit lobortis nisl ut aliquip ex ea

Hans Reichel, the German designer of FF Dax who died in 2011 at the age of 62, was known principally as an experimental guitarist and alternative stringed instrument inventor (also termed an experimental luthier). However, as a young man he studied graphic design and worked as a typesetter, an association that lead to the design of just a few typefaces between 1983 and 2005. These were mainly published by the FontFont digital type foundry and include FF Dax, which, since its original release and as the adapted and improved FF Daxline, has been one of the foundry's best-selling faces.

Reichel's concept for FF Dax was, to quote from the FontFont website description, "to combine the clarity of a narrow Futura with a more humanist touch." He goes a long way in achieving a design that departs significantly from a Geometric sans such as Futura by incorporating a moderate degree of contrast and a number of organic letterforms that are clearly reminiscent of handwriting. The omission of spurs (the small extensions at the ends of the stems) for the "d," "g," "m," "n," "p," "q," "r" and "u" is key to the elegant simplicity of Reichel's design. Unusually, the condensed width was

the first of this large family to be released by FontFont in 1995; the normal (but still relatively narrow) FF Dax followed next, with FF Dax Wide released last. In 2004 the six-weight FF Dax Compact (which doesn't include any italic styles) was released, and in 2005 Reichel's final revision, FF Daxline, was designed. This final revision to the FF Dax family was created to improve the functionality of FF Dax as a text face for setting at smaller point sizes. Contrast is lower, uppercase characters are slightly larger, and the overall metrics have been adjusted to create a better consistency between character widths.

The original FF Dax family consists of six weights: Light, Regular, Medium, Bold, Extra Bold and Black. These are available in three widths, condensed, normal and wide, and all have accompanying italic styles. FF Daxline is available in one normal width but has seven weights; Reichel added a thin weight in front of Light, and once again all have an italic style that is an optically correct oblique roman.

FF Daxline Regular

The lack of spurs on many lowercase characters adds to the simplicity of Dax, which comes in three widths

FF Dax Condensed Regular, Regular, and Wide Regular

Mrs Eaves

| **Country of origin:** United States | **Classification:** Transitional Serif
| **Designer:** Zuzana Licko

1996

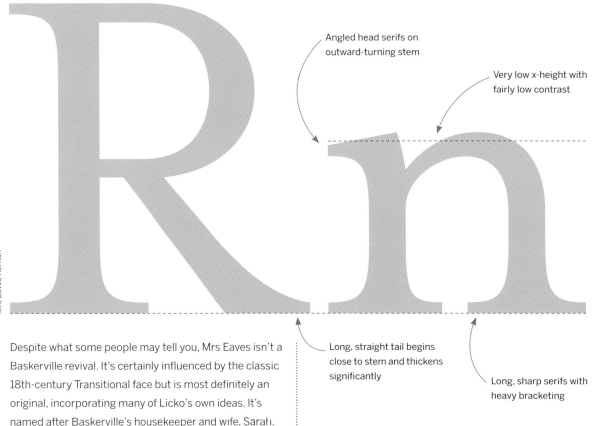

Mrs Eaves Roman

Angled head serifs on
outward-turning stem

Very low x-height with
fairly low contrast

Long, straight tail begins
close to stem and thickens
significantly

Long, sharp serifs with
heavy bracketing

Despite what some people may tell you, Mrs Eaves isn't a Baskerville revival. It's certainly influenced by the classic 18th-century Transitional face but is most definitely an original, incorporating many of Licko's own ideas. It's named after Baskerville's housekeeper and wife, Sarah.

9/12pt Mrs Eaves Roman (Emigre)

LOREM IPSUM DOLOR SIT AMET, CONSECTETUER ADIPISCING ELIT, SED DIAM NONUMMY NIBH euismod tincidunt ut laoreet dolore magna aliquam erat volutpat. Ut wisi enim ad minim veniam, quis nostrud exerci tation ullamcorper suscipit lobortis nisl ut aliquip ex ea commodo consequat. Duis autem vel eum iriure dolor in hendrerit in vulputate velit esse molestie

12/15pt Mrs Eaves Roman (Emigre)

LOREM IPSUM DOLOR SIT AMET, CONSECTETUER ADIPISCING ELIT, sed diam nonummy nibh euismod tincidunt ut laoreet dolore magna aliquam erat volutpat. Ut wisi enim ad minim veniam, quis nostrud exerci tation ullamcorper suscipit lobortis nisl ut aliquip ex ea

In the past, Mrs Eaves has been referred to as a Baskerville revival, but this isn't really the case. It's more accurate to describe Zuzana Licko's design as an interpretation of the 18th-century Transitional serif; it draws on the spirit of the letterforms Baskerville sought to create but at the same time it addresses many of the criticisms leveled at Baskerville's type when it was first released. Critics of Baskerville's typefaces complained that they were too perfect and therefore characterless (in comparison with the popular and ubiquitous Caslon), and that they were hard on the eye and difficult to read for more than a few minutes at a time. One can imagine that Licko felt some personal empathy, having been the target of critics herself during the 1980s when Emigre released a number of experimental bitmap fonts that were radically different to anything else available at the time. There is, of course, no progress without experimentation and in a way Licko was treading similar ground to Baskerville, looking at new ways to design typefaces that could exploit the latest available technology.

From the very start, Licko set out to design a face that didn't attempt to improve on or polish the letterforms that provided her inspiration. Instead, she worked as if she were designing a new face from scratch, taking only the rough proportions of Baskerville's design as a guide. Careful consideration was given to how her typeface would have looked if it were printed using letterpress, and letterforms were designed to "mimic" the effect of ink spread, compensating for the flatness of offset lithography with heavier strokes and serifs with a more gradual transition from the stems. This counters the visually anemic color that can sometimes result from setting other digitized versions of Baskerville at smaller point sizes, and helps explain the quirkily small x-height that characterizes Mrs Eaves. Licko purposely lowered the x-height to reduce the total amount of ink needed to print a paragraph of text, thus providing a slightly more even color overall.

Mrs Eaves is named after Sarah Eaves, John Baskerville's housekeeper and mistress who eventually became his wife and business partner. She worked alongside Baskerville and his staff, helping with typesetting and printing, and continued to run the business after his death. The original family of fonts contained a roman, a true italic, and a bold weight. This has since been expanded to include a bold italic style; there are a raft of alternative characters and ligatures are particularly abundant. In addition, Licko has designed Mrs Eaves XL, which features a larger x-height, shorter ascenders and descenders, and tighter spacing. These characteristics were introduced to improve legibility at smaller sizes and to help create economy of space, making Mrs Eaves XL the better choice for setting longer passages of running text.

Mrs Eaves Roman   *Baskerville 120 Regular*

Bickham Script

| **Country of origin:** United States | **Classification:** Formal Script
| **Designer:** Richard Lipton

1997

Large loop ascenders

Very small x-height
with high contrast

Large loop for crossbar

Teardrop terminals

Bickham Script Regular

Huge selection of
alternative characters

Bickham Script was one of the first typefaces to use the automatic alternative-glyph substitution features of the OpenType format. Both formal and casual scripts benefit enormously from the improved OpenType format that can support up to 65,536 separate glyphs.

18pt Bickham Script Regular (Adobe)

Allographs

36pt Bickham Script Regular (Adobe)

Allographs

72pt Bickham Script Regular (Adobe)

Allographs

Bickham Script, designed by calligrapher Richard Lipton, is something of a trailblazer. Scripts, and in particular formal scripts, have arguably provided type founders and typesetters with their biggest challenge over the years. Achieving a flowing run of consecutive characters with convincing junctions that emulate handwritten calligraphy was difficult to achieve with foundry type or hot metal setting (especially on a Linotype) because of the restrictive metal body. Phototypesetting technology improved things a little as characters could be set much closer together but one still needed the prerequisite amount of ligatures and the key characters for setting scripts, and the number of glyphs that could be included in a single photographic matrix was limited. Even early digital formats with their maximum limit of 256 individual glyphs struggled to accommodate the sufficient number of ligatures required and efforts to produce formal scripts often fell short of the mark. Bickham Script was one of the first fonts to take full advantage of OpenType technology with its built-in capability for automatic glyph and ligature substitution, and is the formal script that all others are measured against.

Richard Lipton opened his own calligraphy studio in Cambridge, Massachusetts, in the 1970s and began working for Bitstream in the early 1980s. His transition to the digital type platform led him to launch his independent digital type foundry in 1991 and Bickham Script was designed for Adobe in 1997. The inspiration (and the font's name) was provided by the work of the 18th-century English calligrapher and engraver George Bickham. OpenType technology was a godsend for scripts of all kinds and the cornerstone of the Pro version of Bickham Script is the inclusion of a huge range of contextual glyphs and ligature variations that are dynamically substituted as words are formed. According to its page at MyFonts, the font contains 1,715 individual glyphs, an enormous number that far exceeds the average amount found in other fully featured fonts. It's a grand statement of a typeface and needs plenty of room to flourish, and a little time spent mastering the OpenType settings of your chosen applications will help you get the most out of its features.

The standard OpenType family contains three weights: Regular, Semi Bold and Bold.

Bickham Script Regular

The increasing flamboyancy of substitute characters is demonstrated ably by the "b," which has at least 12 optional alternatives

Modesto

| **Country of origin:** United States | **Classification:** Glyphic
| **Designer:** Jim Parkinson

2000

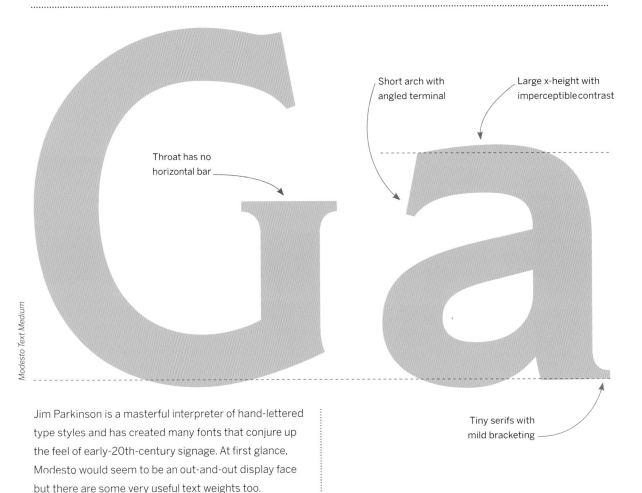

Modesto Text Medium

Throat has no
horizontal bar

Short arch with
angled terminal

Large x-height with
imperceptible contrast

Tiny serifs with
mild bracketing

Jim Parkinson is a masterful interpreter of hand-lettered type styles and has created many fonts that conjure up the feel of early-20th-century signage. At first glance, Modesto would seem to be an out-and-out display face but there are some very useful text weights too.

9/12pt Modesto Text Light (Parkinson Type Design)

LOREM IPSUM DOLOR SIT AMET, CONSECTETUER ADIPISCING ELIT, SED DIAM NONUMMY NIBH euismod tincidunt ut laoreet dolore magna aliquam erat volutpat. Ut wisi enim ad minim veniam, quis nostrud exerci tation ullamcorper suscipit lobortis nisl ut aliquip ex ea commodo consequat. Duis autem vel eum iriure dolor in hendrerit in vulputate velit esse

12/15pt Modesto Text Light (Parkinson Type Design)

LOREM IPSUM DOLOR SIT AMET, CONSECTETUER ADIPISCING ELIT, SED diam nonummy nibh euismod tincidunt ut laoreet dolore magna aliquam erat volutpat. Ut wisi enim ad minim veniam, quis nostrud exerci tation ullamcorper suscipit lobortis nisl ut aliquip ex ea

Before we talk about Modesto we should talk a little about its designer, Jim Parkinson. Born in 1941, he was inspired by a neighbor named Abraham Lincoln Paulsen, who worked as a lettering artist, and resolved to become one himself. He studied at the California College of Arts and Crafts in Oakland and after graduating worked for Hallmark Cards in Kansas City, where he met Hermann Zapf while Zapf was acting as a consultant. He returned to California in 1969 and freelanced for advertising, music business and publishing clients, designing, among many other things, the logo for *Rolling Stone* magazine, and in 1990 he made the quantum leap of going totally digital.

Modesto is one of those faces that's a little difficult to classify accurately. I've listed it as Glyphic because it has those tiny wedged serifs that look like they could be carved or engraved, but it's the hand-painted feel so reminiscent of late-19th- and early-20th-century sign writing that places it in a category of its own. It's named after Modesto, California, where Parkinson's mother grew up, and is a reflection of the designer's background as a hand-lettering artist. Spurred on by the acquisition of a Mac and a copy of the type design software package *Fontographer*, Parkinson decided to begin creating a set of digital fonts based on the style he'd lettered for a new logotype for the Ringling Bros. and Barnum & Bailey Circus. The family started out as two fonts released in 2000, Modesto Regular and Modesto Expanded, and Parkinson has gradually added further weights and styles ever since. To complement the full range of options for Modesto, there are the five "chromatic" Modesto Open fonts and the two-layer Modesto Initials. These fonts were completed around 2004 and are designed to be used together (or indeed separately if desired) to build up display text in combinations of two or three overlaid colors. The metrics of all styles are exactly the same to ensure they align perfectly when set in stacked text boxes.

In 2014, Parkinson added four new italic styles to the standard Modesto family, increasing the number of individual fonts to 10. Modesto Text has three weights, Light, Medium and Bold, with optically corrected oblique roman italics. The display weights named Modesto Poster and Modesto Expanded are single weights with italic styles, and have small caps rather than lowercase characters. Parkinson dropped the term "regular" when he added italics as he didn't like the idea of a font called Modesto Regular Regular, changing it to Modesto Poster to reflect the sign painter roots of the face.

Modesto Initials

Two-color headlines can be made using the "chromatic" font options

Modesto Open

Gotham

| Country of origin: United States **| Classification:** Geometric Sans
| Designer: Tobias Frere-Jones

2000

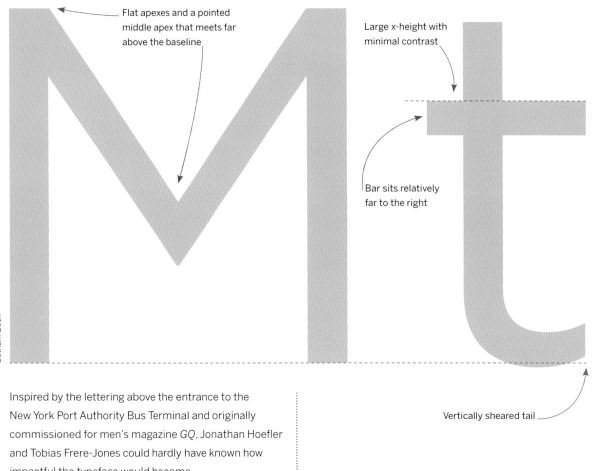

Flat apexes and a pointed middle apex that meets far above the baseline

Large x-height with minimal contrast

Bar sits relatively far to the right

Gotham Book

Vertically sheared tail

Inspired by the lettering above the entrance to the New York Port Authority Bus Terminal and originally commissioned for men's magazine *GQ*, Jonathan Hoefler and Tobias Frere-Jones could hardly have known how impactful the typeface would become.

9/12pt Gotham Book (Hoefler & Co.)

LOREM IPSUM DOLOR SIT AMET, CONSECTETUER ADIPISCING ELIT, SED DIAM nonummy nibh euismod tincidunt ut laoreet dolore magna aliquam erat volutpat. Ut wisi enim ad minim veniam, quis nostrud exerci tation ullamcorper suscipit lobortis nisl ut aliquip ex ea commodo consequat. Duis autem

12/15pt Gotham Book (Hoefler & Co.)

LOREM IPSUM DOLOR SIT AMET, CONSECTETUER ADIPISCING elit, sed diam nonummy nibh euismod tincidunt ut laoreet dolore magna aliquam erat volutpat. Ut wisi enim ad minim veniam, quis nostrud exerci tation

In terms of its public profile, Gotham is a 21st-century Helvetica—but the similarity ends there. Everyone has heard of Helvetica and (unless they say it's Arial) many non-designers are able to identify it. The level of public exposure Gotham has enjoyed, particularly since 2008, is close to that of Helvetica, but outside of the design industry there are fewer people who would be able to identify it if asked. Despite this, Gotham has become one of the most important sans serif typefaces to be released in the last 50 years. Why is this? Perhaps it's because it feels like it's always been here.

Gotham began as a commission from *GQ* magazine; the Hoefler & Frere-Jones digital type foundry (now Hoefler & Co.) was asked to design a sans serif that was "masculine, new and fresh," but they also asked for a face that felt credible and established. Tobias Frere-Jones has acknowledged that, without the *GQ* commission, Gotham might never have come about. At the time he felt that there was probably nothing new to be drawn from the Humanist or Geometric sans serif classifications but was glad to discover that he was mistaken. He took his inspiration from the lettering that the people of New York had been looking at every day for years, the type that adorns the older public buildings around Manhattan; the main source material was

provided by the signage above the facade of the Eighth Avenue Port Authority Bus Terminal. The letterforms of Gotham feel as much engineered as they do designed, a visual trait that helps to give the face its distinctly trustworthy flavor, and it's been said that it's unlike other sans serif faces that are German or Swiss—Gotham's personality is distinctly American.

Gotham's "spotlight" moment arrived in 2008 when it was chosen to replace Perpetua as the principal typeface used for Barack Obama's presidential campaign. Although it would be wrong to suggest that Obama won the election because of a typeface, Gotham's ability to persuade voters to believe the statements set with it has been widely acknowledged as having played a part in the campaign's success. A customized serif version of Gotham was created for Obama's successful 2012 bid for a second term in office, but a commercial release has not yet happened.

Gotham's extended family currently comprises no less than 66 weights and styles. These are spread over four widths: Condensed, Extra Narrow, Narrow and Normal. All weights are accompanied by an oblique roman italic. There is also the four-weight, eight-style Gotham Rounded set of fonts.

Gotham Book Condensed, Extra Narrow, Narrow and Normal

Arnhem

| **Country of origin:** The Netherlands | **Classification:** Transitional Serif
| **Designer:** Fred Smeijers

2002

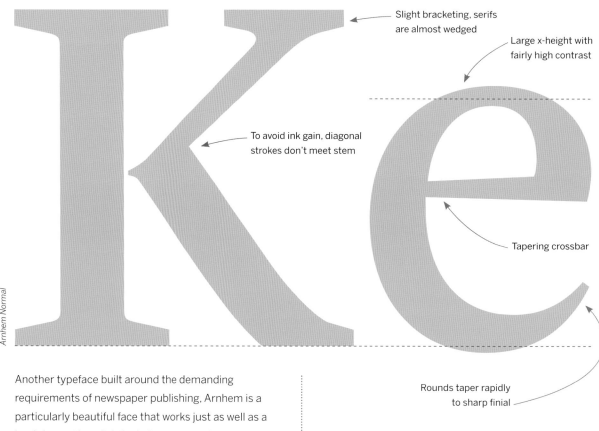

Slight bracketing, serifs are almost wedged

Large x-height with fairly high contrast

To avoid ink gain, diagonal strokes don't meet stem

Tapering crossbar

Arnhem Normal

Rounds taper rapidly to sharp finial

Another typeface built around the demanding requirements of newspaper publishing, Arnhem is a particularly beautiful face that works just as well as a book face with a slightly darker typographic color compared to other similar Transitional serifs.

9/12pt Arnhem Normal (OurType)

LOREM IPSUM DOLOR SIT AMET, CONSECTETUER ADIPISCING ELIT, SED DIAM NONUMMY NIBH euismod tincidunt ut laoreet dolore magna aliquam erat volutpat. Ut wisi enim ad minim veniam, quis nostrud exerci tation ullamcorper suscipit lobortis nisl ut aliquip ex ea commodo consequat. Duis autem vel eum iriure dolor in hendrerit in vulputate

12/15pt Arnhem Normal (OurType)

LOREM IPSUM DOLOR SIT AMET, CONSECTETUER ADIPISCING ELIT, sed diam nonummy nibh euismod tincidunt ut laoreet dolore magna aliquam erat volutpat. Ut wisi enim ad minim veniam, quis nostrud exerci tation ullamcorper suscipit lobortis

The Dutch type designer Fred Smeijers of the independent digital type foundry OurType began working on Arnhem in 1999 in reaction to a commission from the daily newspaper *Nederlandse Staatscourant*. Typefaces for newspapers are designed to operate successfully in a challenging print environment and occasionally style has given way to function. However, in the case of Arnhem, Smeijers has created a face that looks just as beautiful wherever it's used; it's a great example of how the classic features of a typical Transitional serif can be brought firmly up to date through the addition of some lively contemporary (and practical) touches. Its relatively high contrast and unusually large x-height allows Arnhem to be densely set without losing legibility, and its overall color is just on the right side of dark. There are also plenty of little details like the tiny gap between diagonal strokes and stems that help to avoid unwanted ink gain.

A neat trick that I, as an editorial designer, always like to see in a text face, is the duplexing of widths between the separate weights. Switch from Blond to Bold, for example, and the text occupies almost exactly the same horizontal space. Duplexing works best at smaller text sizes so don't expect miracles as increased stroke widths are bound to create slightly wider setting. This creates a great advantage, especially for complex editorial design work, as you can

guarantee that edited text won't reflow if additional formatting is introduced. It's only a good thing if the design of the letterforms isn't compromised, of course, and in the case of Arnhem there are no issues of that kind in evidence.

Arnhem saw its first commercial release in 2002, when the family comprised only four weights with true italic styles: Blond, Normal, Bold and Black. Smeijers opted to call the lightest weight "Blond" rather than "Light" because he felt it was a little too heavy to be classified as a genuine light weight. Typical of a specialist newspaper face, the Normal weight colors quite strongly on the page when set in smaller point sizes and Blond was designed to offer a slightly brighter option for running text. By 2010, Smeijers had designed and released the next generation of Arnhem. He added a Semi Bold weight to the original family, augmenting the OpenType formats with a wealth of extra glyphs, and designed a selection of new titling weights. Arnhem Fine consists of four weights with italics: Normal, Medium, Semi Bold and Bold, and is intended for all settings above 14 point. Arnhem Display is a little heavier with a larger x-height and was designed specifically for newspaper headlines; it was commissioned as part of the redesign of the Dutch financial newspaper *Het Financieele Dagblad* and includes just three weights: Normal, Semi Bold and Bold.

Even at large sizes, the duplexing of character widths works very well

Arnhem Blond and Bold

Neutraface

| **Country of origin:** United States | **Classification:** Geometric Sans
| **Designer:** Christian Schwartz

2002

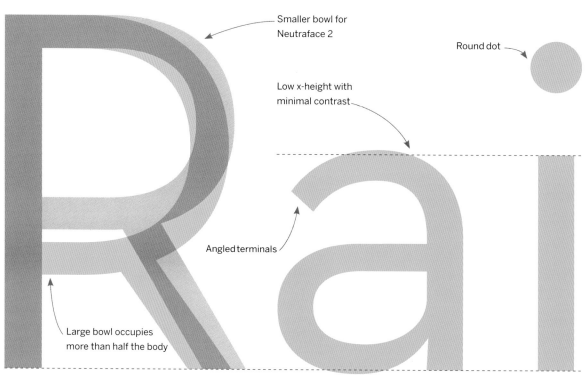

Neutraface Text Book and Neutraface 2 Text Book

Smaller bowl for Neutraface 2

Round dot

Low x-height with minimal contrast

Angled terminals

Large bowl occupies more than half the body

Neutraface's distinctly architectural properties are not coincidental. A joint project between Christian Schwartz and House Industries, the expansive range of Neutraface weights and styles is strongly influenced by the theories of modernist architect Richard Neutra.

9/12pt Neutraface Text Book (House Industries)

LOREM IPSUM DOLOR SIT AMET, CONSECTETUER ADIPISCING ELIT, SED DIAM NONUMMY NIBH euismod tincidunt ut laoreet dolore magna aliquam erat volutpat. Ut wisi enim ad minim veniam, quis nostrud exerci tation ullamcorper suscipit lobortis nisl ut aliquip ex ea commodo consequat. Duis autem vel eum iriure dolor in hendrerit in vulputate velit esse molestie

12/15pt Neutraface Text Book (House Industries)

LOREM IPSUM DOLOR SIT AMET, CONSECTETUER ADIPISCING ELIT, sed diam nonummy nibh euismod tincidunt ut laoreet dolore magna aliquam erat volutpat. Ut wisi enim ad minim veniam, quis nostrud exerci tation ullamcorper suscipit lobortis nisl ut aliquip

Neutraface is named after the Austrian-born American architect Richard Neutra, whose work is marked by his efforts to link the constructed with the natural; he coined the term "biorealism" and designed many residential and commercial buildings that sought to connect the interiors to the outside world. Neutra's attention to detail encompassed the selection of any signage required for his commercial buildings, and it's this source that provides the inspiration for Neutraface. Designer Christian Schwartz worked with Ken Barber and Andy Cruz of House Industries to design the original Display and Text weights, releasing the first of them in 2002. Schwartz consulted with Richard Neutra's son and business partner Dion to help ensure that the characteristics of Neutra's architectural ideals translated truthfully to the design of the typeface, and the result is a Geometric sans that manages to exude a degree of warmth that other more severe sans serif faces such as Futura or Avenir lack. Working from the relatively limited source material, Schwartz designed the full uppercase character set first, then added new lowercase characters that hadn't existed in any previous form.

The principal workhorse faces that sit at the core of the Neutraface family are the Neutraface Display and Neutraface Text variants. Display weights include Thin, Light, Medium, Bold and Titling and do not have italic styles. Text weights (which have a larger x-height, a slightly increased stroke contrast, and more tapering at the junctions to combat ink gain), include Light, Book, Demi and Bold and all have a true italic rather than the oblique roman more common to sans serif faces. The face proved to be very popular following its release and by 2004 Schwartz had designed five condensed weights to add to the original series. Schwartz then identified a demand for what he termed a "more normal" Neutraface and in 2007 added the Neutraface 2 variants. The letterforms broadly share the same overall metrics but Schwartz raised the crossbars on characters such as the "E," "F" and "H," reduced the top-down height of the bowls of the "P" and "R" by a corresponding amount, and substituted in a monocular "g." This serves to remove some of the historical flavor of the original design but retains the overall styling, providing an option that is arguably suited to a broader range of situations. The most recent addition to the family is Neutraface Slab, a set of Geometric slab fonts released in 2009, based on and corresponding to the original sans serif. It retains the minimal contrast of the sans, avoiding the stricter geometry of other similar slabs, so consequently manages to work pretty well as a text face when set at fairly small sizes.

Neutraface 2 comes with a useful set of Display weights, featuring a significantly smaller x-height

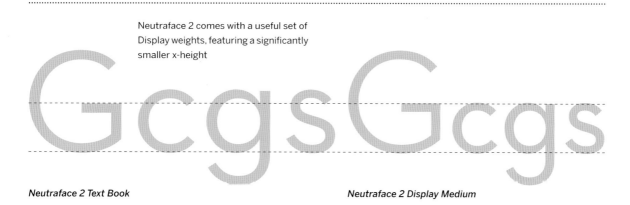

Neutraface 2 Text Book   Neutraface 2 Display Medium

MVB Verdigris

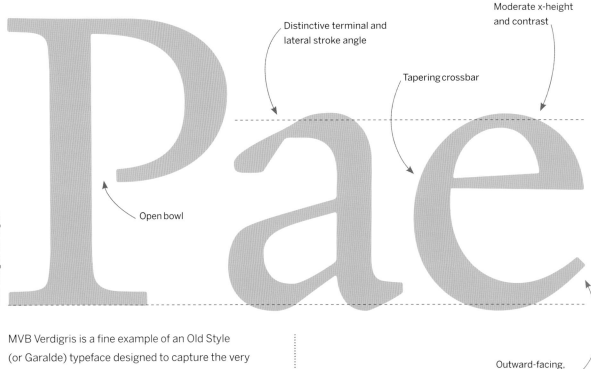

| **Country of origin:** United States | **Classification:** Old Style Serif
| **Designer:** Mark van Bronkhorst

2003

MVB Verdigris Text Regular

Distinctive terminal and lateral stroke angle

Moderate x-height and contrast

Tapering crossbar

Open bowl

Outward-facing, fairly sharp final

MVB Verdigris is a fine example of an Old Style (or Garalde) typeface designed to capture the very essence of a 16th-century metal font. The letterforms are designed to create the sense of an impression rather than simply referencing the original form of the metal type.

9/12pt MVB Verdigris Text Regular (MVB Fonts)

LOREM IPSUM DOLOR SIT AMET, CONSECTETUER ADIPISCING ELIT, SED DIAM nonummy nibh euismod tincidunt ut laoreet dolore magna aliquam erat volutpat. Ut wisi enim ad minim veniam, quis nostrud exerci tation ullamcorper suscipit lobortis nisl ut aliquip ex ea commodo consequat. Duis autem vel eum iriure dolor in hendrerit in vulputate

12/15pt MVB Verdigris Text Regular (MVB Fonts)

LOREM IPSUM DOLOR SIT AMET, CONSECTETUER ADIPISCING elit, sed diam nonummy nibh euismod tincidunt ut laoreet dolore magna aliquam erat volutpat. Ut wisi enim ad minim veniam, quis nostrud exerci tation ullamcorper suscipit lobortis nisl ut

In the 16th century, the period from which this French Old Style (or Garalde) draws its inspiration, punch cutters would introduce tiny adjustments to weight and detailing from one size of type to the next to help ensure that good and consistent typographic color could be achieved between cuts of differing sizes. Their designs reflected the printed impression of the type rather than the type itself, and meant that the design of every cut was inextricably linked to its size. However, the modern one-size-fits-all approach to type design negated this craft-like approach to typeface production and the precise reproduction of modern offset litho meant PostScript fonts based on a single size often failed to deliver at sizes below 10 point or thereabouts, appearing too weak on the printed page. Today, many contemporary digital type designers have returned to the idea of creating optically adjusted fonts for use over specific size ranges, but 10 years ago the practice was less prevalent.

When Mark van Bronkhorst, the owner of Californian digital type foundry MVB Fonts, began work on MVB Verdigris, he initially focused on a design that would excel in the point sizes that we use most often for text setting. He cites the italics cut by Pierre Haultin, which appear in the 1584 edition of Julius Caesar's *Commentaries on the Gallic War,* as his reason for embarking on the project; he felt the letterforms were particularly beautiful in their simplicity but all the same opted to tone down the swashes to create a more contemporary feel for his interpreted face. The roman used in the same edition is Robert Granjon's and acts as the second source of inspiration for MVB Verdigris. Van Bronkhorst drew the roman with a little more typographic color than was typical of other contemporary text faces to counter the printing issues created at smaller point sizes, and in the case of the italic left in a little of what he terms "inkiness" rather than making it look too clean. Despite its original intention, MVB Verdigris actually works very well in a broad range of sizes.

The current family (along with all the usual OpenType niceties) contains Regular and Bold weights for MVB Verdigris Text, both of which have true italics rather than oblique romans. Accompanying these are a pair of useful "mid-caps" fonts—the uppercase characters are slightly smaller than the normal caps and larger than the integral small caps, providing an additional option that works really well when set within running text. The italic mid-caps font is brand new at the time of writing. A pair of high contrast roman titling fonts named MVB Verdigris Big, inspired by the work of 16th-century punch cutter Hendrik van den Keere and designed in 2012, complete the set.

Compared to other Granjon-inspired faces, MVB Verdigris shows a little more "color" on the page

MVB Verdigris Text Regular

Garamond Premier Regular

Brioso

| **Country of origin:** United States | **Classification:** Humanist Serif
| **Designer:** Robert Slimbach

2003

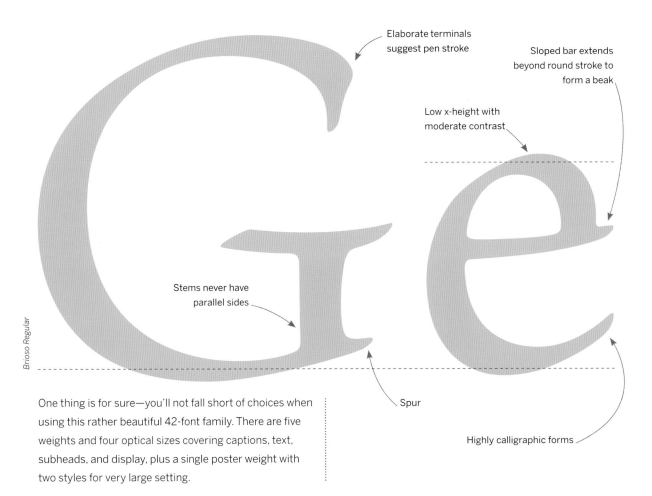

Brioso Regular

Elaborate terminals suggest pen stroke

Sloped bar extends beyond round stroke to form a beak

Low x-height with moderate contrast

Stems never have parallel sides

Spur

Highly calligraphic forms

One thing is for sure—you'll not fall short of choices when using this rather beautiful 42-font family. There are five weights and four optical sizes covering captions, text, subheads, and display, plus a single poster weight with two styles for very large setting.

9/12pt Brioso Regular (Adobe)

LOREM IPSUM DOLOR SIT AMET, CONSECTETUER ADIPISCING ELIT, SED DIAM nonummy nibh euismod tincidunt ut laoreet dolore magna aliquam erat volutpat. ut wisi enim ad minim veniam, quis nostrud exerci tation ullamcorper suscipit lobortis nisl ut aliquip ex ea commodo consequat. Duis autem vel eum iriure dolor in hendrerit in vulputate velit esse molestie

12/15pt Brioso Regular (Adobe)

LOREM IPSUM DOLOR SIT AMET, CONSECTETUER ADIPISCING ELIT, sed diam nonummy nibh euismod tincidunt ut laoreet dolore magna aliquam erat volutpat. Ut wisi enim ad minim veniam, quis nostrud exerci tation ullamcorper suscipit lobortis nisl ut aliquip ex ea

Brioso is Italian for "lively," making it an apt choice for the name of this energetic Humanist serif. It's about as calligraphic as one can get without becoming an out-and-out script, but holds back just enough, blending the directness of hand-lettering with a more disciplined structure that allows this rather beautiful typeface to function surprisingly well when used at smaller point sizes to set running text. It was designed in 2003 by Robert Slimbach, an accomplished calligrapher and typeface designer who has worked with Adobe since 1983.

From the beginning of his career, Slimbach had harbored the desire to design a book face with a handwritten form. He points out in Adobe's published Brioso sampler that Humanist calligraphy dating from the Italian Renaissance, which began during the 14th century and lasted until the 16th, provided the models for the first typeface designers to work from and it's true to say that the model still works today for contemporary interpretations of Old Style faces. Brioso is a very personal design as it's drawn from a series of practice alphabets lettered by Slimbach over a long period of time; during the extended process, he learned how to reconcile the hand drawn with the constructed while applying his acquired knowledge of digital typeface families. The result is a refined version of his own hand-lettering that tidies character shapes, alignments, and spacing into a cohesive family of fonts.

The Brioso family contains no less than 42 fonts arranged over five weights: Light, Regular, Medium, Semi Bold and Bold. The different weights relate to the different widths of pen-nib a calligrapher might use to create letters that carry the differing levels of emphasis. Additionally, each weight is supplied in four useful optical sizes; Caption is intended for use at very small setting, with Text, Subhead, and Display styles available to cover the rest of the bases. There is also a Poster weight with an italic style, which is the lightest and narrowest of all the fonts, and should only be used at very large sizes to ensure the calligraphic details aren't lost. The palette of alternative glyphs, ligatures, ornaments and swashes is particularly extensive, making this a very pleasurable face to work with when an extra flourish or two is required.

Many uppercase characters have swash alternatives

Brioso Italic

Brioso Light Poster

The Poster weights have tiny calligraphic detailing, that can really only be seen at very large point sizes

Akkurat

| **Country of origin:** Switzerland | **Classification:** Neo-Grotesque Sans
| **Designer:** Laurenz Brunner

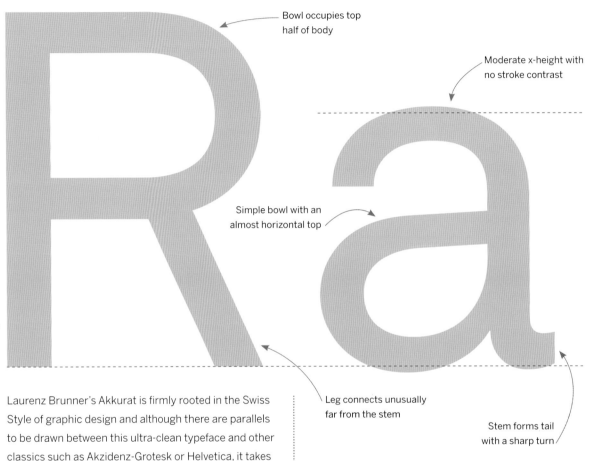

Bowl occupies top half of body

Moderate x-height with no stroke contrast

Simple bowl with an almost horizontal top

Akkurat Regular

Leg connects unusually far from the stem

Stem forms tail with a sharp turn

Laurenz Brunner's Akkurat is firmly rooted in the Swiss Style of graphic design and although there are parallels to be drawn between this ultra-clean typeface and other classics such as Akzidenz-Grotesk or Helvetica, it takes the Neo-Grotesque style to a new level of perfection.

9/12pt Akkurat Regular (Lineto)

LOREM IPSUM DOLOR SIT AMET, CONSECTETUER ADIPISCING ELIT, SED DIAM NONUMMY NIBH euismod tincidunt ut laoreet dolore magna aliquam erat volutpat. Ut wisi enim ad minim veniam, quis nostrud exerci tation ullamcorper suscipit lobortis nisl ut aliquip ex ea commodo consequat. Duis autem vel eum iriure dolor in

12/15pt Akkurat Regular (Lineto)

LOREM IPSUM DOLOR SIT AMET, CONSECTETUER ADIPISCING ELIT, sed diam nonummy nibh euismod tincidunt ut laoreet dolore magna aliquam erat volutpat. Ut wisi enim ad minim veniam, quis nostrud exerci tation ullamcorper suscipit lobortis

The Swiss designer Laurenz Brunner isn't primarily a typeface designer, but in his capacity as a graphic designer he's drawn over 100 typefaces in support of various projects. He studied at the Rietveld Academie in Amsterdam and at the Central Saint Martins in London where, during 2002 and 2003, he designed Akkurat. Initially, Brunner had no plans to publish the face commercially but was persuaded otherwise by Cornel Windlin, one of the founders of Swiss digital type foundry Lineto, and Akkurat was released a year later in 2004. The publisher is an apt choice considering Akkurat follows so closely in the tradition of other classic Swiss Neo-Grotesques, such as Akzidenz-Grotesk or Helvetica. Having said that, Akkurat pushes the pragmatism of the Swiss Style to new levels; its clean lines and precise letterforms make it as much a Geometric sans as it is Neo-Grotesque. It's only touches like the narrow width of the oval-shaped rounds and the binocular "g" that tip it into the latter classification.

The first drawings for Akkurat were done by hand, then painted with acrylic on sheets of A4 paper before they were digitized and refined. It's Brunner's painstaking attention to detail during these stages that gives the face its flavor, which is unusually warm for a sans serif of this kind. Small touches like the short tail on the "l," that binocular "g," and true italics instead of an oblique roman all help to raise its game when compared to its predecessors. These details also add legibility at small point sizes, making Akkurat an excellent choice for running text that simultaneously requires neutrality and approachability.

The six-font Akkurat family is small but perfectly formed with three weights, Light, Regular and Bold, and true italic styles. Since the release of the earliest version, Brunner has revised the character set for the OpenType format. The number of glyphs has increased from 256 to 875, enabling the face to be used to set over 150 languages, and an additional weight, Akkurat Black, has been designed but at the time of writing doesn't appear on the Lineto website.

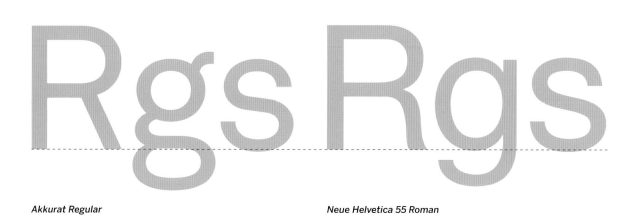

Akkurat Regular

Neue Helvetica 55 Roman

Although Akkurat is a Neo-Grotesque sans, its letterforms achieve a more precise level of geometry

Freight

| **Country of origin:** United States | **Classification:** Humanist Slab/Rational
| **Designer:** Joshua Darden

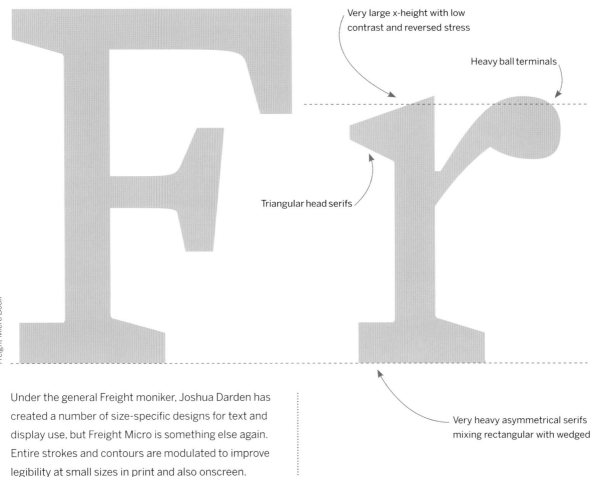

Very large x-height with low contrast and reversed stress

Heavy ball terminals

Triangular head serifs

Freight Micro Book

Very heavy asymmetrical serifs mixing rectangular with wedged

Under the general Freight moniker, Joshua Darden has created a number of size-specific designs for text and display use, but Freight Micro is something else again. Entire strokes and contours are modulated to improve legibility at small sizes in print and also onscreen.

9/12pt Freight Micro Book (GarageFonts)

LOREM IPSUM DOLOR SIT AMET, CONSECTETUER ADIPISCING ELIT, SED DIAM NONUMMY NIBH euismod tincidunt ut laoreet dolore magna aliquam erat volutpat. Ut wisi enim ad minim veniam, quis nostrud exerci tation ullamcorper suscipit lobortis nisl ut aliquip ex ea commodo consequat. Duis autem vel eum iriure dolor in hendrerit in vulputate velit

12/15pt Freight Micro Book (GarageFonts)

LOREM IPSUM DOLOR SIT AMET, CONSECTETUER ADIPISCING ELIT, sed diam nonummy nibh euismod tincidunt ut laoreet dolore magna aliquam erat volutpat. Ut wisi enim ad minim veniam, quis nostrud exerci tation ullamcorper suscipit lobortis nisl

Designed by Joshua Darden in 2004 and published by digital type foundry GarageFonts, Freight is another large typeface family built around a series of size-specific optical variants. Freight Micro sits at the core of the family. It's designed to be set below 9 point in print and for text sizes onscreen, and Darden sums it up nicely in his website commentary as "an exercise in whispering loudly." To help preserve legibility at these small point sizes, Darden has moved beyond the usual ink-trap solutions by modulating entire strokes and contours. A very large x-height provides an additional aid to legibility, and the chunky asymmetrical serifs provide a lively horizontal fluidity. Despite it being designed for use at small sizes, and whether the intention of Darden or not, the unusual forms of the characters also allow Freight Micro to work really well as a display face.

Freight Text does what the name suggests and was designed specifically for running text. Darden tested samples extensively on press during the design process to ensure any potential reproduction issues were ironed out before the fonts were completed. Freight Big is a different proposal altogether and looks a lot more like a traditional Rational serif. It's designed for use as very large headline setting and features a mildly narrow width with fairly tight spacing to preserve horizontal space. Freight Display is Freight Big's less graceful relative; it's still a refined serif but features a slightly lower contrast, making it ideal for more general display use when a warmer tone is required. Darden has also released Freight Sans, a single optical design intended for a broad range of uses at all sizes. It's not necessarily a companion to other Freight styles, but pairs well with Freight Micro and Freight Text.

The different optical sizes of Freight each contain six weights: Black, Bold, Semi Bold, Medium, Book and Light. The italic styles that accompany each are all true italics, which have a distinctly different feel to the roman weights, particularly in the case of the lowercase characters. They were designed concurrently but either style can happily operate with complete independence from the other, which only adds to the intriguing charm of this unusual and versatile family of fonts.

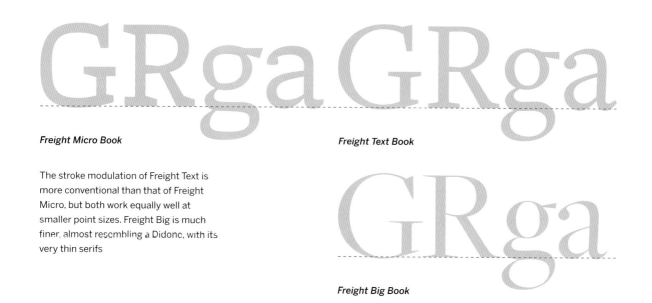

Freight Micro Book

Freight Text Book

The stroke modulation of Freight Text is more conventional than that of Freight Micro, but both work equally well at smaller point sizes. Freight Big is much finer, almost resembling a Didone, with its very thin serifs

Freight Big Book

Bello

| **Country of origin:** The Netherlands | **Classification:** Calligraphic Script
| **Designers:** Akiem Helmling, Bas Jacobs and Sami Kortemäki

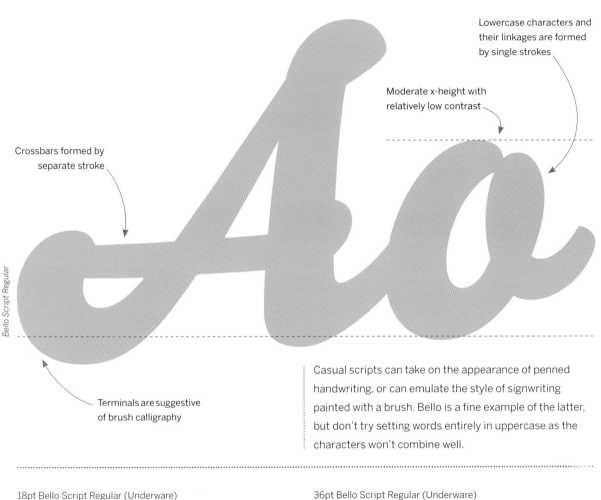

Lowercase characters and
their linkages are formed
by single strokes

Moderate x-height with
relatively low contrast

Crossbars formed by
separate stroke

Bello Script Regular

Terminals are suggestive
of brush calligraphy

Casual scripts can take on the appearance of penned
handwriting, or can emulate the style of signwriting
painted with a brush. Bello is a fine example of the latter,
but don't try setting words entirely in uppercase as the
characters won't combine well.

18pt Bello Script Regular (Underware)

AEQdcgstu

36pt Bello Script Regular (Underware)

AEQdcgstu

72pt Bello Script Regular (Underware)

AEQdcgstu

Bello is one of several award-winning typefaces designed by the pan-European graphic design studio Underware. Theirs is an unusual arrangement in that the three partners, Akiem Helmling, Bas Jacobs and Sami Kortemäki, live in three different cities but work together on a daily basis. Based respectively in Den Haag, Amsterdam, and Helsinki, the partners formed Underware in 1999 and have developed a reputation for innovative type design alongside their other activities, which include running the online typographic resource Typeradio since 2004.

Over the years, a raft of typefaces that attempt to emulate the appearance of sign writing has appeared but few of them manage to capture the vibrancy of the medium as intelligently as Bello. It's based on a large number of hand-drawn sketches; lowercase characters were drawn first with the most common characters such as the "a" and the "e" providing the jumping-off point for the design of and linkages to other characters. The presence of 64 separate ligatures helps to maintain the natural flow of the text and an extensive selection of swash characters can be added to the lowercase at both the beginning and the end of words set in lowercase. As with all fonts of this kind, always ensure that your spacing is set to "metrics" rather than "optical" or the carefully

implemented kerning won't work correctly. As lovely as the Script is, it doesn't work for text set entirely in uppercase and besides, most jobs need a complementary face that can tone down the flourishes for the more straightforward elements of the text, so Underware has included Bello Caps. The authenticity of both fonts is aided by smart touches such as non-lining figures for the Script and lining figures for the Caps, just as a genuine signwriter would have painted them.

The third style included in the complete package performs a neat trick that allows you to create two-color type, where the main body of the text can be one color with a secondary color added to a shadow. The Bello Words font includes 62 common English words so it's a little restrictive in that sense—you can't input whatever text you want—but the choice of words is geared to the kind of projects you might want to use Bello for in the first place, so it's a worthy feature. Downloadable PDFs and full explanations of how to achieve the effect are available on Underware's website but it's easy to create, especially if you have the OpenType version of the font that uses the Discretionary Ligatures function to combine characters correctly.

Bello Caps Regular

When you need something that's a little less showy, or for setting text in upper case, Bello Caps comes in handy

Bello Words

Whitney

| **Country of origin:** United Kingdom | **Classification:** Gothic Sans
| **Designers:** Hoefler & Co.

2004

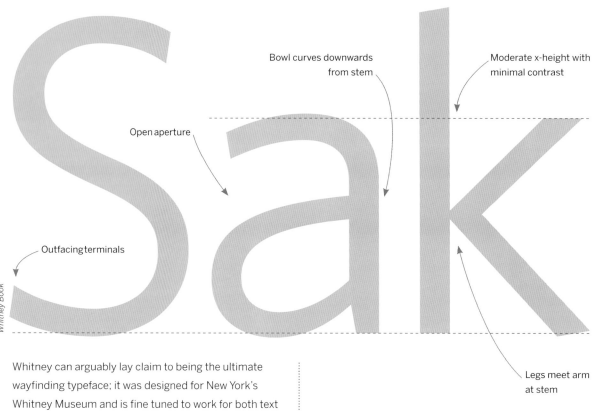

Bowl curves downwards from stem

Moderate x-height with minimal contrast

Open aperture

Outfacing terminals

Whitney Book

Legs meet arm at stem

Whitney can arguably lay claim to being the ultimate wayfinding typeface; it was designed for New York's Whitney Museum and is fine tuned to work for both text and signage. It successfully combines the qualities of both Gothic and Humanist sans in one extensive family.

9/12pt Whitney Book (Hoefler & Co.)

LOREM IPSUM DOLOR SIT AMET, CONSECTETUER ADIPISCING ELIT, SED DIAM NONUMMY NIBH euismod tincidunt ut laoreet dolore magna aliquam erat volutpat. Ut wisi enim ad minim veniam, quis nostrud exerci tation ullamcorper suscipit lobortis nisl ut aliquip ex ea commodo consequat. Duis autem vel eum iriure dolor in hendrerit in vulputate velit esse molestie

12/15pt Whitney Book (Hoefler & Co.)

LOREM IPSUM DOLOR SIT AMET, CONSECTETUER ADIPISCING ELIT, SED diam nonummy nibh euismod tincidunt ut laoreet dolore magna aliquam erat volutpat. Ut wisi enim ad minim veniam, quis nostrud exerci tation ullamcorper suscipit lobortis nisl ut aliquip ex ea

Whitney is a triumph of both form and function as it succeeds as a typeface for signage, and works really well for editorial setting. It was designed at Hoefler & Co. (or Hoefler & Frere-Jones, as the firm was known before the much publicized split between Jonathan Hoefler and Tobias Frere-Jones occurred in 2014), in response to a commission from New York's Whitney Museum. The brief required a new design able to work as a corporate face across the board for printed matter and for all the public signage throughout the museum's buildings. This isn't an easy thing to achieve, as typefaces suitable for use in exhibition catalogs and other marketing material need to flourish in the relatively cramped environment of the printed page, while type designed for wayfinding needs open forms legible from a variety of distances (signs have to be read close-up too).

For over 100 years, Gothic sans serif faces have been a go-to style for editorial designers; Morris Fuller Benton's News Gothic is a classic example of a workhorse sans that has never really gone out of fashion but perhaps lacks some of the detailing that we've come to expect today from our high-performance OpenType fonts. On the flip side, when we think of the archetypal signage face, one of the first to come to mind is Frutiger with its Humanist leanings

designed to provide that famous legibility. Whitney manages to bridge the divide between these two styles of sans serif and introduces an overtly contemporary feel at the same time. It has a fairly compact form so is space efficient, but its moderately large x-height and very open apertures and large counters mean it's legible at any point size from 6 to 600. It's unusual for one design without a variety of optical sizes to work so well across quite so many applications.

There are six weights of Whitney ranging from Light to Black, all with a true italic style, small caps, lining and Old Style figures, and a wealth of alternative glyphs. It's a great example of OpenType technology implementation with no less than 13 stylistic set options, all of which are well documented on the Hoefler & Co. website. There's also a six-weight family of condensed romans for compact headlines, and the very useful Whitney Index styles in four flavors, black round and square, and white round and square. These are brilliant for labeling maps and diagrams, saving you the fiddly job of aligning a text box above a bullet to create combined character groups.

Whitney Book

News Gothic BT

The classic letterforms of News Gothic are taken to a new level with the contemporary liveliness of Whitney

Ministry Script

| **Country of origin:** Argentina | **Classification:** Calligraphic Script
| **Designer:** Ale Paul

2005

Many characters are formed by one continuous stroke

Loop ascenders can be exchanged with alternative standard strokes or swash characters

Low x-height with high contrast

Thousands of kerning pairs ensure fluid junctions between characters

Ministry Script

Berta

Ministry Script, a highlight of the extensive collection of script fonts designed by the team at Sudtipos, is a landmark typeface. It has over 1,000 characters but, more importantly, no less than 99, 814 separate kerning pairs. Could that be a record?

18pt Ministry Script (Sudtipos)

Ragtor28

72pt Ministry Script (Sudtipos)

Ragtor28

36pt Ministry Script (Sudtipos)

Ragtor28

The Argentinian digital type foundry collective Sudtipos was jointly founded in 2002 by Ale Paul, Ariel Garofalo, Claudio Pousada and Diego Giaccone. It's the first collective of its kind in Argentina and is well known for its large selection of accomplished script faces. Ministry Script, drawn and digitized by Ale Paul in 2005, is a highlight of the Sudtipos collection. He designed it to be "a time capsule that marks both the Euro-American ad art of the 1920s and 1930s, and the current new-millennium acrobatics of digital type." The advertising reference is important here, and indeed for all scripts designed in this casual hand- or brush-written style. During the first half of the 20th century, the majority of text was set on either a Linotype or a Monotype machine, but for the most part advertisements were put together using a lot of hand-lettered type.

Paul didn't want to create a revival—he preferred the idea of creating a face that preserves the spirit of the 1920s but is firmly rooted in the 21st century, a face capable of doing what vintage calligraphy could do before ramping things up. He set out to design as many different variants of each character as current technology can handle, taking the handling capabilities of Adobe *InDesign* and Adobe *Illustrator* as his benchmark applications for OpenType implementation. Ten years on, OpenType technology has, of course, improved and spread to other software options, but Adobe's flagship applications are still out in front.

Paul states that "never before has a script typeface given you so many creative options." One might assume this is merely marketing speak but in the case of Ministry Script it's not a hollow claim. There is only one weight but that shouldn't be off-putting; my personal feeling is that extra weights of a script face (often the Bold) are sometimes less successful than the more natural-looking Regular weights. If the one weight is balanced perfectly then there's no need for extra options. What Ministry Script does have in spades are characters, over 1,000 in fact, including heaps of contextual and stylistic alternatives, swash characters, and ligatures, and Paul has calculated that there are no less than 99,814 separate kerning pairs. It's a lot to navigate, so Sudtipos provide a comprehensive 43-page downloadable guide with character maps and a personal and detailed explanation of the design process behind Ministry Script.

The use of OpenType Swash characters can be applied to individual characters

Verlag

| **Country of origin:** United States | **Classification:** Geometric Sans
| **Designers:** Hoefler & Co.

2006

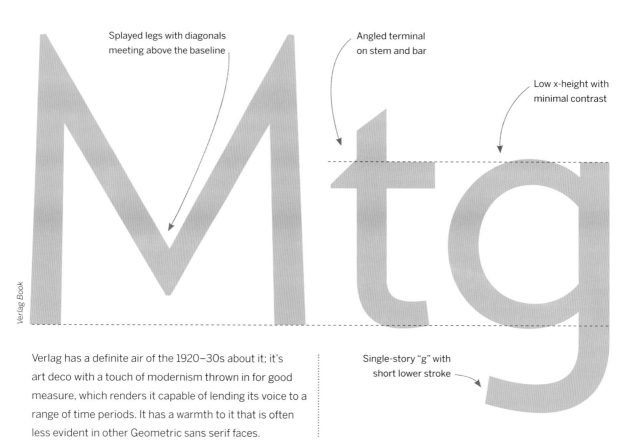

Splayed legs with diagonals
meeting above the baseline

Angled terminal
on stem and bar

Low x-height with
minimal contrast

Verlag Book

Verlag has a definite air of the 1920–30s about it; it's
art deco with a touch of modernism thrown in for good
measure, which renders it capable of lending its voice to a
range of time periods. It has a warmth to it that is often
less evident in other Geometric sans serif faces.

Single-story "g" with
short lower stroke

9/12pt Verlag Book (Hoefler & Co.)

LOREM IPSUM DOLOR SIT AMET, CONSECTETUER
ADIPISCING ELIT, SED DIAM NONUMMY NIBH
euismod tincidunt ut laoreet dolore magna aliquam erat
volutpat. Ut wisi enim ad minim veniam, quis nostrud exerci
tation ullamcorper suscipit lobortis nisl ut aliquip ex ea
commodo consequat. Duis autem vel eum iriure dolor in
hendrerit in vulputate velit esse molestie consequat, vel illum

12/15pt Verlag Book (Hoefler & Co.)

LOREM IPSUM DOLOR SIT AMET,
CONSECTETUER ADIPISCING ELIT,
sed diam nonummy nibh euismod tincidunt
ut laoreet dolore magna aliquam erat
volutpat. Ut wisi enim ad minim veniam, quis
nostrud exerci tation ullamcorper suscipit
lobortis nisl ut aliquip ex ea commodo

A couple of spreads earlier in this book we looked at Hoefler & Co.'s Whitney, a typeface designed for New York's Whitney Museum. Verlag is also the product of a commission from a museum but it's a different kind of proposal, referencing the pre-war modernism of the Guggenheim Museum's iconic art deco lettering. The team at Hoefler & Co. (or Hoefler & Frere-Jones, as it was in 2006) created a family of 30 fonts from the original six designed specifically for the museum, and in the process created a typeface that can quite reasonably be seen as a 21st-century Futura. I'm not for a second suggesting Verlag is a replacement, or even an interpretation, although there's much to suggest that Paul Renner's classic Geometric sans is a clear source of inspiration. However, if you want Futura but need a little more flexibility and bit of extra sparkle, Verlag can provide it.

Verlag has a degree of warmth and elegance to it that is often lacking in other Geometric sans serifs. This doesn't come from any Humanist touches as Verlag's geometry remains strict and stroke contrast is minimal, but elements of the design give this face a touch more character than one might expect. The angled terminals on the bars of the "f" and "t" feel less severe than those featured on other Geometrics such as Futura or Erbar, and the short lower stroke of the "g" feels very modern and snappy. Also, the bowl of the "R" extends slightly above the cap height, a small detail that somehow makes the character feel a lot more organic.

The full Verlag family consists of 30 fonts split into five weights and three widths, all with italic styles. Weights range from Extra Light to Black, and widths are Normal, Condensed and Compressed. Although the italics appear to be oblique romans at first glance, there are a few details here and there that go beyond mere optical corrections, such as the extended descender of the lowercase "f." It's often the case that condensed, and certainly compressed, widths lack italic styles so their inclusion is a welcome addition.

Verlag Book

Futura ND Book

Rounded bowls and angled terminals make Verlag feel less severe than other Geometric sans faces, such as Futura

Archer

| **Country of origin:** United States | **Classification:** Geometric Slab
| **Designers:** Hoefler & Co.

2008

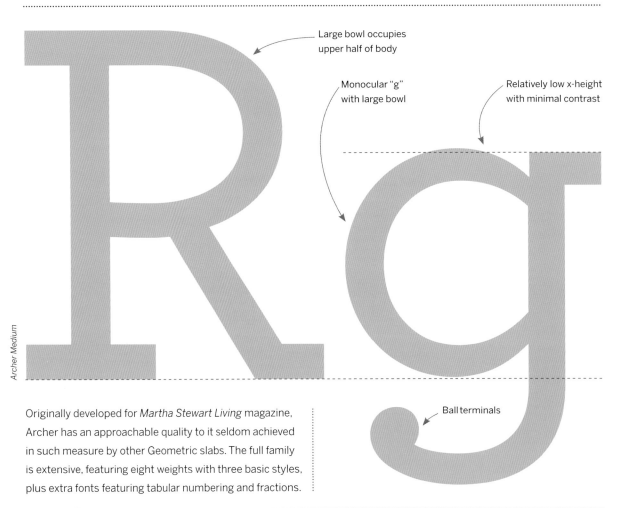

Large bowl occupies
upper half of body

Monocular "g"
with large bowl

Relatively low x-height
with minimal contrast

Archer Medium

Ball terminals

Originally developed for *Martha Stewart Living* magazine,
Archer has an approachable quality to it seldom achieved
in such measure by other Geometric slabs. The full family
is extensive, featuring eight weights with three basic styles,
plus extra fonts featuring tabular numbering and fractions.

9/12pt Archer Book (Hoefler & Co.)

LOREM IPSUM DOLOR SIT AMET, CONSECTETUER
ADIPISCING ELIT, SED DIAM NONUMMY NIBH
euismod tincidunt ut laoreet dolore magna aliquam
erat volutpat. Ut wisi enim ad minim veniam, quis
nostrud exerci tation ullamcorper suscipit lobortis nisl
ut aliquip ex ea commodo consequat. Duis autem vel
eum iriure dolor in hendrerit in vulputate velit esse

12/15pt Archer Book (Hoefler & Co.)

LOREM IPSUM DOLOR SIT AMET,
CONSECTETUER ADIPISCING ELIT,
sed diam nonummy nibh euismod
tincidunt ut laoreet dolore magna
aliquam erat volutpat. Ut wisi enim ad
minim veniam, quis nostrud exerci tation
ullamcorper suscipit lobortis nisl ut

Archer is one of those typefaces that appeared to be everywhere in the few years after its initial release, and its popularity can be explained with a few key points related to the design. As a Geometric slab you might expect Archer to be engineered and chilly, but it's not; it has a gently feminine quality to it with curved forms that are seldom found in typefaces from this classification. It's an open and airy typeface with large bowls and counters but the biggest injection of character is provided by the ball terminals, an unusual addition for a Geometric slab. This was new, very fresh and quite unique, and designers immediately loved it.

Archer was designed in response to a commercial brief for a new editorial typeface. *Martha Stewart Living* identified the need for a fresh new face for the monthly magazine and asked Hoefler & Frere-Jones (now Hoefler & Co.) for advice. Their answer was a new kind of slab serif; a kind of hybrid that draws inspiration from both Grotesque (or Antique) and Geometric slabs to create a face that is by turns approachable but not flippant, and attractive but not decorative. The Grotesque and Geometric styles of slab serif have prevailed for the last 200 years with little to challenge their domination. Grotesques typically have a moderate contrast, bracketed serifs, an "R" with an upturned tail, and ball terminals. They're

visually more accessible but there's a price to pay for this; they carry a distinct retro air that isn't always appropriate. Geometrics have minimal contrast, unbracketed serifs and terminals cut at right-angles to the strokes. They feel a lot sharper, of course, and are less prone to feeling dated, but lack the personality of a Grotesque. Archer takes a Geometric form but adds those cheerful ball terminals back in to many of the lowercase and even a few of the uppercase characters, creating an inviting design that works well for both text and headline setting.

The Archer family is extensive with eight weights in a single width, all with true italics. As one would expect from a Hoefler & Co. face, the character set is extensive and from the beginning was designed to answer the everyday typographic challenges set by complex editorial content. *Martha Stewart Living* is regularly packed with lists, recipes, diagrams and tables, so Archer contains everything a typesetter might need. There are lining and Old Style figures; tabular figures that are duplexed to avoid unwanted text wraps when table entries are set bold; a huge selection of fractions including fifths, sixths and eighths; contextual punctuation; and a set of circled indices from zero to nine, which are indispensable when setting text that features numbered steps.

Archer Book

Neutraface Slab Book

Archer's ball terminals make the face more cheerful than other equally stylish Geomteric slabs

Vitesse

| **Country of origin:** United States | **Classification:** Humanist Slab
| **Designers:** Hoefler & Co.

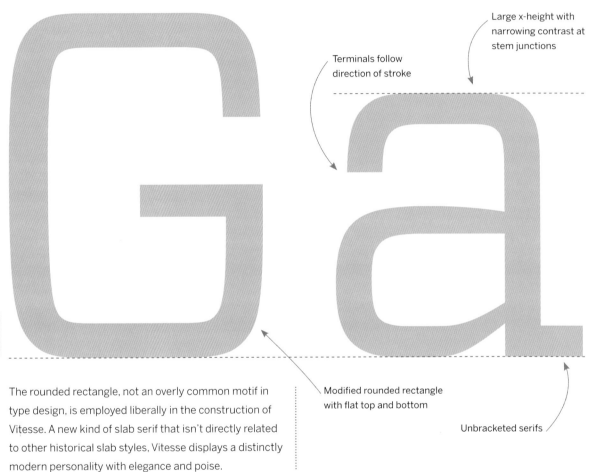

Large x-height with narrowing contrast at stem junctions

Terminals follow direction of stroke

Vitesse Book

The rounded rectangle, not an overly common motif in type design, is employed liberally in the construction of Vitesse. A new kind of slab serif that isn't directly related to other historical slab styles, Vitesse displays a distinctly modern personality with elegance and poise.

Modified rounded rectangle with flat top and bottom

Unbracketed serifs

9/12pt Vitesse Book (Hoefler & Co.)

LOREM IPSUM DOLOR SIT AMET, CONSECTETUER ADIPISCING ELIT, SED DIAM nonummy nibh euismod tincidunt ut laoreet dolore magna aliquam erat volutpat. Ut wisi enim ad minim veniam, quis nostrud exerci tation ullamcorper suscipit lobortis nisl ut aliquip ex ea commodo consequat. Duis autem

12/15pt Vitesse Book (Hoefler & Co.)

LOREM IPSUM DOLOR SIT AMET, CONSECTETUER ADIPISCING ELIT, sed diam nonummy nibh euismod tincidunt ut laoreet dolore magna aliquam erat volutpat. Ut wisi enim ad minim veniam, quis nostrud exerci tation ullamcorper suscipit

As mentioned on the previous spread, Hoefler & Co. know a thing or two about reinventing the slab serif. Archer melds the Grotesque and Geometric styles to great effect using visual notes from the 19th and the 20th centuries, but Vitesse is something different again. The Hoefler & Co. team have come up with something fresh in Vitesse, which they think of as a 21st-century slab serif. Humanist slabs like Vitesse are not a new invention in themselves; the ground-breaking face PMN Caecilia, designed by Peter Matthias Noordzij in 1991, is considered to be the earliest Humanist slab and Freight Micro is another fine example of the style. However, Vitesse offers something quite different as it's built around a different form, the rounded rectangle.

Nineteenth-century slabs are commonly based on elliptical forms, and the circle is a frequent jumping-off point for 20th-century typeface designs. It was the alternative and relatively untried (at least for a slab serif) geometry of the rounded rectangle that sparked the Hoefler & Co. team's interest. It's surprising that this shape hasn't appeared more often in type as it's a familiar architectural feature and crops up frequently in everything from furniture to fabric design. It's a flexible form that can feel very engineered although retaining a degree of organic dynamism, but at the same time presents several key challenges to a type designer. Most notably, great care has to be taken to ensure the "D" and the "O" are distinct from one another; typefaces with this kind of engineered look must walk a careful line between simplicity and complexity. Underplay the serifs and legibility is degraded, overplay them and the subtleties of the design are lost. Hoefler & Co. have got this right with Vitesse, leaving off seriffed details where they're not needed in order to retain the familiar forms of the more complex characters. The personality afforded by the rounded rectangle—actually a more complex form with flat surfaces at top and bottom and subtly curved sides in the case of Vitesse—provides this face with something quite unique when compared to other Humanist slabs.

The Vitesse family is a fairly straightforward offering for a Hoefler & Co. typeface. There are six weights in one width, including Thin, Light, Book, Medium, Bold and Black; all have italic styles that are optically correct oblique romans. The OpenType versions of the fonts use Hoefler & Co.'s Latin-X character set, which facilitates text setting in over 140 languages. Vitesse also has a sans serif sibling, Forza, designed specifically as a companion face following a commission from *Wired* magazine.

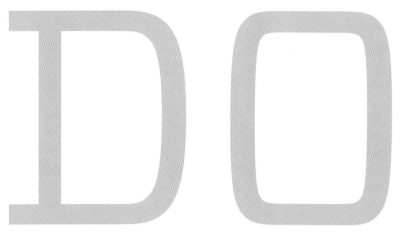

The danger of engineered typefaces like Vitesse is that certain characters can look very similar, particularly at smaller sizes. Careful control over details such as the serifs will combat the problem

Vitesse Book

Heron Serif

| **Country of origin:** United States | **Classification:** Grotesque Slab
| **Designer:** Cyrus Highsmith

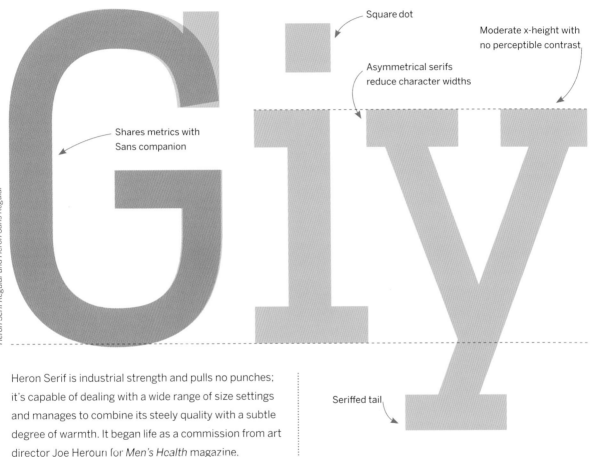

Heron Serif Regular and Heron Sans Regular

Square dot

Asymmetrical serifs
reduce character widths

Moderate x-height with
no perceptible contrast

Shares metrics with
Sans companion

Seriffed tail

Heron Serif is industrial strength and pulls no punches; it's capable of dealing with a wide range of size settings and manages to combine its steely quality with a subtle degree of warmth. It began life as a commission from art director Joe Heroun for *Men's Health* magazine.

9/12pt Heron Serif Light (Font Bureau)

LOREM IPSUM DOLOR SIT AMET, CONSECTETUER ADIPISCING ELIT, SED DIAM NONUMMY NIBH euismod tincidunt ut laoreet dolore magna aliquam erat volutpat. Ut wisi enim ad minim veniam, quis nostrud exerci tation ullamcorper suscipit lobortis nisl ut aliquip ex ea commodo consequat. Duis autem vel eum iriure dolor in hendrerit in vulputate velit esse

12/15pt Heron Serif Light (Font Bureau)

LOREM IPSUM DOLOR SIT AMET, CONSECTETUER ADIPISCING ELIT, SED diam nonummy nibh euismod tincidunt ut laoreet dolore magna aliquam erat volutpat. Ut wisi enim ad minim veniam, quis nostrud exerci tation ullamcorper suscipit lobortis nisl ut aliquip ex ea

It seems that magazine commissions have at least equaled newspapers as one of the richest sources of new typeface designs these days. Heron Sans and its companion Heron Serif were created in answer to a brief from Joseph Heroun as part of a redesign of *Men's Health*. The brief called for letterforms that felt industrial and machine-like with a touch of warmth and refinement, and Cyrus Highsmith of digital type foundry Font Bureau has achieved just this with both the Heron styles.

It's a typeface that looks solid and ready for action; thanks to its monolinear qualities with no visible contrast, all its weights and styles, including the boldest weights, articulate a consistent visual feel. Bold weights can sometimes feel softer and more approachable because of increases in the contrast of the strokes, but Heron Serif resists this—every member of this family is tough as old boots. That's not to say that it's an unattractive face as it has a great deal of personality and poise, and touches like the asymmetrical serifs and oval rounds, which are quite narrow and flat-sided, stop Heron Serif from nudging over into Geometric sans territory. As a publication face, Heron Serif succeeds at both headline and text setting, although the generally dark color of the face may dictate the use of the lightest weight for text setting at small sizes.

Heron Serif is a large family with five weights and two widths; weights range from Light through Regular, Medium, Semi Bold and Bold. Italic styles are true italics rather than oblique romans for both the normal and condensed widths. The Heron Sans family contains the exact same range of weights and styles and has very similar metrics to its seriffed companion. Stroke angles vary a little here and there to compensate for the lack of serifs but the two faces can be used concurrently to good effect. Heron Sans is arguably the better choice for text as it can be set a little tighter and colors less darkly but Heron Serif catches the eye more readily.

Heron Serif Regular

Heron Sans Regular

The metrics of the serif and sans serif weights of Heron are practically identical, and some characters are identical

Selva

| **Country of origin:** Germany | **Classification:** Blackletter
| **Designer:** Gunnar Link

2012

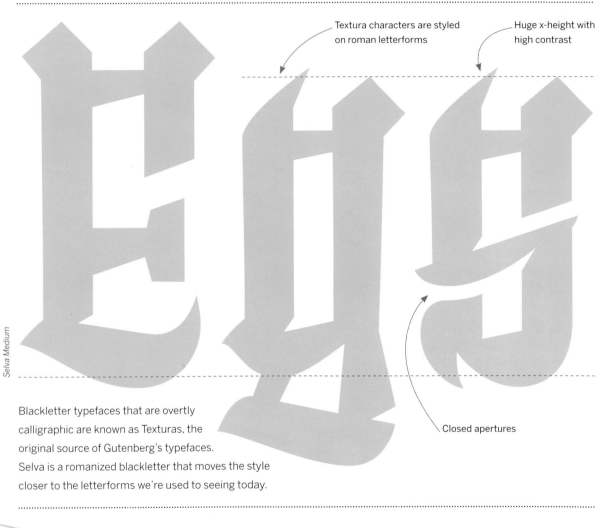

Textura characters are styled
on roman letterforms

Huge x-height with
high contrast

Closed apertures

Selva Medium

Blackletter typefaces that are overtly
calligraphic are known as Texturas, the
original source of Gutenberg's typefaces.
Selva is a romanized blackletter that moves the style
closer to the letterforms we're used to seeing today.

18pt Selva Medium (Gunnar Link)

AGHLQakpy24

36pt Selva Medium (Gunnar Link)

AGHLQakpy24

72pt Selva Medium (Gunnar Link)

AGHLQakpy24

While I was compiling the list of the 100 typefaces that form the backbone of this book, Florian Hardwig kindly drew my attention towards this typeface, and I thought, "What better way to end the story." We began in the 1440s with Gutenberg and his movable type in the blackletter style, and we're ending with a 21st-century blackletter, Selva, by the German designer Gunnar Link.

Except Selva isn't strictly a blackletter. At first glance, it looks like a Gothic Textura— Textura being a subset of blackletter, formed from the most calligraphic blackletter faces— but it's far from being a revival. Link describes it as a modern interpretation of 14th-century calligraphy, which in itself was the original source of the letterforms cut and cast by Gutenberg. The principal differences with Selva are directly evident in the letterforms, which are closer to the kind of shapes we're used to seeing today; this is what's termed a romanized blackletter. Other examples of romanized blackletter faces include TypeTogether's Eskapade and Underware's Fakir, but Selva retains enough of the Textura to keep it hovering more centrally between blackletter and roman letterforms. Link has included a couple of key alternative lowercase characters, the "f" and the "h" (accessed automatically by invoking the single OpenType stylistic set option), which extend below the baseline just as a traditional Textura would and help retain a more historical feel when desired. He's also stuck closely to using fairly homogenous letterforms for certain characters such as the "D," "O," and "U," which makes it a little tricky to identify on their own, highlighting the very reason that type design shifted to a roman form in the 15th century. However, when used contextually the characters become much easier to identify, proving that Link's carefully crafted characters can fulfill their romanized function and look decoratively beautiful at the same time.

The family contains four weights, Regular, Medium, Bold and Black. There is of course no italic, this being a Textura, although it's not unheard of in contemporary romanized blackletter faces. However, I think it's to Link's credit that he wasn't tempted to conform to the notion that every typeface family has to have a range of weights that all have italics, regardless of any historical points of reference.

Selva Regular

When seen as individual Textura letterforms, it's not always easy to distinguish a "D" from an "O" or "U"

Glossary

Aperture

The opening between the exterior and interior of a glyph.

Apex

The upper point at which the stems of a character meet to form a junction with an angle of less than 90 degrees; for example, the uppermost point of a capital "A."

Arch

A curved stroke that extends from a straight stem but does not form a bowl; for example, the top of a lowercase "f" or the bottom of a lowercase "j."

Arm

A stroke that extends either horizontally or diagonally from a vertical stroke; for example, the top of an uppercase "E" or the strokes of an uppercase "K."

Ascender

The part of a lowercase character that extends or ascends above the x-height of the other lowercase characters in a typeface; for example, the top part of the lowercase "h" or "d."

Ball terminal

A circular termination at the end of an arm in characters such as lowercase "a" or "r."

Beak

A sharp projection that usually appears at the end of the arch of a lowercase "f," as well as in the characters "c," "j," "r" and "y."

Bowl

The curved stroke enclosing the rounded or elliptical shape formed in characters such as "B" or "a." Bowls can be closed or open, as seen in the uppercase "P" of Garamond.

Bracketed serif

A serif transitioning from the stem of a character in one unbroken curve; for example, the Transitional typeface Baskerville has bracketed serifs.

Cap height

The height measured from the baseline to the top of uppercase letters in a font. This will not necessarily equal the height of the ascenders.

Color

The tonal value or visual weight of a block of text, expressed as a grayscale. There are many factors that can influence typographic color, including letterform style, stroke width, weight, size and leading.

Counter

The space formed within characters such as "c" or "g." They can be open or closed and shouldn't be confused with bowls, which are in fact strokes.

Crossbar

The horizontal bar that connects two strokes in characters such as an uppercase "A" or "H."

Cross stroke

The horizontal stroke that cuts across the stem of lowercase characters such as "f" or "t."

Crotch

The pointed space formed when an arm or an arch meets a stem; for example, in the inner top corner of an "F." Crotches can be either obtuse (more than 90 degrees) or acute (less than 90 degrees).

Descender

The part of a lowercase character that extends below the baseline of the other lowercase characters in a typeface; for example, the bottom portion of the lowercase "p" or "y."

Double-story

A lowercase "a" with a closed bowl and a stem with a finial arm above, or a lowercase "g" with a closed bowl and ear above a linked loop; for example, Adobe Jenson features a double-story "a" and "g."

Ear

The small projection that appears on lowercase characters such as "g" in certain typefaces.

Expert characters

These have become increasingly outmoded since the advent of the OpenType format, because all characters can now be incorporated into a single font for each weight, but there are still plenty of older-format fonts in use today. Designed for Type 1 PostScript fonts, expert characters are non-standard letterforms extra to the standard character set, which may incorporate a swash or accent, or be an alternative form of a standard character.

Extenders

A common term used interchangeably for both ascenders and descenders.

Eye

A fully closed bowl, as seen in a lowercase "e."

Finial

A tapered, curved terminal at the end of a stroke; for example, at the bottom of a "C." Swashes and ornamental flourishes are also commonly called finials.

Font

All the characters or glyphs for one style (or font file) within a font family. The terms "font" and "typeface" are often interchanged, but technically there's a difference. This is best illustrated through the use of an example: Gotham is a typeface family; Gotham Bold Italic is a font.

Font family

All of the point sizes, weights and styles of one set of typefaces. A typical family consists of at least four styles; the most common are roman, italic, bold, and bold italic. However, it's now common to find superfamilies with 10 or more weights and styles ranging from thin to heavy.

Glyph

Each individual character in a font is a glyph; for example, symbols and all of the alternative forms for characters are individual glyphs.

Legibility

The measure of how easy it is to distinguish one letter of a typeface from another. The design of the typeface bears primary responsibility for the level of legibility, not the typographic styling of a layout.

Ligature

A single glyph composed of two or sometimes three characters paired together in certain combinations. Common examples are "fi," "fl" and "Th," with the exact configuration dependent on the choice of typeface.

Loop

A closed counter that extends below the baseline and connects to a bowl by a link. A double-story "g" features a loop.

Lowercase

The uncapitalized characters of a typeface. The term derives from the fact that small letters were kept in the lower compartments of a type case when metal type was composed by hand. Historically, lowercase letters were known as minuscules.

OpenType

A font format developed jointly by Adobe and Microsoft. The primary advantage over previous formats is the ability to include up to 65,536 glyphs in a single font, plus advanced typographic features that allow the automatic substitution of alternative characters or glyphs in supporting applications such as InDesign or Illustrator. Font files are cross-platform and can be installed under both Mac OS and Windows.

Point

A unit of measurement expressing font size. A point equals 0.0139 inches (0.0353 cm).

Point size

The height of the body of a typeface in points.

Readability

Readability isn't necessarily dependent on the legibility of the chosen typeface. It's primarily the responsibility of the designer. A highly legible font used poorly in a layout will not produce good readability.

Serif

In a serif typeface, the small stroke that completes the arms, stems, tails and descenders of individual characters.

Single-story

A lowercase "a" with a closed bowl and no finial arm above, or a lowercase "g" with a closed bowl, stem, and tail; for example, Futura features a single-story "a" and "g."

Spur

The small projection that occurs at the terminals of some characters, such as the uppercase "S" of Arnhem.

Stem

The main vertical strokes of a character, such as the upright strokes on either side of a capital "H."

Stress

The vertical, diagonal and occasionally horizontal emphasis suggested by a character's stroke. Horizontal stress is also referred to as reversed stress.

Stroke

The structural component of any character that is neither vertical nor horizontal. Stems are sometimes called vertical strokes, while crossbars can be called horizontal strokes.

Swash

An ornamental stroke extension used to add a decorative element to a standard character or glyph.

Tail

The descending stroke on characters such as the "Q" or the bottom of the leg of an "R."

Terminal

The end of a stem or stroke.

Typeface

A set of characters, independent of individual point size, but with common design characteristics, classification, serif style and so on. The terms "font" and "typeface" are often interchanged, but there is a difference. This is best illustrated through the use of an example: Optima Nova is a typeface family; Optima Nova Light Italic is a font.

Unbracketed serif

A serif that joins the stem of a character at a 90-degree angle. Unbracketed serifs are a characteristic of Rational serif faces such as Bodoni or Geometric Slabs such as Rockwell.

Uppercase

The capitalized characters of a typeface. The term derives from the fact that capital letters were kept in the upper compartments of a type case when metal type was composed by hand. Historically, uppercase letters were known as majuscules.

Wedge serif

A serif that transitions from the stem of a character at an angled slope without curves. Linotype's distinctive Neue Swift is a fine example of a font with wedge serifs.

Weight

The thickness of a glyph's strokes. Type terminology uses the term "weight" to describe individual fonts within a typeface family.

Width

Width can indicate whether a typeface has been either expanded or compressed when used as part of a font's name; for example, "condensed" or "extended." It can also be used as a general term to describe the average space occupied by a font's characters.

x-height

The height of a lowercase "x." The "x" is used to define this measurement because it has no ascenders or descenders and no part of the character extends below the baseline.

Bibliography

Blackwell, Lewis. *20th-Century Type.* London: Laurence King Publishing, 2004.

Bringhurst, Robert. *The Elements of Typographic Style.* Vancouver: Hartley and Marks Publishers, 2004.

Carter, Sebastian. *Twentieth-Century Type Designers.* London: W.W. Norton and Co., 1995.

Cheng, Karen. *Designing Type.* London: Laurence King Publishing, 2006.

Coles, Stephen. *The Anatomy of Type: A Graphic Guide to 100 Typefaces.* New York: Harper Design, 2012.

Garfield, Simon. *Just My Type: A Book About Fonts.* London: Profile Books, 2010.

Jaspert, W. Pincus; Berry, W. Turner and Johnson, A. F. *Encyclopaedia of Typefaces.* London: Cassell Illustrated, 2008.

Lawson, Alexander. *Anatomy of a Typeface.* New Hampshire: David R. Godine, Publisher, Ltd., 1990.

Loxley, Simon. *Type: the Secret History of Letters.* London: I.B. Tauris & Co. Ltd, 2004.

McGrew, Mac. *American Metal Typefaces of the Twentieth Century.* New Rochelle: The Myriade Press, 1986.

Macmillan, Neil. *An A–Z of Type Designers.* London: Laurence King Publishers, 2006.

Meggs, Philip and Carter, Rob. *Typographic Specimens: The Great Typefaces.* New York: John Wiley & Sons, Inc., 1993.

Sutton, James and Bartram, Alan. *Typefaces for Books.* London: The British Library Publishing Division, 1990.

Online reference

Typedia: typedia.com

Typophile: typophile.com

Typographica: typographica.org

The Font Feed: fontfeed.com

Luc Devroye: luc.devroye.org/fonts.html

The Type Directors Club: tdc.org

Eye magazine: eyemagazine.com

Print magazine: printmag.com

I Love Typography: ilovetypography.com

The Foundries

....

Adobe: adobe.com

Alter Littera: alterlittera.com

Commercial Type: commercialtype.com

Dutch Type Library: dutchtypelibrary.nl

Elsner+Flake: fonts4ever.com

Emigre: emigre.com

Enschedé: teff.nl

Font Bureau: fontbureau.com

FontFont: fontfont.com

GarageFonts: garagefonts.com

Gunnar Link: gunnarlink.net

Hoefler & Co.: typography.com

House Industries: houseind.com/fonts/

Lineto: lineto.com

Linotype: linotype.com

LucasFonts: lucasfonts.com

Mark Simonson: marksimonson.com/fonts

Monotype: monotype.com

MVB Fonts: mvbfonts.com

Neufville: neufville.visigroupe.net

Our Type: ourtype.com

P22: p22.com

Parkinson Type Design: typedesign.com

Production Type: productiontype.com

SoftMaker: softmaker.com

Storm Type Foundry: stormtype.com

Sudtipos: sudtipos.com

Underware: underware.nl

(URW)++: urwpp.de

Index

Aicher, Otl 171

Akkurat 226–7
  Akkurat Black 227

Akzidenz-Grotesk 62–3
  Akzidenz-Grotesk Next 63

Albertus 100–1
  Albertus MT 101

Aldus 109, 128

ALOT Gutenberg A 12

Amber 135

Amelia 134–5

Americana 140–1

Antique Olive 132–3

Archer 238–9

Arnhem 12, 218–19
  Arnhem Display 219
  Arnhem Fine 219

Arrighi 77

Atalante 71

Austin 41

Austin, Richard 41, 47

Barber, Ken 221

Barnbrook, Jonathan 193

Barnes, Paul 41, 167

Barney, Gerry 159

Baron, Fabien 185

Base Nine & Twelve 206–7

Baskerville 38–9

Baskerville, John 13, 23, 39, 211

Bates, Keith 95

Bauer, Konrad F. 117

Bauhaus 54, 87, 89
  see also ITC Bauhaus

Baum, Walter 117

Bayer, Herbert 153

Belizio 49

Bell 40–1

Bell Centennial 154–5

Bell Gothic 155

Bello 230–1
  Bello Caps 231
  Bello Words 231

Bembo 26–7
  Bembo Book 27

Benguiat, Ed 69, 147, 151, 153, 166

Benton, Linn Boyd 53, 56, 59

Benton, Morris Fuller 25, 56, 59, 61, 65, 71, 73, 75, 103

Benton Sans 75, 166, 204–5
  Benton Sans Book 205

Berlow, David 49, 73, 167, 197

Bertsch, Fred 81

Besley, Robert 49

Bickham Script 212–13

Black, Roger 167, 197

Bloemsma, Evert 133

Bodoni 42–3
  Bauer Bodoni 43
  ITC Bodoni 43

Bodoni, Giambattista 43

Bookman 68–9
  ITC Bookman 69

Bookmania 69

Bourcellier, Laurent 37

Brainerd, Paul 162

Brioso 164, 224–5

Bronkhorst, Mark van 223

Brunner, Laurenz 227

Bullen, Henry Lewis 35, 57

Burgess, Starling 99

Burke, Jackson 75

Burns, Aaron 147, 157

Caledonia 106–7

Calvert, Margaret 123

Camelot 79

Carnase, Tom 147

Carter, Matthew 47, 155, 157, 166, 203

Caruso, Victor 73, 89, 153

Caslon 34–5
  Adobe Caslon 35
  Caslon Old Style 35

Caslon, William 35

Cassandre, Adolphe Mouron 105

Caxton Initials 151

Centaur 25, 76–7

Century 56, 58–9
  Century Old Style 59
  Century Schoolbook 59
  ITC Century 59

Chappell, Warren 173

Cheltenham 60–1
  Cheltenham Old Style 61
  ITC Cheltenham 61

Citizen 165

Clarendon 48–9
  Craw Clarendon 49

Cleverdon, Douglas 55, 91

Cloister 25

Coles, Stephen 10, 14

Consort 49

Cooper, Oswald 65, 81

Cooper Black 80–1
  Cooper Black Italic Swash 81

Copperplate Gothic 70–1

Cornelia 107

Cruz, Andy 221

Darden, Joshua 229

Davis, Stan 135

De Vinne, Theodore L. 59

Deck, Barry 177

Devroye, Luc 105, 135

Dickinson, Samuel Nelson 47
Didot, Firmin 45, 185
digital fonts 161–3
DIN 96–7
    DIN Next 97
    FF DIN 97
Does, Bram de 189
DTL Fleischmann 190–1
Dwiggins, William Addison 107

Eckmann, Otto 67
Eckmannschrift (Eckmann) 66–7
Eidenbenz, Hermann 49
Engravers 64–5
    Engravers Bold 65
    Engravers Roman 65
    Engravers Titling 65
Enschedé, Izaak and Johannes 191
Excoffon, Roger 113, 133

Fella, Edward 177
FF Balance 133
FF Dax (FF Daxline) 208–9
FF Meta 175, 182–3
    FF Meta Serif 183
FF Scala 178–9
    FF Scala Pro 179
Figgins, Vincent 197
Filosofia 165
Fishman, Janice 43
Fleischmann, Johann Michaël 191
Folio 116–17
Forza 241
Fournier 36–7
    Fournier ODP 37
Fournier, Pierre-Simon 37
Fox, Benjamin 49
Franklin, Benjamin 23, 35, 39, 73

Franklin Gothic 56, 72–3
    ITC Franklin Gothic 73
    URW Franklin Gothic 73
Freight 228–9
    Freight Big 229
    Freight Display 229
    Freight Micro 229
    Freight Sans 229
    Freight Text 229
Frere-Jones, Tobias 47, 166, 167, 195,
    205, 217
Frutiger 129, 148–9
    Frutiger Next 149
    Neue Frutiger 129, 149
Frutiger, Adrian 33, 119, 129, 139, 143,
    149, 181
Futura 88–9
Futura ND 89

Garamond 28–9, 57
    Garamond 3 29
    Garamond Premier 29, 164
    Monotype Garamond 29
    Simoncini Garamond 29
    Stempel Garamond 29
Garamond, Claude 29
Garofalo, Ariel 235
Gataud, Roxane 37
Giaccone, Diego 235
Gill, Eric 55, 85, 91, 95
Gill Sans 55, 90–1
    Gill Sans Infant 91
Giza 196–7
    Giza NineFive 197
    Giza OneOne 197
Glypha 143
Goldsmith, Holly 43
Goodhue, Bertram Grosvenor 61

Gotham 166, 216–17
Gothic (term) 73
Goudy, Frederic W. 25, 56, 71, 77, 79,
    107, 151
Goudy Old Style 78–9
    Goudy Old Style Italic 79
Granjon, Robert 13, 31
Griffin, Patrick 49
Griffith, Chauncey H. 33, 93, 155
Griffo, Francesco 13, 22, 27
Grimshaw, Phill 113
Groot, Luc(as) de 181, 201
Gulliver 169
Gutenberg, Johannes 12, 20–1, 51

Handy, John 39
Helmling, Akiem 231
Helvetica 120–1, 129
    Neue Helvetica 121
Heron Serif 242–3
    Heron Sans 243
Hess, Sol 33, 47
Hiepler, Gerd 159
Highsmith, Cyrus 47, 166, 195,
    205, 243
Hoefler, Jonathan 164, 185, 199
Hoefler & Co. 49, 166, 233, 237,
    239, 241
Hoffmann, Eduard 49, 121
Hofrichter, Dieter 63
HTF Didot 184–5

Interstate 166, 194–5
Isbell, Richard 141
Italian Old Style 25
ITC Avant Garde Gothic 146–7
    ITC Avant Garde Gothic Pro 147
ITC Bauhaus 152–3

ITC Galliard 156–7
   ITC Galliard eText 157
ITC Officina Sans 174–5
ITC Tiffany 150–1

Jackaman, Steve 49
Jacobs, Bas 231
Jannon, Jean 13, 29, 57
Janson 32–3
   Janson Text 33
Jenson 24–5
   Adobe Jenson 25
Joanna 55, 94–5
   Joanna MT 95
Johnson, Lawrence 35
Johnston, Edward 55, 128
Jost, Heinrich 43

Kabel 54, 86–7
   ITC Kabel 87
Kaiser, Erhard 33, 191
Keere, Hendrik van den 223
Kennerley Old Style 79
Kindersley, David 123
Kinneir, Jock 123
Kircher, Ernst Wilhelm 45
Kis, Miklós 33
Kis Antiqua Now 33
Klingspor, Carl 54, 67, 83
Knockout 198–9
Kobayashi, Akira 97, 109, 131, 149
Koch, Rudolf 54, 83, 89, 101, 128
Koreman, Marie-Thérèsè 89
Korger, Hildegard 33
Kortemäki, Sami 231
Kotulla, Martin 135

Lange, Günter Gerhard 63
Lanston, Tolbert 13, 52
Lardent, Victor 99
Laserwriter 162
Levée, Jean-Baptiste 37

Lexicon 188–9
Licko, Zuzana 165, 207, 211
Lining Plate Gothic 71
Link, Gunnar 145
Linotype machines 13, 52–3, 113, 121, 137
Lipton, Richard 213
Litho Antique 103
Lubalin, Herb 147

Majoor, Martin 179
Malin, Charles 85
Manutius, Aldus 22, 27
Marder, Clarence C. 71
Martin, William 107
Mason 192–3
   Mason Sans 193
Mathieu 37
Matteson, Steve 137
Mauricio, José Alberto 83
Meier, Hans Eduard 145
Melior 110–11, 128
Memphis 92–3
Mergenthaler, Ottmar 13, 52
Meridien 119, 129
Metro 107
Miedinger, Max 121
Miller 47
Minet, Yoann 37
Minion 164
Ministry Script 234–5
Mistral 112–13
Modesto 214–15
   Modesto Expanded 215
   Modesto Initials 215
   Modesto Open 215
   Modesto Regular 215
Möllenstädt, Bernd 63
Monotype Ehrhardt 33
Monotype machines 13, 52, 53, 113, 127
Montaigne 77

Morison, Stanley 27, 31, 41, 55, 57, 85, 91, 95, 99, 101
Morris, William 25
Mrs. Eaves 165, 210–11
   Mrs. Eaves XL 211
Multiple Master fonts 187
MVB Verdigris 222–3
   MVB Verdigris Big 223
Myriad 164, 186–7

Neue Haas Grotesk 120–1, 129
Neutraface 220–1
   Neutraface Slab 221
New Caledonia 107
News Gothic 56, 74–5
Niccoli, Niccolò de' 22
Nicholas, Robin 171
Noordzij, Gerrit 181, 201
Noordzij, Peter Matthias 181, 189

OCR-A and OCR-B 138–9
Optima 128, 130–1
   Optima Nova 131

P22 Bayer Universal 153
Pagemaker 162
Palatino 108–9, 128
   Palatino Nova 109
Pantograph 56
paper 23, 39
Parker, Mike 157
Parker, Wadsworth A. 69
Parkinson, Jim 43, 215
Paul, Ale 235
Peignot 104–5
Peignot, Charles 129
Perpetua 84–5
Phemister, Alexander 69
Phinney, Joseph W. 25, 61
phototypesetting 125–7
Pierpont, Frank Hinman 31, 85, 99, 103

Plantin 30–1, 99
  News Plantin 31
  Plantin Headline 31
Plantin, Christophe 31
PMN Caecilia 180–1
Pool, Albert-Jan 97, 181
Porchez, Jean François 137
Porter, Mark 167
PostScript 162, 163
Pousada, Claudio 235

Ransom, Will 65, 79
Reichel, Hans 209
Renner, Paul 54, 89, 115
Renshaw, Bud 73
Rickner, Thomas 203
Rimmer, Jim 145
Rockwell 102–3
Rogers, Bruce 25, 33, 57, 77
Rogosky, Wolf 159
Ronaldson Old Style 151
Rosenberger, August 109
Rossum, Just van 175
Rotis 170–1
  Rotis II Sans 171
Royal Grotesk 63

Sabon 136–7
  Sabon eText 137
  Sabon Next 137
Sabon, Jacob 137
Sans Serif 87
Savoie, Alice 171
Schäfer, Ole 175
Schraubs, William 103
Schrift 54
Schwartz, Christian 41, 121, 167, 183, 221
Scotch Roman 46–7
  Scotch No.2 47
  Scotch Roman Italic 47
  a 244–5

Sentinel 49, 117
Serifa 129, 142–3
Simonson, Mark 69
Slimbach, Robert 25, 29, 164, 173, 186, 225
Smeijers, Fred 12, 219
Solus 95
Source Sans 75
Sowersby, Kris 183
Spartan 71, 89
Spiekermann, Erik 167, 171, 175, 183
Stan, Tony 59
Stern 145
Stone, Sumner 43, 164
Štorm, František 39, 45
Swift 168–9
  Neue Swift 169
Syntax 144–5
Syntax Next 145

Taglienti, Giovanni 27
Template Gothic 176–7
Theinhardt, Ferdinand 63
Thesis family 200–1
  TheAntiqua 201
  TheMix 201
  TheSans 201
  TheSerif 201
Times New Roman 98–9
Trade Gothic 75
Trajan 172–3
  Trajan 3 173
  Trajan Pro 173
Transport 122–3
Transport New 123
TrueType 163
Trump, George 115
Trump Mediaeval 114–15
  Trump Gravur 115
Tschichold, Jan 115, 137
Twombly, Carol 35, 164, 173, 186

type
  anatomy 16–17
  classification 14–15
typesetting 13, 19–21

Unger, Gerard 169, 171, 175
Univers 118–19, 129
  Univers Next 119

VAG Rounded 158–9
VanderLans, Rudy 165, 177
Verdana 202–3
Verlag 236–7
Vitesse 240–1
Vox, Maximilian 14

Walbaum 44–5
  Walbaum 120 45
  Walbaum Grotesk 45
Walbaum, Justus Erich 45
Warde, Beatrice 29, 57
Warde, Frederic 57, 77
Weiss Antiqua 54, 173
Whitney 232–3
  Whitney Index 233
Wiebking, Robert 65, 77
Wilhelm Klingspor Schrift (Gotisch) 82–3
Wolf, Rudolph 93
Wolpe, Berthold 101
woodblock printing 19–20

Zapf, Hermann 33, 109, 111, 128, 131, 215

Acknowledgments

I'm once again incredibly grateful for the cooperation and generosity of the type foundries and independent type designers that have allowed me to use their typefaces in this book. These foundries are listed with their URLs on page 251 and I would urge readers to visit the websites to take a look at the wealth of quality faces which couldn't be featured for reasons of editorial continuity, and of course space. Many individuals helped me to complete this project, but to single out a few (in no particular order) I'd like to thank Allan Haley, the team at Hoefler & Co., Zuzana Licko and Rudy VanderLans at Emigre, Mark Simonson, Mark van Bronkhorst, the team at Lineto, Jim Parkinson, Jean-Baptiste Levée, František Štorm, the team at Underware, Joshua Darden, Gunnar Link, Ale Paul, José Alberto Mauricio, Luc Devroye, Kris Sowersby, Florian Hardwig and Laurenz Brunner. If I've omitted anyone from the list, please accept my apologies.

My thanks go to Stephen Coles who has provided a wealth of insightful advice as well as the foreword. His book *The Anatomy of Type* (or *The Geometry of Type* in its UK edition), which I had the pleasure of designing for Stephen and Quid Publishing, was a reference mainstay throughout the writing of this title. If you haven't read Stephen's book I highly recommend it.

Many thanks to the team at Quid Publishing: James Evans and Nigel Browning for their ongoing support and enthusiasm for books about typefaces, and Chris Turton for his editorial input and support throughout the process.

Bringing this book together has been quite a journey and I'm sure there were times when I might not have been the best person to spend time with, so I must in particular thank my wife Sarah, who has once again endured sharing a life with someone whose world occasionally revolves around typefaces.

Quid Publishing would like to give special thanks to the following: Commercial Type / Dutch Type Library / Elsner+Flake / Enschedé / Font Bureau / Garage Fonts / Gunnar Link / Hoefler & Co. / House Industries / MVB Fonts / Neufville / OurType / Parkinson Type Design / Storm Type Foundry / Underware / (URW)++

Photo p.124 © Mary Evans Picture Library